Dacia

Land of Transylvania, Cornerstone of Ancient Eastern Europe

Ion Grumeza

Hamilton Books
A member of
The Rowman & Littlefield Publishing Group
Lanham • Boulder • New York • Toronto • Plymouth, UK

Hamilton Books
4501 Forbes Boulevard
Suite 200
Lanham, Maryland 20706
Hamilton Books Acquisitions Department (301) 459-3366

Estover Road
Plymouth PL6 7PY
United Kingdom

Library of Congress Control Number: 2009922257
ISBN: 978-0-7618-4465-5 (paperback : alk. paper)
eISBN: 978-0-7618-4466-2

Cover photo: Dacians (right) fighting the Romans (left) while King Decebalus (above the wounded warrior) watches the battle. At the top, in the middle, fly two Dacian dragon-wolf standards. In the upper right corner, Trajan and two generals witness the outcome of the battle. Source: *The Column of Trajan* (2000) by Filippo Coarelli. By permission of Colombo Duemila, S.p.A. (Rome)

Contents

A Note to the Reader

Ancient names that were written using letters that are close to the English alphabet are duplicated here to the extent that is possible. Since many Romanian names are spelled with the letters ţ and ş, I have replaced these with the phonetic *ts* and *tz*, e.g. Moţ appears as Motsi; Constanţă, as Constantza; and Niş, as Niss.

Wherever possible, these names are followed by their modern version and the latter is enclosed within parentheses, e.g. Potaissa (Turda). Often two or more names are placed in sequence, e.g. Keltoi/Celts, Getae/Getians, etc. Also, they are frequently repeated for easier identification.

Large geographic areas like Banat, Oltenia, and Muntenia for which there are no ancient equivalents are identified with the words "what is/are today."

To facilitate the description of Dacian and Eastern European geography, I have designed maps that either alternate between ancient and modern names of rivers and specific locations or use both of types of names (including the Romanian and English names). To this end, I have also marked the Romanian border, as established in 1947, on the maps as well.

Unless otherwise indicated, all dates are understood to fall within A.D.

Preface

The history of Dacia, the powerful and rich ancient land that is now Romania, is little known, especially that of the period of 500 B.C. to A.D. 500. Yet, this kingdom was once the cornerstone of Eastern Europe. The historic changes, wars, economy, and traditions of this Transylvanian land permeate the geopolitics of today's Balkan countries. Thus, to understand what is happening today in modern Eastern Europe, we need to understand the history of this area.

As a Romanian whose roots go back to Dacian times, I have undertaken the task of sorting through its disparate and often confusing historical records in order to present a more accurate story of its ancient people. Historical accuracy is by no means easy to achieve. At best, there are written records, but these are sometimes in archaic languages and require skill in linguistics and a sense of place and time in order to make critical connections between the various texts. Moreover, such documents often contradict each other, thereby prohibiting accurate interpretation.

The Dacians left no written language so the researcher is not provided with the types of readily available testimonies or clues that the Greeks and Romans abundantly provided. "Reviving" their history requires that one rely on narratives based on the memories of contemporary travelers from outside the region. Herodotus, "the Father of History," is, for example, a primary source of information about many ancient lands. He traveled widely, but in the case of Dacia and Eastern Europe he relied on the tales of other travelers whose Homeric-like remembrances were often imprecise or inflated. As to the clues he provides about different lands and natives considered barbarians, including the Geto-Dacians, they allow us to know at least something of the lives and times of these people.

Written legends, myths, and diaries are also sources of data, as are art findings, ruins, graves, and heaps of ancient garbage unearthed in archaeological digs. In some cases, the evidence of history is still out in the open. Indeed, it often so much a part of everyday experience that its importance is overlooked.

Sometimes, too, history is purposefully revised or accidentally misinterpreted. Names are a case in point: some languages often had more than one spelling for a name, and repeated translations, ending in English, tended to generate misunderstandings. The mistransmission of information such as this, be it biased or innocent, can lead to historical errors. And, when such errors are passed on, they become undisputed "facts." The result is often academic confusion. The ongoing debate about such details can often benefit from fresh analysis of available evidence.

Fortunately, part of the Dacian legacy is written in stone. One of Rome's famous tourist attractions is Trajan's Column, built to commemorate the most profitable invasion in the history of the Roman Empire. Yet, few are familiar with the country of Dacia, whose defiant military history adorns the column. Still fewer are aware that Dacian warriors destroyed many of the invading elite Roman legions and effectively kept other mighty conquering armies at a respectful distance for centuries.

Ancient Dacia encompassed today's Romania as well as the lands adjacent to it. The Dacians are one of the few indigenous peoples in Eastern Europe who have never left their inherited lands. In the years before Christ, Dacia was the only civilized society north of the Danube and Rhine rivers. The Dacians are believed to have had a 360-day calendar long before the Egyptians, Greeks, and Romans did. Their society was based in a monotheistic religion and they were a tribal federation with tremendous national pride, a quality that matched the land's plentiful natural resources, high social standards, and military power.

Conveniently nestled inside and around the Carpathian Mountains, Dacia controlled both the lower Danube and the west coast of the Black Sea. It therefore dictated the terms of travel north of the Balkan Peninsula and also owned the road toward Scythia (Ukraine). Its geographical location made it a crossroads for more than fifty super-tribes, including the Alani, Celts, Germans, Goths, Sarmatians, Scythians, and others.

Before A.D. 100 Dacia was a kingdom with two million people. Its immense natural resources of gold, silver, copper, and especially salt attracted the envy of Rome. Indeed, twelve emperors tied their destiny to Dacia, one of the greatest honors being to attach the epithet *Dacicus Maximus* to their royal title.

Eventually, Dacia became the gateway for the entry of Asian barbarians from Eastern Europe into the Balkan Peninsula. This gave the Dacians the negotiating power with which to choose their allies against the Roman Empire. It was therefore only a matter of time until Rome would send its legions to subdue the land and incorporate it into its multi-continental empire. But Rome had to engage in three major campaigns and apply the might of numerous legions led by the most capable generals in order to invade this rich and independent kingdom, which was the third military power of ancient Europe.

Ultimately, only part of Central Dacia (today's Banat and Transylvania) was annexed by Trajan in A.D. 106. Most of the original country remained free and served as a buffer zone against the barbarian hordes moving in from the east. By then the Romans could not afford another invasion, nor could they fully garrison occupied Dacia. During the period of their domination of Dacia Felix, the Romans gained such wealth from plundering their new colony that no major wars were carried on for the next one hundred years, except for purposes of defense. This was the longest period of relative peace in Roman history.

After A.D. 275 the Romans withdrew from the occupied territory, weary of battling the tenacious Free Dacians and the barbarian invaders who had taken refuge there. However, when Rome could no longer exploit Dacia's abundance to support its legions, it lost control of its barbarian borders. At no point after this did the Roman legions claim decisive victory in any battle north of the Danube.

The Dacians never migrated and they remained preeminent in the southern part of the ancient Eastern Europe. Yet, the forces of history caused their descendents to be subject to many political changes. In the Middle Ages, the Daco-Romanian people were subjugated by the Ottoman, Austro-Hungarian, and Russian empires. In the twentieth century, Nazi Germany and the Soviet Union amputated parts of Romania's ancient land of Dacia and brutally imposed Communism on all the Eastern Europe nations. After the Red Empire collapsed, those nations were subjected to a bloodless economic invasion of capitalistic opportunism, which in some aspects was as traumatic as the actions of the Huns and Tartars. In the absence of a dictatorial regime which could enforce the peace, old tensions based in longstanding territorial disputes resurfaced and ethnic wars erupted in the Balkan Peninsula. Similar conflicts had occurred over the last two thousand years.

Today, Romania is part the European Community and supports NATO; it thus tries to both please and take advantage of the new masters of Europe. Only time will tell if this is a repeat of the Roman times when Dacia played the major powers against each other in order to survive and eventually prosper.

Acknowledgments

Special thanks are owed to Colombo Duemila, publisher of *The Column of Trajan* by Filippo Coarelli (Roma, 2000) for allowing me to use their remarkable photographs of the friezes on Trajan's Column to illustrate many of the historical events described here, as well as to The Beinecke Rare Book and Manuscript Library of Yale University, New Haven, Connecticut, for giving me access to centuries-old volumes that contained two of Ptolemy's maps and to Sterling Memorial Library at Yale University, New Haven, Connecticut, for making its Romanian sources available for this project.

Also, I would like to express my gratitude to the University of Chicago Press for granting permission to use the map "The World According to Herodotus, B.C. 440," from *Herodotus, The History* (1987), translated by David Grene, and to Oxford University Press for granting permission to use map 24, "The Extension of the Hellenic Civilization Overland 171 B.C." (pp. 122-143) from *A Study of History, Vol. XI: Historical Atlas and Gazetteer* (1959) by Arnold J. Toynbee.

Introduction: The Story of the Column

Trajan's Column stands inside the area of the Roman forum, commanding the admiration of tourists just as it did nineteen hundred years ago. At that time, however, everyone knew that the 110-foot marble monument with its hundreds of chiseled images immortalized the Roman campaigns against the Dacians.

The story of the column begins in A.D. 98 after Marcus Ulpius Traianus came to the throne. He was the first of a series of emperors who were adopted by the Caesars. Born in 53 near Seville, Spain, this would-be conqueror came from an aristocratic family with a military tradition. His father commanded Legion X Fretensis which conquered Judea and later became the Governor of Syria, where his son, Trajan/Traianus, served as a tribune.

Trajan's great capacity for leadership evidenced itself first in Germany when he marched on foot alongside his soldiers. He faced the greatest military challenge of his life during a Dacian war in which he played a marginal role under Domitian—and this before he became emperor of Rome. Simple, modest, honest, and brave, this competent leader was above all a committed imperialist. Extending the Roman Empire toward the cardinal points was his mission to the last day of his life, and he excelled in accomplishing it.

When Trajan was named emperor, everything seemed to go according to his wishes—except for the fact that the impudent Dacians showed no respect for the might of Rome. Decebalus, the Dacian king who defeated each Roman legion sent to capture him, aimed to rule the Balkan Peninsula and Eastern Europe. That was unacceptable to Rome because it was in competition for the same territories.

Well aware of the danger posed by the Dacians, the new emperor's first military task was to inspect the garrisons and legions stationed on the Danuvius (Danube) line, the unofficial Roman border with Dacia. There Trajan strategized to invade the rebellious kingdom. He brought in additional troops to protect Moesia (today's Bulgaria and Serbia), and he sent a delegation to negotiate with Decebalus asking him to peacefully accept the conditions imposed by Rome. Trajan's primary demands were that the Dacians not cross into the land south of the Danube River and that they deliver a yearly tribute in the form of gold, salt, and other goods greatly needed by the Roman Empire to pay its legions and to ensure the luxurious lifestyle of its citizens.

At that time, Dacia had attained economic and military strength as well as ethnic, religious, cultural, and commercial homogeneity. It was a kingdom that already rivaled any European power. Therefore, Decebalus felt he was in a position to defy orders from Rome. He considered the Romans to be too far away and their legions too weak and busy to fight a war with Dacia. Unafraid of Trajan, he bluntly turned down all of his proposals. Furthermore, he continued to invade Moesia and raid the Roman settlements there, intensifying the fury of Rome.

Emperor Trajan decided to crush the Dacians, but he kept in mind that their territory exceeded that of Britannia, Gallia, Spain, Thracia, and even Italy. Their military power rivaled that of Germany and Egypt. Like Parthia, which controlled the silk and spice trade, Dacia controlled a valuable commodity, but one that was far more important—gold. With the empire's treasury emptied by so many wars, the submission of intractable Dacia was a priority.

First, Trajan tried again to intimidate Decebalus by using diplomatic means, this time sending his most valued adviser, Lucius Licinius Sura, to negotiate with him. But the discussion came to a sudden halt when the consul presented Rome's conditions. Angry Decebalus countered by demanding that Roman-occupied Getia (today's Dobrudja in Romania), Moesia, and even Pannonia (today's Hungary) be returned to Dacia.

Revolted by the king's arrogant attitude, the consul returned to Rome with a single recommendation for Trajan, namely, to eliminate the Dacian power altogether. Trajan agreed and summoned some of his best legions to take part in the invasion of Dacia. It did not concern him that Dacia had one hundred thousand fanatical warriors, half of them skilful horsemen, and a five hundred-year tradition of undefeated military engagements. In the Roman view, this would be just another war against a barbarian country that would end in a quick victory.

In the second half of the year 100, Trajan ordered an exploratory military survey of the Dacian forces from the western part of Getia. Cavalry and light infantry scouting units were sent to map important points of resistance. Without having engaged in any decisive battles, the Roman expeditionary corps reached the foot of the Carpathian Mountains. Once there, they were harassed by Dacian horsemen, and, limited in their movements due to lack of access roads and threatened by the oncoming winter, soon the Romans were forced to retreat. Decebalus did not hesitate to proclaim victory for himself.

Encouraged by this success, the Dacians crossed the frozen Danube and continued their devastating raids against the outlying Roman garrisons and settlements. But these seasonal victories came at a price. Their actions further infuriated Rome, and Trajan and his generals used the rest of the winter to complete their war preparations.

Trajan left Rome with great pomp in April 101. One month later, two columns of Roman legions arrived on the banks of the Danube. They rested and waited for the final units and supplies to arrive at designated points and prepared to invade Transylvania on two fronts.

The chiseled scenes on the Column of Trajan do an admirable job of illustrating important events in the wars between Trajan and Decebalus. Much like a modern film, the story begins at the base of the Column and shows how the Roman troops crossed the Danube using pontoon bridges.

Once on the other side of the river, they found themselves in the vast forests in enemy territory, a land shrouded in mystery. The Column shows Trajan inspecting his troops, military councils planning future battles, and legions building new forts to facilitate a lasting occupation. The spiraling carvings display animals sacrificed to Roman gods to ensure their blessings. There are also depictions of advancing troops cutting trees to penetrate the dense forests of Transylvania, and of others building bridges over the streams for easier access for the remaining troops and their heavy war equipment. Scouts are shown bringing the first prisoners before Trajan, among them a bearded Dacian clothed in the traditional national costume.

At this preliminary stage, the campaign went according to plan, but what had been decided in Rome was not going to happen. The Column documents the sudden turn from a peaceful march to a full cavalry charge as the Romans begin their first assaults on important fortified Dacian cities. One frieze after another in the longest sequence of the Column depicts them charging forward and the Dacians fighting back under their beloved dragon standard—a wolf head with jaws wide open, connected to a winged hollow serpent. In the remainder of the battle scenes, only the Dacians are shown as having fallen to the ground while the Roman auxiliaries massacre villagers and set fire to their households.

The story continues upward and around the column. A delegation of Dacian citizens is shown trying to plead for mercy from the Emperor who is determined to continue fighting. In the next frame, the legions are depicted as chasing the retreating Dacians while well groomed civilians, looking like anything but barbarians, are led to ships to be taken into captivity. Just like their fighting men, the women are portrayed as dignified and contemptuous of the invaders.

It is thought that the "editing" of these vivid scenes accords with real events and probably followed the description of Trajan's *Commentarii*, his lost war memoirs.

The second advancing Roman column headed towards Sarmizegethusa, the Dacian capital, but the weather turned bad and the Romans were trapped in mud that would soon freeze. In order to spare both sides an agonizing campaign, Trajan sent envoys to Decebalus but he again refused to negotiate a truce. He knew too well that the enemy hesitated to fight in freezing weather: their clothing was tailored not to keep them warm, but to accommodate battle movements. Because of the fact that winter was fast approaching, the campaign lulled to a stop and the Romans prepared to camp in their newly built forts and wait for spring. This was exactly what Decebalus had counted on.

In the heart of the winter, the Romans were hit by a shocking turn of events: Dacian allies—the Buri and the Sarmatian Roxolani—crossed the frozen Danube into Dobrudja and Moesia Inferior and attacked the empire's garrisons. Once these raiders made it across the river, they rammed the Roman strongholds while Getian archers took aim at the defenders in the ramparts.

Overnight, the Romans faced a second front more than 500 kilometers/310 miles to the east. There the invaders, led by Sarmatian warlords, sacked the non-Dacian settlements. The Column dedicates many scenes to these Roxolani warriors clad in fish scale-like body armor. For purposes of sensationalism, the sculptors also chiseled their horses as outfitted in similar armor.

Trajan collected his last reserves and, taking advantage of the fact that the Danube was half-frozen, rushed them off by boat. At the same time his cavalry dashed down the riverbank to repel the devastating attacks of the Dacians and their allies. One scene shows the mounted emperor taking charge of the attack and the Romans galloping over the fallen Sarmatians in full armor. The next eight scenes reflect savage hand-to-hand combat in which half naked Roman auxiliaries battle the Dacians who protect retreating civilians, many of whom are holding children. The encounter was evidently so horrifying that creators of the Column felt the need to also include an image of the first wounded Romans. Their military arrogance was obviously put to its first real test here.

Eventually the Dacians and their allies were pushed back, and the Romans took control of the blood-soaked battlefield (later known as Adamclisi) where four thousand legionaries died. All of this was chiseled into another war monument, one that was commissioned by Trajan and still stands today in the middle of the Dobrudja plains, hundreds of miles from Rome.

The Emperor generously rewarded his troops who were now ready to join the summer attack in Transylvania aimed against Sarmizegethusa. More of them crossed the Danube under the command of Hadrian, the adopted son of

Trajan and his successor. The final assault against the Dacian capital resulted in Decebalus's request for an armistice. The king negotiated an agreement that left him in power even as he formally agreed to accept the suzerainty of Rome. As a client king he was treated more like an ally and paid annually for his friendship and also trusted with turning Dacia into a solid buffer against the continually invading Asian tribes who tended to attack the Roman Empire.

While Trajan was being acclaimed by the Senate, taking the title of *Dacicus Maximus* and celebrating victory, Decebalus was proceeding to make his nation stronger and stop the plundering invaders at the eastern border. For the next three years, he pretended to do what he was asked. He did, however, have a hidden agenda—a plan to fight the Romans again. He used this period to build a stronger army, one that was intended to free the rest of the Dacian lands from Roman occupation and push the legions out of Balkan Peninsula once and for all.

But Trajan had his own plans for the future of Dacia. He ordered Apolodor, his favorite architect, to build a bridge across the Danube River. It would connect the Roman Empire with this rich kingdom that he wanted so badly. The bridge came to be the longest one in the ancient world. It was instantly declared the eighth wonder of the world and immortalized on a commemorative coin. It anchored the power of Rome between the banks of the Danube at Drobeta/Turnu-Severin.

The reaction of Decebalus to this permanent and intimidating Roman fixture was predictable. He had his squadrons burn the Roman garrisons which had been built in Dacia and he hired spies to assassinate Trajan. By the end of year 104, the Dacians were striking again in full force across the frozen Danube, demolishing the Roman settlements there and taking their civilians and soldiers prisoners, including the commanding general, Longinus, hostage.

Rome was outraged and Decebalus was declared an "enemy of the Republic." When Trajan announced another war against the Dacians, the entire senate applauded him, a rare event in itself. Preparation for this new war exceeded that undertaken for any other in the history of the Roman Empire. Rome's military reputation was at stake, and the plunder of Dacia would bring tremendous benefits.

In June 105, Trajan used the famous bridge to re-invade Dacia with increased military force. This time he was determined to eliminate Decebalus and make his kingdom a province of Rome. But, once again, the plans made in Rome did not match the reality on the ground in Dacia. The events of this second war are also illustrated on the Column, and its historical consequences are reviewed in a subsequent chapter of this work.

Today's visitors to the ruins of the famous Forum can see the relief carvings of the Column with their many unique details; this is information that otherwise would have been lost forever. The uniforms and the equipment of the combatants, the dramatic fighting scenes, the personal triumphs and tragedies, the treatment of the prisoners, the labor of the Roman engineers, and military reviews are all immortalized there. It also shows that the Dacians were not savage barbarians. Certainly their love for their children is made clear throughout the various frames of the Column, scenes of tenderness which are unique to a war monument.

Above all, the Column testifies to the millennial existence of the Dacians and their contribution to the continuity of the Romanian nation. It also immortalizes the forefathers of today's Romanians and serves as a "birth document" written in stone. So imposing was the Column that neither the Vandals nor other invaders of Rome dared to destroy it, given its majesty and its message. Despite the deterioration in the condition of the Roman Forum, Trajan's Column has remained a symbol of the once powerful Eternal City that dominated the civilized world but could subdue only part of Dacia—and that not for long.

Who were these Dacians and their allies? Who were the other tribes with names and destinies, e.g. the Thracians, that confused even ancient historians? What was their role in European history? Why was Eastern Europe so important for the Roman Empire? And, how does this ancient history impact our modern era? These are the questions I hope to address here. Hopefully, by doing so, I will be able to illuminate some of the important details of life in a world that has vanished, but is in many ways also still with us.

Chapter One

The Geographic Configuration and Historic Development of Dacia

The end of the Ice Age and the period of the Biblical floods reduced the land of continental Europa to its present shape with its several peninsulas. Like the Caspian and Aral seas, the Black and Mediterranean seas were unconnected inland lakes which had a lower water surface than they do today. Most likely the Mediterranean was an immense low lying valley between Europe and Africa, and the water level of the Black Sea was at least 130 meters/426 feet below that of the Atlantic Ocean. Glacial melt increased the ocean's volume and forced its water to break through what is today the Straits of Gibraltar and flood the low land of the Mediterranean and its chain of lakes. The ripple effects of this geo-climatic event may have occurred as early as twelve thousand years ago when they continued through the Balkan Bosporus and the salty water entered the Black Sea at a steady pace.

Stone Age humans tended to live near water since it provided an easier life for them; this was the case for most of the early inhabitants of the Balkans. The flood advanced roughly 2.4 kilometers/1.5 miles each day, giving the Neolithic people on the nearby plains time to flee from the lower lands and take refuge in the mountains.[1] While there is evidence that the Carpathians were inhabited by humans before the flood, it is likely that at least some of the people who fled the rising waters helped populate the mountain valleys and pastures of what would come to be called Dacia.

The first of these future Dacians settled in a territory that had a mix of high and low lands. The semi-circle formed by the Carpathian Mountains provided excellent shelter in the elevated plateau of Transylvania, whose name means "the land beyond the forests." With its mild climate, forests abundant with fruits and animals, fertile soil, and ores of salt, gold, and other subterranean riches, Transylvania was populated with groups of wanderers who were forced to share living space and cooperate during their fishing and hunting expeditions.

Gradually, these randomly organized clans came to establish closer racial and blood ties and learned to fight against natural and human enemies. By the middle of the last millennium before our era, they had united into permanent tribes named Daii, Daoi, Dacs, Dacii, Dagae, or simply Dii, names which are all derived from *daos*, an ancient Greek word for wolf, the animal most worshipped by the Neolithic Dacians. Their religious and social centers were in Transylvania, which became the hearth of the future Dacian kingdom. At this point, the isolated but hospitable Dacian society was thriving; it had a plentiful tribal life and little need for the outside world.

No other epic natural disasters occurred in Europe except the eruption of Tera/Thera (Santorini) in 1630 B.C., despite a popular belief held by some Hellenic philosophers that the Danube River could flood the entire known world. That prophecy never materialized, however, and the abundant European land attracted long estranged Aryan tribes who migrated from the Caucasus and the Sea of Azov region back to their ancestral tribal lands. Among them were the Scythians, described by Strabo as "the most straightforward of men and the least prone to mischief"[2]; they were the masters of the Eastern European steppes for hundreds of years. But they were slowly pushed southward by the Sarmatians who, in turn, were pushed westward by Asiatic tribes advancing towards the Caspian Sea.

The fair skinned and blue-eyed, mounted Scythian herders proceeded along the coast of the Black Sea and entered the Dacian lands after crossing the Bug, Dniester, and Prut rivers. They settled below the Danube Delta, were quickly assimilated into local society and became known as the Getae/Getians (for reasons explained below) of Little Scythia or Scythia Minor. In modern day Romania, this is the area of Dobrudja.

The Sarmatian Moetsi from the Maeotis Lake (Sea of Azov) crossed the Carpathians and, settling in the Maramures region, became Motsi, the pillars of the future Dacian nation. Some of the Motsi of Transylvania later migrated south the Danube where they became known as Moesi; the land they populated would be called Moesia (today's Bulgaria). Thus the Dacian roots were in part Sarmatian, while the Getians' were mostly Scythian.

The year 500 B.C. found the Da(v)oi/Dacians in the center of the Carpathian-Danubian-Pontic region, beginning a process of territorial expansion aimed at keeping away unwanted hordes of invaders and also at dominating the nomads of adjacent lands. This was a relatively easy task given that the Celts were busy colonizing Gaul, the Germans had not yet settled between the Oder and the Rhine, and the main body of Iranian Sarmatians and Caucasian Scythians were still canvassing the Eurasian steppes for water and shelter.

The Greeks and Romans were too distant and concerned with their own wars to pay attention to Dacian exploits. To them, the Dacians were the barbarian Getians of the western Black Sea shore, a people whom they misnamed Thracians after the tribes at the northern border of Greece.

The Dacians first moved along the Danube River and southward from there into lands that were sparsely populated by wandering Celtic, Illyrian, and Thracian tribes. Tribes of Getians occupied the region between the final turn of the Danube and the Black Sea (where Dobrudja is today), and soon the Dacian Moesi took over the land between the Danube River and the Haemus (Balkan) Mountains. It was a rapid conquest by the Dacian horsemen, and their families followed and quickly settled on the lands. Ironically, Moesia, the new land of the Getians, became more known to historians than Dacia and its forested Transylvanian mountains.

As for the Thracians who lived below the Balkan Mountains, they were busy defending themselves against their powerful Greek and Macedonian neighbors. They could hardly afford campaigns of retribution against the Dacian invaders of Moesia. Given that they faced little opposition, the Dacians grew bolder and stronger and came to dominate the land between Sarmatia and Thracia in a well defined corner of Eastern Europe.

Even though they were engaged in other conquests and not concerned about the tribal maneuverings in the Danubian regions, the Greeks, Romans, and other imperial powers were interested in Dacia's well known rich natural resources and its geographical position at the crossroads of Eastern Europe. This area was the primary conduit to both the Near and the Far East, and where the barbarians pouring out of Asia had to be restrained. Dacia's natural barrier, the Danube River, made an ideal buffer zone for the western and southern European civilizations.

Many ancient chroniclers ceased their efforts when it came to objective narration of areas beyond the Danube line, the northern border of the Balkan Peninsula. Beyond that lay the unknown and dangerous barbarian world of Transylvania and the Dacians. When the Greeks and Romans explored northward along the shore of the Black Sea, they came upon some of the many trading posts run by Thracians. As they returned home, these travelers brought with them names they had picked up from the Thracians — and this word of mouth information came to substitute for actual geographic knowledge. Hence the Dacians and Getians were mistakenly thought to be Thracians, just as many of the ethnic tribes of the Italic Peninsula were known as Romans. Sarmatians, Scythians, and other names were also used to refer to Dacians. Based on scant contemporary references, the confusion about Dacian identity therefore began very early in antiquity.

The world map made by Herodotus showed most of the Balkan Peninsula occupied by the Thracians. South of the Ister (Danube) River, he placed Getae, framed by the Pontus Euxinus (Black Sea) and the land of Illyrians.[3] Dacia was not shown on his map, and, surprisingly, neither was the name of any Greek/Hellenic state to which he belonged.

Herodotus was fascinated by the Ister, "which is the largest of any river we know of, flows with always the same volume, summer or winter. It is the furthest to the west of any of the Scythian rivers."[4] He believed it to be "one of the rivers of the Scythians"[5] that began from the Celtic land, crossed all Europe and flowed with five mouths into the Euxinus at Histria. Thus he added two more extensions to the mouth of the Danube.

Many Dacian rivers can be still identified on the basis of his geographical descriptions, such as the Maris (Mures), Tyras (Dniester), and Hypanis (Bug). The Maris was identified as flowing perpendicularly into the Danube; in reality, it is the Alutus (Olt) River that does so. The true Maris flows east-west out the Carpathians where it meets the Tisza River, not the Danube. All of the other rivers and, so the locations of the tribes in their vicinity, were erroneously described as well; cartography had not yet been invented.

Even though he was a great admirer of the Sarmatians about whom he wrote in great detail, Herodotus forgot to put them on his map as well. Once again, this shows that the great historian was confused about Dacia and overlooked it, believing it to be only Getia/Getae. In fact, the two phonetic names are almost interchangeable, and Daco-Getian super-tribes constituted the majority of the population of Dacia.

As for the Thracians (also called Thraki), whom he printed in the largest letters across the Balkans and so many other historians incorrectly believed them to be the Dacians' tribe of origin, certain facts need to be separated from legend and myth. The Thracians did not live near the Danube in Moesia, as is often thought, but well south of the Haemus (Balkan) and Rhodope mountains, near the tip of the Balkan Peninsula. According to Herodotus, "a Thracian tribe, the Dolonici, held the Chersonese" and even threatened Athens.[6]

At that time, the Thracian Chersonese was the name for the Gallipoli Peninsula, located in the heart of Greece. Moreover, part of the Aegean Sea was called the Thracian Sea, and the future Straits of Constantinople were known as the Thracian Straights. No Thracian names were to be found attached to the Danubian area or to regions north of it.

It is therefore clear that the Thracians had little interest in the land of Moesia; instead, their goal was to dominate the Hellenic world as it extended into Minor Asia. Most of their tribes already lived in what is today Turkey. The Thracians were neither numerous enough nor militarily capable of fighting on a second front towards the Danube against the Daco-Getians. As for the

Greek city states, they were too busy fighting their fratricidal wars to attend to Dacia. Basically, Getia and Moesia were part of Dacia because no other military power had conquered these territories.

Thucydides, a contemporary of Herodotus, was described as the son of a Thracian leader. He became the commander-in-chief of an army that failed to save the city of Amphipolis (a former Thracian settlement near the Aegean Sea) from a Spartan siege in 422 B.C., a fact that demonstrates that the Thracians were indeed influential in Greek affairs. On the other hand, in so far as they exiled Thucydides for twenty years, the Athenians also showed their contempt for him as an unworthy foreigner who failed to fulfill his generalship. Ironically, it took such a foreigner to write about the Peloponnesian War, the first history book on European warfare.

Like many historians of his time, Thucydides located Scythia below the mouth of the Danube, a few hundred miles south of its actual location. However, this was not entirely incorrect since Getae (today's Dobrudja) was often named Scythia. He paid detailed attention to the map of the Balkan Peninsula and correctly placed the Thracian tribes between the Haemus, Rhodope Mountains, the Euxinus, and the Peloponnese, some 321 kilometers/200 miles south of the Danube River.

He was familiar with the Getian territory that lay between the Danube and the Haemus and was bordered on the east by the Black Sea. He wrote that the people there were neighbors "of the Scythians and are armed in the same manner, being all mounted archers,"[7] and described the Getians as superior fighters in comparison to the Thracians. He also acknowledged the existence of "many of the independent Thracian hill tribes, swordsmen called Dii."[8] Like other paid Scythian warriors, these tribes lived on Mount Rhodope and came to fight for the Odrysian king of Thrace against the Macedonians. Still, they were not Thracians.

These brief descriptions of events offer a striking piece of evidence to support the historic claim that the Dii (often named as Dacae, Daii, Daoii, and Dakii) were Dacian warriors, well known for their mercenary services in the Balkan Peninsula. They freely moved through what was named Thracia because in fact it was their land and they certainly did not want the Macedonians to occupy it. However, in 336 B.C. Alexander the Great defeated the Thracians and so caused them to lose their independence. This was never the case for the Dacians. They consistently remained untouched by the Macedonian powers.

Alexander's general, Lysimachus, became the Thracian king. He quickly realized he could not rule over the Getians in Moesia who were governed by their king, Dromichete. In a key battle that probably took place at Odessos (Varna), a Getian city, the Dacians defeated the Thracians. Lysimachus and his son were taken prisoners and brought to Helis (Sboryanovo), the Getian capital. The captured Lysimachus was treated so well that Dromichete married his daughter, and the Getians regained full control over Moesia. That did not make Dromichete a Thracian leader.

To summarize these developments, when the Greek historians described "Upper Thracia" as the most beautiful mountain region of the Danube, they were surely talking about the Carpathian Mountains and most likely Transylvania, both of which were within the area of Dacia. Yet, ironically, the Dacians were the mysterious people of the impenetrable northern lands, barbarians who inspired fear but were not worth mentioning in history records.

This confusion and lack of information about Dacia was perpetuated by the Romans three hundred years later, when Strabo described how Alexander the Great invaded the country of the Tribalians/Tribalii (today, this area of the Danubian Banat lies between Romania and Serbia) and observed that it extended as far as the Ister and the island of Peuce.[9] Alexander "did, however cross over the Ister into the country of the Getae, took their city and other things."[10] The Roman historian went on explain that Syrmus, their king, refused to give the Macedonians access to the island, and by offering gifts and flattering the invaders, he obtained "the friendship of great men."

Julius Caesar (100-44 B.C.) confirmed in his *De Bello Gallico* (Book VI) that the Hercynian forest along the Danube River bordered Dacia. Because he was too busy and too exhausted to fight the Celts and Germans for eight years, he never crossed into Dacia, but his thoughts often wandered in that direction, where the richest of the European salt and gold mines were located.

It took an outstanding foreigner who lived among the Daco-Getians and was not an historian to write extensively about them. Ovid (Publius Ovidius Naso), the Roman poet, was exiled in A.D. 9 to Tomis (today's Constantza in Romania). He proved to be equally misinformed, to say the least, about where he spent the last nine years of his life. The sum total of this unhappy bard's knowledge of his new home was acquired in Rome, so it is no wonder he confused geographic and historical facts about Dacia and Getia. It is clear from his poems that he believed himself to be exiled on "this far Sarmatian coastline." He thought he was living "away by the Danube, on Scythian soil,"[11] but was aware that he sent letters from "the Getic shore."

He subsequently wrote that he arrived at Tomis "via Scythian waters" and lived among "the barbarous Goths." He mentioned "wild Thracian mustangs"[12] and complained about his life on the "Black Sea's sinister shore." At other times, he was convinced that he sent his letters "from where the Danubian estuary joins the [Black] sea,"[13] a geographical error of at least 120 kilometers/75 miles—the distance between Tomis and the Danubian Delta. However, he did know where Thracia was. And, when he was terrified that savage barbarians might raid Tomis, he wrote that he hoped that King Kotys/Cotys (the Thracian king) "just over the frontier, in a neighbor state" would come to his aid.[14]

The Getian land of his banishment was cold and inhospitable, "a dangerous frozen hell-hole," Ovid complained, exaggerating the climate of Tomis. No doubt it was freezing in the winter, but the city shared the same latitude as Florence, and Ovid there experienced just about the same climate as he had in his native Sulmo in the Abruzzi region. The climate in the rest of Dacia was comparable to that of central Italy, except for winter when land toward the north and into Eastern Europe was subject to freezing temperatures. Thus, another stereotype was passed on to Rome, one that was picked up by Juvenal who used "the Getic snow" as a term of comparison for cold in his *Fifth Satire*.

At this point, the most viable explanation for all the geographical and historical errors that were made would be that Transylvania, the central section of Dacia, was out of reach of the Hellenic and Roman empires. It was a land of dense and impregnable forests in which the Greek, Macedonian, and Roman armies were not stationed, and for which no precise military maps were available. The commercial routes followed only the Black Sea shore towards the Sea of Azov, while the Dacians had full control of the last portion of the Danube. They went across the river and south of it to exchange goods, thus keeping intruders away.

Strabo, who chronicled his knowledge in forty-three books including his famous *Geography*, knew where Thracia was, as can be seen by his repeated references to "the Thracian Chersonse" (Gallipoli Peninsula). He described the flow of the River Istrus (Danube) crossing "the whole Germany (which begins at the Rhine), all the country of the Getans, and the country of the Tyregetans, Bastarnians, and Sarmatians as far as the River Tanais and Lake Maeotis [Azov Sea]; and it leaves on its right the whole of Thrace, Illyria, and, lastly and finally, Greece."[15]

He also placed "the land of the Getae" near the German Suevi, "stretching as it does along the Ister on its southern side and on the opposite side along the mountain-side of the Hercynian Forest (for the land of the Getae also embraces a part of the mountains), afterwards [it] broadens out towards the north as far as the Tyregetae."[16]

Strabo confirms that the Dacians battled the Iapodes (a mix of Celts and Illyrians living in what are today's Croatia and West Slovania) over the city of Segestica (Sisak). He also corroborates the claim that, during the reign of Caesar, the Dacians fought the invading Boii "until they perished, tribe and all."[17] Strabo was here referring to the military expeditions of King Burebista (reigned 82-44 B.C.) who defeated the Boii and Taurisci/Teurisei who lived in the land of today's Bohemia and Slovakia. We can deduce from this that Burebista was responsible for extending the Dacian borders from west to east, from the Vltava to the Bug rivers, and north into Transcarpathia (Ukraine).

Yet Burebista's main attacks were aimed toward the south, as his Dacian warriors "would cross the Ister with impunity and plunder Thrace as far as Macedonia and Illyrian country," [18] explained Strabo. In fact Burebista established his court at the present Balcik (believed to be Zargedaua) and pushed the frontier of his kingdom to Apollonia (now Sozopol). Moesia had to belong to the Dacians if Burebista was to reach Thracia and plunder it.

Like the historians who preceded him, Strabo connected Thracia to the Danube, even though it had nothing to do with that great river. He left a generous territory above the Danube for Getarum Terra (the land of Getians) that reached from the Black Sea to Bohemia.

Fifty years after Ovid's death, Pliny the Elder hardly talked about Dacia in his *Natural History*. In a subchapter on the Danube region, he concluded that most of the races are Scythian and only mentioned the Getae and the Sarmatae as exceptions to this. Thrace (Thracia) was cited for its carbonated waters, but no connection was made between it and the Dacians.

Pliny the Younger (A.D. 61-122) was a professional politician whose adulation for Trajan was limitless. Flattering words for the emperor fill most of his *Panegyricus* text. Even though Trajan was able to conquer only a portion of Dacia, the ever laudatory Pliny expounded on the important battles "with the spoils of plundered provinces and gold wrung from our allies, but with our enemies' arms and the chains of captured kings."[19] Nevertheless, he repeatedly neglected to mention the name of Dacia, which was the object of the entire tribute. Pliny also did not refer to Decebalus, the Dacian king whose suicide allowed Trajan to keep the titles of *Dacicus* and the Father of the Roman Nation.

Tacitus was a well traveled, high ranking Roman officer. He knew the difference between Dacia and Sarmatia, although he believed that the Danube discharged its water through six channels into the Pontic Sea. This historian described the borders of the German tribal federation in his book *Germania*: "The whole vast country of Germany is separated from Gaul [France], from Rhaetia [Switzerland] and Pannonia [parts of Austria, Croatia, Hungary, Serbia], by the Rhine and the Danube; from Dacia and Sarmatia, by a chain of mountains, and, where the mountains subside, mutual dread forms a sufficient barrier."[20] The barrier he refers to could have been the Tatra Mountains and the Hercynian Forest, a safe buffer zone between the Germans and Dacians. Actually, these two nations shared and controlled almost the entire flow of the Danube River.

Cassius Dio (ca. A.D. 150-235) was another Roman historian who, in eighty books written in Greek, also stubbornly avoided acknowledging Dacia. When he described the Caesar-Anthony-Octavian military conflicts in which Dacia was heavily courted and prepared to become a key player, Dio mentioned only Greece, Macedonia, and Thrace.[21] Nevertheless, he once was the appointed governor of Upper Pannonia and certainly was aware of the Dacian population living in his province, which, by that time, was bordered by Roman-occupied Dacia.

He wrote one of the most precise paragraphs ever about these perpetual enemies of Rome:

> I call the people Dacians, the names used by the natives themselves as well as by the Romans, though I am not ignorant that some Greek writers refer to them as Getae, whether that is the right term or not; for the Getae of whom I myself know are those that live beyond the Haemus range, along the Ister.[22]

It was obvious that only Daco-Getians lived north of what are today the Balkan Mountains and the Danube River.

Despite this plethora of confusing names and references, it is clear that by the first century A.D. Dacia was a well established kingdom in its own right, and not part of Thracia, Scythia, or Sarmatia. On the other hand, due to rapid decline of these three mega-tribes, the name of Thracia was replaced with Moesia; the name of Scythia, with Saka; and Sarmatia with Sourmamatae. By the time of Tacitus, the empires of Sarmatia and Scythia were long gone, and Thracia had been a Roman province since the year 46.

In the middle of the sixth century A.D., Jordanes wrote his early history of the Goths and located the hearth of the Gothic land in Scythia (with its presumptive capital at Tomis) and also in Moesia (with its capital at Marcianopolis now Devnya, Bulgaria)). Both of these Roman provinces were originally part of the Dacian tribal federation, which had kept its name and continued to control its main territory north of the Danube. He identified the Goths with the Scythians who by this time had vanished from history, and with the Getians, who were essentially the Dacians' twin brothers. Unwittingly but correctly, Jordanes, himself a Moeso-Goth, denied that Thracia had anything to do with his ancestors' land of Gothia (formerly called Dacia) that he described in his book. Jordanes mentioned Thracia in the context of the Gothic raids south of the Balkans: "After the Goths had thus devastated Asia, Thrace next felt their ferocity."[23] It was obvious that Thracia was not close to Dacia and that it was also far away from Asia. However, that did not mean that the Thracian people had vanished or that some had not populated parts of what are today Bulgaria, Greece, and Macedonia. They just were not Dacians.

Jordanes referred to Dacia again when describing the Visigoths' settling south of the Danube River around 376 when "they finally sent ambassadors into Romania to the Emperor Valens."[24] This is the first time that the name "Romania" was mentioned in a surviving ancient document. It clearly referred to the ancient Dacian land. Jordanes called the Visigoths "Getae," and vice versa, but he was not confused about the geography of the Balkans.

He wrote that Valens "received the Getae into the region of Moesia."[25] And he also confirmed: "They [the Visigoths] themselves, as we have said crossed the Danube and settled in Dacia Ripensis, Moesia and Thrace by permission of the Emperor."[26] Once again, this proves that Dacia and Thracia were different countries containing different peoples.

Confusion over Dacia was passed down over the next fifteen centuries. In 1922, Professor M. Rostovtzeff from the University of Wisconsin wrote about ancient South Russia, commenting: "Little is known about the conditions on the Dnieper and Danube. The region seemed to have been the meeting-place of several currents: a Thracian current of Getians or Dacians, who took Olbia in the middle first century B.C."[27] In just a few words, he further transmitted the old errors that had labeled the Getians and Dacians as Thracians.

He then went on to describe the same territory as "extremely varied and complex," as having been invaded by Celtic and Germanic tribes. He then concluded: "Moreover, the revival of a Thracian state, that of the Dacians, in the first century B.C. and the first A.D., led to constant invasions of South Russia by Thracians. One of these brought about the capture and sack of Olbia."[28] The Russian historian accurately acknowledged the existence of the Dacians and their land, but he omitted any mention of Burebista, the Dacian king who sacked Olbia. Burebista also raided Tyras on the mouth of Nistru (Dniester) River and incorporated both city colonies into Dacia. Centuries later, Tyras would become Cetatea Alba (White Fortress) in the later Moldova.

As noted, Rostovtzeff, like so many historians before him, perpetuated the ongoing confusion about the Dacians and Thracians and their role in Eastern Europe. The Dacians, who practically owned the last leg of the Danube River, had invaded south Russia. At that time the Thracians were living on the other end of the Balkan Peninsula, hundreds of miles away from the Danube and so were in no position to bypass the Dacians and raid what, for them, was far away Olbia.

It was another eighty years before the British historical professor and eminent researcher, Arnold Toynbee, would at last do justice to the history of the Getians and Dacians by showing them on his map of 171 B.C. as occupying most of the Balkan Peninsula. Only Macedonia and the Greek states were included in the southern tip of the peninsula. Thracia was nowhere to be found on the map. He placed the Scythians and Sarmatians above the Sea of Azov and the Caspian Sea.[29] For Toynbee, there was no confusion about who was who in Eastern Europe.

Dacia was about twice the size of today's Romania and was centered around Transylvania. Additionally, far reaching Dacian tribes (or tribes controlled by them) occupied adjacent territories that made the kingdom five times as large as today's Romania. Referred to as the "people of Ister," and even called "Istriani," the Dacians never hesitated to demonstrate their ownership of the great Danube River. They considered all the lands alongside it to be theirs, extending west into the Pannonian fields beyond Vindobona (today's Vienna).

They also took full advantage of any population gap and controlled portions of the vast Hercynian Forest (of Bohemia and Moravia), extending their reach as far as Zavist (today's Prague) along the Vltava River. Because they encountered tribes with low population densities who were able to pose little opposition, they were able to extend their mini-empire north toward the Vistula River and into what is now Galicia. Thus the only geographical borders of Dacia were the Pontus Euxinus in the east and the Haemus (Balkan) mountains in the south.

When the Romans expanded toward the Danube, the Dacians fearlessly attacked and destroyed the legions' garrisons in Moesia, ensuring that it remained unoccupied at least during the winter. This defiance continued until the end of the first century A.D. In the centuries that followed, Dacia continued to be subjected to numerous destructive barbarian invasions as well as internal and external wars

The Dacians did not have a written language, nor did they duplicate the Greek and Roman tradition of leaving monuments to attest to the grandeur of their civilization. But the remains of their settlements left ample information for posterity. The numerous archeological sites that now exist throughout Eastern Europe evidence this. Written documents, maps, and other information support the fact that Dacian federation of tribes did exist and confirm that they were not a migratory population. In fact, most of these settlements are still in existence today in and around modern Romania.

The maps of Dacia in the first century A.D. reflected an astonishing number of fortified places nicknamed *davas* that may be related to the Sanskrit word *deva* meaning divine. Many Dacian locations ended with the suffix *dava*, probably roughly equivalent to the Germanic suffix *burg*, meaning castle/fortress or town. Thus, for example, Sucidava meant "the shrine locale in the town of Suci," home of the Suci tribe, while Buridavensi was the tribe of Buri with its capital at Buridava.

As a further note of linguistic interest, over centuries *davas* often had *v* changed into *b* or *u*. Names incorporating *daba*, *daua*, and *dara* are also taken to mean a Dacian sacred place. The Romans replaced *dava* or *daba* with *diva* (goddess), and the Greeks, with *polis*/city; Ptolemy often replaced *dava* with *dana* and *bara*.

Earlier Dacian settlements prior to the fourth century B.C. have been found in more than ten locations, including modern Zimnicea on the Danubian shore, Cotnari in Moldova, Tulcea county, Dobrudja, and other places in Transylvania. Ptolemy's map of these lands offers splendid proof of the Dacians' existence by marking their settlements and clearly spelling out more than thirty of their main cultural centers (substituting *dava* with *dana* and *dara*). Among them are the easily recognizable Acrobadara, Angustia, Argidava, Docirana/Docidava, Dierna, Carisdava, Marcodava, Napuca/Napoca, Nentinava, Petrodava, Rhamidava/Ramidava, Tibiscum, Utidava, Ziridava, and Zusidava.

Ptolemy pointed out that many *civitates Daciae* (Dacian cities) were not shown on his map. Among them were the new capital Sarmizegethusa (the old Sarmizegethusa Regia is clearly marked east of the Tibiscus River) and the nearby fortress Singidava (Hill Fortress), with Zuribara/Zurobava above lower Maris River. Other locales he mentioned include Hydata, Lizisi, Paloda, Patruissa, Pinum, Pirum, Triphulum, Sandana/Sandava, and Zemiziriga; most have survived under different names in present day Romania, Upper and Lower Moesia (Central and Northern Bulgaria), and Scythia Minor (Dobrudja), which was densely populated by the Dacians at that time. [30]

North of the Danube, however, he missed the second most important city in Dacia, Buridava (Stolniceni-Valcea), as well as others, but he did mention the settlement of Clepidava "above the Tyras (Dnister) river near Dacia,"[31] thereby correctly identifying the eastern border of Dacia. The Dacian settlements extended into what are today Galicia and Bukovina, with Carsadava located east of Cernovitz, Dogidava, and Patridava.

This entire region of Eastern Dacia was also known as Moldova, a land of *molto* (many) *dava* (sacred places). There were clusters of fortifications like those in Petrodava (Piatra Neamt) and Utidava (Targul Ocna). Lined up along the Hierasus (Siret River) were Piroboridava (Nicoresti), Zargedava/

Zargidava (Brad), and other settlements. Between the Siret and the Prut rivers were large forts that today are known as Cotnari, Poienesti, and Stanesti.

The Prut line was guarded by Tamasidaua/Tamasidava (Reni) and Vtidava. Between the Nistru and the Dnieper, Ptolemy showed the thriving Setidava and Susudava. Even though the Dacians controlled the eastern region before and after many commercial posts were built, at that time cities still carried typical Greek names, such as Aliobrix, Harpis, Heracleea, Halmyris, Ophiussa, Niconium, Tomos/Tomis, Troesmis (Iglita), and Tyras (Cetatea Alba). The Black Sea island of Leuce (Isle of Snakes) also belonged to the Dacians as part of the Getia (Dobrudja) area.

Located in Valahia/Wallachia (Muntenia) were the strong fortresses of Arcina, Argidava on the Ordessos (Arges) River, Cumidava (Rasnov near Brasov), Jidava (near Campulung Muscel), Netindava, and Zucidava. The Oltenia region abounded in *davas*, like Buridava, Rusidava (Dragasani), and Arutela (Bivolari) on the Alutus (Olt River), and Pelendava (Craiova) on the Roboses (Jiu) River.

The Transylvanian mountains and their crossing passages were guarded by other fortresses that sheltered the elite of the Dacian population. These towns included Acrobadava/Acrobadara, Deva, Napoca, Porolissum (Zalau), and others. Near today's Sighisoara were Ramidava (Rupea) and Sandava, while inside the Tibiscus (Timis) River enclosure were Aizis, Arcidava, Berzobis, Jidova, Partiscum, and Tapae. The Maris (Mures) Valley and Banat were controlled by strongholds in Germisara, Ziridava (Pecica), Zizdava, and a web of *davas* in the northern area around Sarmizegethusa. To the northwest was Zurobara.

The shores of the Danube were well monitored from the Dacian fortresses Acidava, Buricodava, Dausdava (the Shrine of Wolves), Diacum, Drobeta (Turnu Severin), Nentinava (Oltenita), Sucidava (Corabia), Tirista, Tsierna/Dierna (Orsova), and what is today Zimnicea. Downstream there were also other fortresses: Axiopolis (Cernavoda), Barbosi, Buteridava, Capidava (Topalu), Carsium (Harsova), Durostorum (Silistra), Sacidava/Sagadava (Dunareni), along with still others in the areas of Braila, Galati, and Ialomita in today's Romania.

The mouth of the Danube was controlled by the key fortified ports of Aegyssus (Tulcea), Dinogetia, Noviodunum (Isaccea), Peuce, Troesmis, and Zisidava. Inside the Dobrudja region were the fortified garrisons of Argamum, Basidava, Caesum, and Istros. The Dacians controlled most of the southern shore of the Black Sea, and their cities of Alboris, Callatis (Mangalia), Dionysopolis (Balchic), Histria, and Tomis (Constantza) were much sought after destinations for both foreign tradesmen and ambitious military leaders.

South of the Danube (in what are now Bulgaria and Serbia) the names of other Dacian settlements were well known, including Aedava/Aedadeba, Acrobadara, Basidava, Bregedava, Danedebai, Dinogetia, Egeta, Genucia/Genucla, Giridava (Pleven), Hydata, Mesambria, Moesorum, Muriedava, Odessus (Varna), Petrada, Patruisa, Sagadava, Scaidava, Sukidava/Tanatis, and Zaldapa.

Also in densely populated Dacian Moesia were Acmonia, Amutrium, Drupheis Kuimedava, Rhuconiu, Tiristum, Zisnedeva/Zisnudeba, and other cities. Many other *davas* were scattered throughout Bulgaria, such as Dausadava and Perubidava, and it is known that Pulpudeva became Philippolis/Plovdiv, and Rexidava became Marcianopolis (today's Reka Devnya).

In Dalmatia, there were Kuimedava and Therimdava, while Aiadava/Aidaba, Brecedava, Desudava, and Itadava/Itadeba were located in today's north eastern Macedonia. Gildova/Gildoba was in the former Thrace; a town with the name of Getidava was alongside the Vistula River, and Setidava was on the Warta River.

Over time, the suffix *dava* changed into *oara*; for example, Timesiennsis in Greek was Timisdava (the shrine on the Timis River), and became Timisoara in today's Romania. It is possible that the original name of capital Sarmizegethusa (the Romanians write and pronounce Sarmizegetusa) was Sarmizegetdava, the holy place of the Dacian population. South of the Danube, the Thracian places ended in *bria, para* and mostly in *dizas* (fortress). D*ava* was later Slavonized as *ovo*, hence today's Karlovo, Ostrovo and Tarnovo.

No one will ever know exactly how many Dacian settlements actually existed as they have not all been accounted for. What is known is that King Burebista moved his capital from Argidava into the Sebes Mountains, which were considered sacred. Probably Deceneus and the high priests already lived there, and the king's presence with his army represented a demand to consolidate the Dacian nation. Also, this new location was closer to salt and precious metal mines.

Burebista named his new capital Sarmizegethusa Regia, and its ruins can still be seen today in Gradistea Muncelului. It was located only 1,200 meters/3,937 feet above sea level, so the city did not have a natural means of defense. It therefore became more of a religious center than a military stronghold. Unlike other fortresses which were built of limestone, the walls of Sarmizegethusa were made of andhesite/andesite, an ancient and very hard volcanic rock that is known today as "dacite."

There is no doubt that the *davas* belonged to the Dacians, and only a few of these geographical names belonged to the Thracians. Still, the fact that the Thracians were an Asian family of tribes located at the southern tip of the Balkan Peninsula, above Greece and next to Macedonia, 321 kilometers/200 miles from Dacia, did not prevent ancient and modern historians from loosely using the Thracian name to describe most of the tribal formations of the Eastern Europe.

Sarmatia was another mistaken name often used for Dacia, even though Dacia was another 322 kilometers/200 miles south from its border and Ptolemy regarded the Vistula River as the border between Germania and Sarmatia. Similarly, the name of Chersonese was commonly applied to the Crimean, Gallipoli, and Jutland peninsulas, even though one is in Ukraine, one in Greece, and the other in Denmark.

Indeed, many of the small Sarmatian and Thracian tribes lived in the tribal federation of Dacia, along with Celts, Germans, Scythians, and others; still, they did not rule the Carpatho-Danubian territory. In fact, by the middle of the first century A.D. Sarmatia, Scythia, and Thracia had vanished altogether as countries, while Dacia was economically and militarily stronger than ever and proving itself to be a formidable adversary of the expanding Roman Empire.

Thus by the year A.D. 100 more than 400,000 square kilometers/154,400 square miles (today Romania measures 237,500 square kilometers/91,700 square miles) were dominated by the Dacians who numbered two million. Numerous interconnections between tribes made the people of Dacia increasingly strong and expansionist. The end result was a Daco-Getian kingdom that measured more than 2,000 kilometers/1,243 miles in circumference.

Five distinctive regions of Dacia can easily be identified using today's landmarks: Central Dacia included Banat, Crisana, and Transylvania; Northern Dacia covered Bucovina, Galicia, Maramures, and lands north of them; Eastern Dacia began east from the Siret River and covered Moldova, Bessarabia, Transnistria, and all the territories beyond the Dniester up to the Bug line; Western Dacia extended over the Tisza River across Hungary to the Vltava and Sava rivers; and Southern Dacia began at the Meridional Carpathians and the Danube Delta and extended across the Danube and through Bulgaria down to the Balkan Mountains.

To summarize, the Dacians controlled the territories of what now are Romania, Moldova/Bessarabia, Western Ukraine, Bukovina, Hungary, parts of Austria, Croatia, Serbia, the Czech Republic, Slovakia, and the northern half of Bulgaria. Their lands included the modern cities of Belgrade, Budapest, Lvov, Prague, Varna, and Vienna.

Topographic descriptions and footnotes on Ptolemy's map of Dacia include few Roman names, which indicates that he did his cartographic work before the year A.D. 104 He identified Oescus and Rhetiaria/Ratiaria as Danubian bridgeheads, and he also outlined the Dacian territory between the Danube, Tibiscus/Timis and Tyras/Nistru rivers—a smaller country than the kingdoms of Burebista and Decebalus. But the impact of the Roman takeover of a segment of Dacia was enormous and felt at all levels of the society, especially because so many settlements were built. This was a common trademark of Roman occupation. The conquerors also rebuilt many of the Dacian cities ravaged by the two wars of occupation.

Along the Danube, a line of newly fortified towns featured Axiopolis, Carsum, Durostorum, Prista, Regianum, Sitiuenta, Tramarisca, Trimannium, and Tribolarum. Legion I Italica was stationed in Novae, and Legion IV Flavia in Singidunum.

The rest of occupied Dacia included Acmonia, Amutrium, Apulum, Fratesia, Praetoria Augusta, Rucconium, Tiasum, Ulpianum, Triphulum, Zeugma, Zermizirga, and Zurpbara. The most important towns were not even on Ptolemy's map, such as Noviodunum (Isaccea), Pirum (Pitesti), Romula (Resca), and Thyanus which fourteen hundred years later would be known as Bucharest, the capital of today's Romania.

Dacia established such a powerful legacy that even after the Romans left the country they gave parts of Moesia the names of Dacia Aureliana, Dacia Nova, Dacia Ripensis, and Dacia Mediterranea, a fact that provides still more incontrovertible evidence to the effect that today's Bulgaria and part of Serbia were Dacian lands before and after the Roman invasion of Banat and Transylvania. In the present day Czech Republic, the eastern part of Moravia is called Wallachia,[32] just like Wallachia of the Romania land of the Dacians.

Whether or not it was properly cited in geography and history books, the name of the Dacians lived on, eventually to be chiseled onto Trajan's Column in the middle of Rome. Their unique land never changed its geographical position, and its distinct population played a major historical role in the development of the Carpatho-Danubian civilization at the crossroads of the ancient world of Eastern Europe.

NOTES

1. The Learning Channel, 25 August 2000. Geologists searched the submerged coastline of the Black Sea and discovered an uneven bottom filled with the remains of sweet land and water plants dating back some seven thousand years.

2. Strabo, *The Geography of Strabo*, trans. Horace Leonard Jones (London: William Heinemann; New York: G.P. Putnam's Sons, 1924), vol. 3, 199.

3. Herodotus, *The History*, trans. David Grene (Chicago: University of Chicago Press, 1987), 294-295.

4. Herodotus, *History*, 4.48.

5. Herodotus, *History*, 4.51.

6. Herodotus, *History*, 6.34.

7. Thucydides, *History of the Peloponnesian War*, trans. Rex Warner (New York: Penguin Books, 1972), bk. 2, 151.

8. Thucydides, *History of Peloponnesian*, bk. 2, 151.

9. It was the Paicul lui Soare/Ada Kalech Island, not the Peuce Island in the Danube Delta where presumably Alaric, king of Visigoths, was born. When the Danubian dam was built in 1964, a reservoir covered the island.

10. Strabo, *Geography*, trans. Jones, 201

11. Ovid, "Tristia," *The Poems of Exile*, trans. Peter Green (Berkeley: University of California Press, 2005), bk. 5, 1. 22

12. Ovid, "Black Sea Letters," *Poems*, bk. 5, 2.63-3.8; bk.1, 2.109.

13. Ovid, "Black Sea Letters," *Poems*, bk. 3, 5:1-2.

14. Ovid, *Poems*, bk. 2, 9.2-5.

15. Strabo, *The Geography of Strabo*, ed. G. P. Goold, trans. Horace Leonard Jones, Loeb Classical Library (1917), vol. 1, 493.

16. Strabo, *Geography*, trans. Jones, vol. 3, 174-175.

17. Strabo, *Geography*, trans. Jones, vol. 3, 311.

18. Strabo, *Geography*, trans. Jones, vol. 3, 211.

19. Pliny, *Letters, Books VIII – X and Panegyricus*, vol 2 of *Letters and Panegyricus*, trans. Betty Radice (Cambridge: Harvard University Press; London: William Heinemann, 1975), 363.

20. Tacitus, *The Germania of Tacitus*, vol. 5, *History*, The Latin Classics (New York: Vincent Parke & Company, 1909), 354.

21. Cassius Dio, *Roman History*, trans. Ernest Cary, (Cambridge: Harvard University Press; London: William Heinemann, 1955), bk. 50, 449.

22. Dio, *Roman History*, bk. 67, 329.

23. Jordanes, *The Gothic History of Jordanes*, ed. and trans. Charles Christopher Mierow (Cambridge: Speculum Historiale, 1966), 108.

24. Jordanes, *Gothic History*, 131.

25. Jordanes, *Gothic History*, 132.

26. Jordanes, *Gothic History*, 133.

27. Michael Ivanovitch Rostovtzeff, *Iranians & Greeks in South Russia* (Oxford: Clarendon Press, 1922), 116.

28. Rostovtzeff, *Iranians & Greeks*, 145.

29. Arnold J. Toynbee and Edward D. Myers, *A Study of History*, vol. 11, *Historical Atlas and Gazetteer* (London: Oxford University Press, 1959), 122, map 24.

30. On his world map, Ptolemy contoured only three continents: Asia, Europe and Africa. His geographical knowledge was based on charts of Marinus of Tyre (A.D. 70-130), a Phoenician cartographer and mathematician. Because of the Roman wars in Europe Ptolemy clearly showed the River Vistula as the border between Germania and Eastern Europe. He also showed the Danube crossing Dacia, whose name he wrote in large capital letters.

31. Ptolemy, *The Geography* (New York: New York Public Library, 1932), bk. 3, ch. 5.

32. Rick Steves and Cameron Hewitt, *Rick Steves' Eastern Europe* (Berkeley: Avalon Travel, 2008), map 2.

Chapter Two

The Ancient World Surrounding Dacia

Dacia played a pivotal role in the history of ancient Eastern Europe because its core tribal confederation never migrated or allowed itself to be pushed off its land by Asiatic invaders and European powers. Transylvania continued to be the hearth of Dacia as the latter extended its boundaries in all four directions and became a large kingdom in its own right. Its tribal people united under a flag bearing the image of a wolf-dragon. To understand the history of Dacia, however, one needs to first become acquainted with the tribes, nations, and empires that once populated the Balkan Peninsula and lands between what are today the Vistula, Vltava, Danube, and Bug rivers, and beyond.

The most accurate ancient map of Eastern Europe in 171 B.C.[1] is a simple one that places the Persians east of the Caspian Sea, the Sarmatian tribes between the Caspian and the Sea of Azov, and the Scythians above them to the west. The Daci/Dacians and the Getae/Getians (or Geatae/Getons) are accurately shown dominating Danubian Eastern Europe. Byzantium was further south at the tip of the Balkan Peninsula.

At that time, the Scythian road referred to the commercial route around the Pontus Euxinus (Black Sea). It came from the Balkan Peninsula and crossed Scythia (Ukraine) between the Hypanis (Bug) and Borysthenes (Dnieper) rivers. Numerous historical sources confirm that the Sarmatians and Scythians were settled between Asia and Europe, and that they made up the main tribal population of the incipient Eastern Europe.

Centuries earlier, historian Herodotus (ca. 484-ca. 425 B.C.) drew a map that placed Scythia and Getae in the same area. His sketches, however, greatly distorted the shape and location of the three continental seas around them. It is likely that during his travels, he met the two tribal groups whom he correctly noted were on opposite banks of the Ister (Danube) River. He also wrote that the Scythians and Sarmatians were separated by the Tanais

(Don) River. He described the Scythians as living along the Black Sea and explained that this is why they were known to "the Greeks of the trade port on the Borysthenes River and the other ports on the Pontus."[2] He refers to the "Royal Scythians" from the Maeotis/Maeetian Lake (Sea of Azov) and other Scythians from the Ister River; these people were most likely the parent tribes of the Moesi and Getians who controlled the Danube and Black Sea ports of the west coast.[3]

The western Eurasian migration pushed the Scythian tribes throughout Eastern Europe toward the Danube River. Many of them ended up in Dacia, one being the Getae/Getians, an offshoot of the Massagetae from the Caspian Sea, who settled in what is today Dobrudja.

Herodotus's information was fairly accurate with one important exception—he failed to mention the Dacians, having mistaken them for the Thracians. This error would, unfortunately, be passed on by future historians, and to this day much of the remarkable Dacian history has been hidden between the lines of the legends, myths, and arbitrary judgments of their biased neighbors.

Dacian history goes back to a time that preceded Herodotus by many centuries, a period in which the Scythians used their tremendous horsepower to control and expand into Asia Minor. In 650 B.C. Syria and Palestine began to revolt against the Assyrian occupation, and the Scythians smashed their rebellion. The city of Beth-Shan in Palestine was renamed Scythopolis since the Scythian mercenaries spread terror throughout the land of the Bible for a period of ten years.

Scythian expansion was halted by King Cyrus, who created the Persian Empire in 530 B.C. With a population of thirteen million people and the most feared army in the ancient world, Cyrus wanted to extend his rule into Europe, and, in attempting to do so, he pushed the Scythians out of Asia. Ancient historian Jordanes wrote: "Then Cyrus king of the Persians...waged an unsuccessful war against Tomyris, queen of Getae."[4] According to Herodotus, her Messagetae soldiers with their battle-axes (*sagaris* "bent swords") were the fiercest of all barbarians and "got the upper hand." An example of this is the fact that they avenged the Persian execution of the queen's son, who had been taken prisoner by the Persians. Jordanes went on to explain: "After achieving this victory and winning so much booty from her enemies, Queen Tomyris crossed over that part of Moesia which is called now Lesser Scythia—a name borrowed from great Scythia—and built on the Moesian shore of Pontus the city of Tomi named after herself."[5] Today the ancient city of Tomis is known as Constantza in Romania.

How large was the Getian kingdom if the army of Queen Tomyris defeated the Persians near the Araxes (Volga) River? And, was she also the queen of the Massagetae who killed Cyrus in a final battle? Questions such as these suggest the need for a new and closer look at the Getians and their role in Eastern Europe.

In the next few centuries, the Scythians settled west of the Tanais (Don) River. It remained their eastern border. Jordanes wrote: "Now Scythia borders on the land of Germany as far as the source of the river Ister and the expanse of the Morsian Swamp."[6] This shows that the Scythians' western border extended as far as the source of the Danube River in the Black Forest, or 2850 kilometers/1771 miles into the heart of central Europe; it also extended south to Pannonia and Croatia.

Jordanes went on to name many other landmarks of the Scythian Empire, including the Scythian Taurus (Caucasus Mountains), Lake Maeotis, the straits of Bosporus (Crimea), and others. According to him, the Scythian borders reached the rivers Vistula, Tyras, Hypanis, and Ister, and the Pontus Euxinus. These therefore defined the borders of the land of Dacia. Given the fact that Dacia had no fixed borders, the Dacians and the Scythians shared the ownership of many of these overlapping Eastern European territories, with the Getians being the masters of the western coast of the Black Sea.

The Battle of Marathon in 490 B.C. destroyed the myth of Persian military invincibility, and eventually the Hellenistic and Persian empires self-destructed. The fall of these titans made possible the rise of the young Macedonian Empire at the southern tip of the Balkan Peninsula. The Dacians were then courted by the great emperors who wanted to keep them from joining the enemy camp. But they remained neutral to the extent that this was possible in those uncertain times. Their main concern was to keep their lands free of any invaders.

While visiting the eastern barbarian regions, Herodotus met the Thracians and the Getians on the shores of the Black Sea, which had long been the location of Greek commercial colonies. One of the things he noted was that their clothes were made of hemp fiber and that they had a tendency to respond to violence with more violence. From Thucydides (ca. 460-ca. 395 B.C.) we learn that in 430 B.C. ninety thousand Athenians were stricken by a plague, thus diminishing the Greek military power and its thwarting expansionist ambitions as far as Eastern Europe was concerned. It is likely that his long trip north of the Danube saved Herodotus's life, and that this deadly epidemic saved Dacia from a Greek invasion.

During this same time period, in the area south of the Danube many tribes were united by Sitacles/Sitalkes who was known to the Macedonians as the Thracian king. Thucydides, who was himself a descendent of a Thracian royal family, confirmed this. Sitalkes possessed such great military strength that he was able to force the Athenians to negotiate with him for part of

Greece in exchange for his helping them fight against Sparta. By the time his son Seuthest became a ruler (Seuthopolis was a royal city named after him), Thracia was larger and more prosperous; it aspired to take over the Hellenic world, but not Eastern Europe.

Herodotus analyzed the Persian wars and included in his nine volumes of history many rich facts about the social and military condition of the Eastern European tribes of his time. In 513 B.C. Darius I invaded the Balkan Peninsula with three army corps (out of the total of six which he possessed). According to Herodotus, they numbered some seven hundred thousand men. Among them were tens of thousands of horsemen and chariots, transport wagons, and countless animals to be used for hauling equipment and for food.

The Persian army was the largest and the most powerful the ancient world had seen. Its military formations crossed the Bosporus on a pontoon bridge and invaded nearby Thracia. Darius received numerous peace delegations from the tribes that were settled on the shores of the Black Sea in this area, but despite their pleas and efforts at resistance, he occupied most of Thracia. This horse-breeding land was important for supplying the emperor's army. At this point in time, the combined Greek army (mainly formed of the Spartans) numbered some 110,000 soldiers and probably three hundred warships. To the relief of these modest forces, the Persian invasion was headed northward, not southward toward the Hellenic cities.

Since they were facing annihilation, the Thracians decided not to fight. This made it easier for the Persians to cross their country into the small kingdom of the Odryssians. Thracia thus became a colony of Persia. Marching north into Moesia, the formidable Persian military expedition entered into the Getae/Getian section of Dacia.

Once again Jordanes's testimony must be read in the context of the veridical facts about the relationship between Dacia and Thracia. He wrote of Darius: "Crossing on boats covered with boards and joined like a bridge almost the whole way from Chalcedon to Byzantium, he started for Thrace and Moesia."[7] However, Thrace was south of Moesia and the two could not possibly overlap and be inhabited by the same people. At first the Getian horsemen charged the Persian scouting patrols and even forced them to turn back. Encouraged by this success, the Getians chased after them—only to run headlong into the colossal Persian military columns marching full force toward their country.

The valiant Getians realized that they had no hope of overcoming the Persians. If they joined them, they would be protected from Thracian aggression and maintain hegemony over the cities of Callatis (Mangalia), Histria, and Tomis, all of which are located in today's Romania. The Getian leaders therefore decided to ask for peace and submit to Persian rule.

Darius was tempted to take over the Dacian gold mines of Transylvania about which he had heard so much, but his troops never entered the Carpathians. Perhaps the numerous packs of Dacian horsemen who patrolled the base of these mountains dissuaded him. It is also likely that the Thracian chieftains had already warned Darius of the unrelenting and powerful Dacian forces. Going after Transylvania would be a diversion that could be costly. Instead, the king pressed north towards Scythia.[8]

The Persian fleet was as multinational as its army and included six hundred large galleys with two hundred men each. The armada navigated along the coast of the Black Sea with orders to move into the Danube. The warships advanced up the river and probably dropped anchor at the mouth of the Pyretus (Prut) River. There, the Ionian engineers built a bridge of tied boats across the Danube. The Persian infantry advanced along the shore of the Black Sea until it reached the Tyras (Dniester) River where its soldiers built a military camp and rested for three days.

Darius had confidence in the strength and the morale of his troops as they made their way to conquer Scythia, and so ordered the destruction of the bridge. He envisioned returning to Persia by marching around the Sea of Azov. But many of his generals advised him to leave the bridge in place for at least sixty days to ensure their having an alternate route across the river. Darius agreed, and he entrusted the Ionians with guarding the invaluable bridge. The generals' advice was prescient. The Persian armies advanced for three days into the heart of Eastern Europe where they met up with the strong and determined Scythian cavalry who were ready to die rather than admit defeat.

These warrior pastoralists (named Sakas by the Persians and Sacae by the Latins) were masters of equestrian archery and could also charge with a heavy lance. The lance was solidly propped against the saddle, so its striking and penetrating force was greatly enhanced during a wild gallop. A straight double-edged iron sword with a sharp point encased in a metal scabbard and a quiver and bow-case combination completed their arsenal. All their weapons were heavily ornate; gold was not spared and increased their beauty and value.

The Scythian strategy was simple: they withdrew to a distance of one marching day and set everything in the path of the invaders on fire. They attacked only during the night. Their battle tactics were equally simple: they used the ax blade formation to splinter and induce heavy losses among the enemy infantry. They disengaged from the battle in reverse order, avoiding strangulation of the spearhead units. Many Sarmatian tribes joined the fight against the Persians, knowing that if the Persians subjugated the Scythians, the Sarmatians would be next.

The retreat of the Scythians deceived the Persian armies into thinking it was an opportune time to enter the steppes. However, they did not know that the flat and empty land offered neither food nor shelter. As soon as he realized he had fallen into a trap, Darius halted the movement of his troops—probably near what is now Odessa. Although he was still committed to conquering Scythia, the confident king ordered the construction of eight forts to serve as a military base there and symbol of Persian conquest. But, with each passing day, as the number of wounded and sick Persians increased, so too did the demoralized troops' and worried generals' desire for battle diminish.

Still sure of himself, the Persian king then sent envoys to ask the Scythians to surrender. But slavery, like defeat, was unknown to them and they continued to fight. The Scythian hit and run attacks became bolder and stronger. Herodotus tells us that in the Persian camps the only defense during the night was the braying of donkeys and mules. The Scythians did not know of these animals and were terrified by such "evil" sounds, as were their horses.

Unlike the Persian horses and donkeys which could not withstand the freezing weather, the small and shaggy Siberian horses of the Scythians could survive the incredibly harsh winter of that area. The first snowfall made the Scythians instant winners in the ongoing battle. Recognizing that the brutal climate and terrain would work against him in the approaching winter, Darius led his huge army out of unfriendly Scythia. He left just in time to prevent it from perishing in the snowstorms of the Ukraine steppes.

Since he had not given up hope of future conquest, Darius left a Persian garrison in the Oarus area (most probably this is not related to the Oarus/ Volga River since it is located beyond the Don River). However, the remainder of the Persian army consisted mainly of sick soldiers who were too weak to march back to their own country. Those who had not been killed by the Scythians were surely doomed by the Siberian winter. Nothing is known of their fate.

Darius proceeded straight back to the Danube. Meanwhile, the Ionians had demolished roughly one third of the vital bridge in an attempt to keep the Scythians from using it. With the Persians approaching, they repaired it just in time for the evacuation of the retreating troops. The Scythian campaign lasted less than two months and ended at the start of the winter of 512 B.C. The weakened Persian army again hurriedly crossed the lands of the Getians and the Thracians which were already under the control of Darius. He left eighty thousand Persian soldiers to garrison Thracia and part of Macedonia, while Getia remained unoccupied.

Declaring himself to be content with his "conquests," the emperor returned with the rest of his "victorious" troops to Persia. Because no Persian troops were stationed north of the Danube, Dacia and her people remained free. The military power of the Scythians stayed unchallenged. Still, they did not raid the western territories of Dacia.

A hundred years later, many Thracian tribes were united by King Teres of the Odrysses kingdom, an ally of Athens. But other "Thracian" tribes refused Athenian patronage, choosing instead to ally themselves with the Getians who dominated the Lower Danube territories. It is possible that those tribes were not actually Thracian, but only under Thracian domination, since they finally freed themselves from it with the help of the Getians. They all faced another massive military invasion.

In 340 B.C. King Philip II (the father of Alexander the Great) led the Macedonian troops into the northern Balkan Peninsula. At first, Philip negotiated with the Thracian King Kotys I in an attempt to establish a truthful alliance. He was, however, eventually forced to take up arms in order to annex the province of Nestos, where he stationed his troops. Jordanes explained this by quoting the historian Dio: ". . . Philip, suffering from need of money, determined to lead out his forces and sack Odessus [Varna], a city of Moesia, which was then subject to the Goths by reason of the neighboring city of Tomi."[9]

Considering that Jordanes identified the Getians with the Goths (to him Gothia was Dacia and vice-versa), Odessus and Tomis could not possibly have been part of Thracia, nor could Philip have considered it a friendly territory. It was the Dacian wealth that lured him to move in that northern direction in order to conquer faraway Scythia. The latter had abundant granaries upon which the Greeks and Macedonians depended. The Macedonian army would have passed through Eastern Dacia as it proceeded toward Scythia.

It is known that Philip and his troops marched through the Danubian land of the Tribalii/Tribalians, an area that had Celtic roots. Their cavalry was impressive, and in 339 B.C. Philip took back with him twenty thousand mares, a number that confirms the wealth of Dacia. An equal number of young women and children were also taken by the invaders. The king was determined to control this plentiful land and so occupied parts of Moesia, and probably Dobrudja as well.

Some historians believe Philip married Meda (Jordanes named her Medopa), the daughter of Getian king Kothelas (Jordanes named him Gudila, king of the Goths), and that for this reason the takeover was peaceful. One Macedonian corps may have entered Transylvania in search of its gold mines. This would explain why royal coins were suddenly minted in large quantity and with such exceptional quality. The king also rebuilt Eumolpias, an old Thracian settlement on the Hebrus/Maritsa River, and renamed it Philippopolis, known today as the Bulgarian city of Plovdiv.

We do not know how much of the territory of Eastern Europe was occupied by this Macedonian expedition, but in a 339 B.C. battle Philip killed Ateas, the ninety-two year old king of the Scythians. His defeat marked the beginning of the end of the Scythian military power that controlled what is today's Ukraine. Philip's assassination in 336 B.C. did not stop the Macedonians from becoming a world military power. Attracted by the gold, silver, copper, and salt of Dacia, his son Alexander continued the campaign his father had begun.

By defeating Sparta, Alexander, who was already named "the Great," assured his hegemony in the southern Balkans. Now at the age of twenty, the emperor decided to conquer the rest of the peninsula, including Dacia. For that, he already had five thousand Scythian horsemen incorporated into the famous phalanx (a wedge-shaped formation), a tactic that was actually copied from the Scythians. In May 336 B.C. he occupied Thracia, founded Alexandropolis (today's Syrthemeya) as a new capital, and continued to march north.

Because the proud Daco-Getians refused to submit to his will, the young emperor decided to invade their lands and incorporate them into his empire. But in attempting to cross the Danube the next year, he was halted by a large group of Tribalian warriors who lived in the main Dacian lands of what today are Banat and southwest Oltenia. Before facing their invaders, these warriors sheltered their families on the Danubian islands, most likely in what is today the Calafat-Vidin area of Romania. The as yet undefeated Tribalians took a position on the south bank and planned to ambush the Macedonians in a dense forest.

Alexander's scout units detected the trick and lured the Dacian swordsmen out of their protective forest. A few phalanxes cut off their retreat, and the Macedonians slaughtered more than three thousand men. It is not clear if King Syrmos/Syrmus/Sarmis of the Tribalii was among them. The rest escaped to tell the story of this cruel defeat.

Given that he was confronting no other military obstacles, Alexander led his armies to the bank of the Danube. His plan was to build a pontoon bridge, but in that area the great river was flowing too fast; it was also filled with whirlpools. He decided to march downstream and reaching a section which was wide and calm. On the opposite bank, the Dacians with four thousand horsemen and twelve thousand foot soldiers were following the enemy in parallel formation, screaming obscenities at them and further intimidating them with insulting gestures.

The first attempt to cross the Danube did not succeed for the Macedonians: no bridge could be built under the rain of arrows hurled at them by the native bowmen. Crossing the great river with primitive boats would have caused Alexander's troops to be decimated. He therefore planned an ingenious assault—he provided his men with rafts made of animal skins inflated with hay (an Assyrian invention from the eighth century B.C.). Under the cover of night some fifteen hundred cavalrymen and four thousand infantrymen crossed the Danube and took cover in fields containing tall grain. Among them was Alexander, who led an early morning attack against the Dacian camp at what is now Zimnicea.

His men had difficulty flattening the grain with their spears in order to create a path for the few phalanxes of three hundred soldiers each. Utterly surprised by such a massive silent invasion, the Dacians retreated into the mountains, taking with them their families and the rest of the population from the fortified villages. The important fortress located only miles from the Danube and marked by Ptolemaios with the name "Getae," the city of the Getians, was also quickly abandoned. The vengeful invaders plundered and burned it, razing it to the ground.

Meanwhile, the Macedonian fleet had sailed from Byzantium along the coast of the Black Sea, entered the Danube, and dropped anchor near today's Giurgiu in Romania. Having received these newly arrived re-enforcements, Alexander led his phalanxes into Dacia. He was pleased to find there a population clad not in animal furs, but in fine wool and linen, living in well built settlements. The emperor saw that the Daco-Getians did not belong to the barbarian world he so detested.[10]

With his intact army moving unopposed along the Danube, Alexander set up a military camp and wisely waited for the news to reach all the tribes of Dacia and Getia. The first to come and ask for peace were the already defeated Tribalians. Their proud, tall, and handsome envoys were not impressed by the stocky young prince who behaved in keeping with his position—arrogantly.

Alexander was, however, impressed by the collection of fine swords and the peace proposal the Tribalians offered him. He was aware of their Celtic heritage and also of their reputation for fearlessness and so asked them what they feared the most. The envoys answered that they were afraid of only one thing—that the sky would fall on their heads. Alexander reflected on this statement in silence, anticipating the hard battles against these unafraid warriors that might await him. Eventually, after having received numerous gifts and focused on his other military priorities, he continued his military expedition in the opposite direction, toward the tribes of the Ionian and Adriatic coast. Simultaneously, he ordered only one expeditionary corps to head toward the Black Sea.

The Macedonian commanders had accurately estimated the intensity of the rivalry between the cities of Callatis, Histria, and Tomis and so were able to overtake them without a fight. Instead, they promised economic advantages—lower taxes, free trade, and military protection. After collecting a substantial tribute, Alexander ordered the foundation of Axiopolis to be built on the Dacian Danube bank (today the city of Cernavoda in Romania). Satisfied with the results of his peaceful expedition, he moved his troops south to invade Asia. Overall, however, his invasion of Eastern Europe turned out to be a military failure, and the peoples of Dacia and Getia continued to live their lives as they previously had done.

Macedonian hegemony was now assured in most of the Balkans, and the young emperor was free to engage in what became his legendary biblical conquests and move towards India. He proceeded to establish one of the largest empires the world had ever seen. He partially conquered three continents and destroyed the empire of Darius III; still, he never united the people he ruled, primarily because he died prematurely in 323 B.C. The history of his military campaigns has, however, provided mankind with a wealth of information about the ancient world.

Due to their somewhat remote geographic location, the Dacians were not forced to confront the large imperial armies that destroyed each other in endless wars. Meanwhile, the wars between the Persians and the Greeks resulted in glorious victories and major defeats for both sides, but did not affect the Dacians. Moreover, numerous deserters from these embattled armies found refuge in Dacia.

Left by Alexander to govern Thracia, General Zopyrion was also lured by the lands north of the Danube and, in 331 B.C. he attempted to continue Macedonian expansion. He led his phalanx of thirty thousand men beyond the Prut River into Eastern Dacia (today's Republic of Moldova and western Ukraine), where Sarmatian and Scythian warriors had dispersed themselves, and attacked the fortress of Olbia. It was a hollow victory, though, because the brutal Scythian winter killed most of Macedonian soldiers stationed in Eastern Europe. Those who retreated were massacred by the Getians, and the ambitious general was killed as well.

Lysimachus, a former body guard of Alexander, took over the Thracian lands and in 308 B.C. founded Lysimachia as its new capital. (It is located in modern Gallipoli in the Gulf of Saros, Greece.) Proclaiming himself the king of Thracia, he lost no time in assuming full possession of the Getic shore after he occupied the cities of Callatis, Odessus, Histria, and Tomis. When the first three revolted, the king and his Macedonian troops, aided by the Thracians, crushed the rebels.

This defiant action infuriated King Dromichete/Dromichaites, who reigned over southern Moldova and part of what are today Romanian Wallachia/ Muntenia, Baragan, and Dobrudja. This area comprised almost half of the Dacian territory. His kingdom was densely populated and mostly held together by a strong and homogeneous tribal army; it struck back and liberated these four cities. This historical fact alone suffices to prove that the Daco-Getians were not Thracians; they were never allies, nor did they share a common land.

Such aggressive impudence made Lysimachus determined to begin a campaign to recover the possessions he had lost and, furthermore, to conquer the entire Dacian territory. When, in 291 B.C., the Thraco-Macedonian army crossed the Danube, it was brutally defeated by the Dacians who captured the king and his son. They were treated royally; still, the humiliated Lysimachus was freed only after the Macedonians agreed to stop harassing the Getians and after Dromichete married Lysimachus's daughter.

At the same time as the successors of Alexander were busy destroying each other and the Macedonians were fighting factional wars, the Daco-Getians remained free. They continued to use their gold and salt as bargaining chips in their negotiations to retain control of the Danube and the Black Sea territories. But who were the Thracians, a name Jordanes practically ignored in his Gothic history?

The Thracians (who had more than 150 tribal locations) were the other powerful Balkan people living south of the Haemus (Balkan) Mountains. Ancient historians believed them to be closely related to the Dacians—possibly their parent tribe. Thus in many historical documents, the Thracian name replaced that of Daco-Getians in order to avoid complicated explanations as to who was who in the lands north of Greece and Macedonia.

This misnomer was widely accepted until Strabo (63/64 B.C.-ca. A.D. 24) clearly stated that "Thracians...settled in Boetia" (in central Greece) and that "Pieria and Olympus and Pimpala and Leibethrum were in ancient times Thracian places and mountains, though they are now held by the Macedonians."[11] Nevertheless, "certain parts of Thessaly [were held] by the Thracians"[12] and the Thracians also held much of Macedonia[13]. During Homeric times, the latter was referred to as Thrace.[14] Also their land covered "the Thracian Chersonesus which forms the Propontis and the Melas Gulf and the Hellespont [Dardanelles]; for it is a cape which projects towards the southeast, thus connecting Europe with Asia by the straight, seven stadia wide."[15] Furthermore, the Sea of Marmara was nicknamed the Thracian Bosporus, and the Aegean Sea was called the Thracian Sea. In fact, some of the Thracian tribes "crossed over into Asia and their name was changed to Phryges."[16]

All of this supports the claim that the land of the Thracians was mostly in what are today's Greece and Turkey, not in Moesia, which is now Bulgaria. Certainly the Thracians did not live in the Daco-Getian areas. Strabo's work therefore confirms that the Thracians did not extend north of the Haemus Mountains since he cites their territorial aim to have been domination of Greece, Macedonia, the straits of the Aegean, and the Sea of Marmara.

Because these were times in which there was some amount of migration, it is reasonable to assume that some Thracians could have been living in Moesia and south of the Danube, but that most of their twenty-two tribes (identified by Strabo) were settled on the southern tip of the Balkan Peninsula or across the Sea of Marmara in Asia Minor. That is why the Greek historians were so familiar with their name and excluded others that were less known.

In the middle of the sixth century A.D., historian Jordanes, a Gothic military secretary of an Alani tribe who had strong Gothic ties, accurately documented the extension of the Getian land south of the Danube: "Our ancestors called his [King Telefus's] kingdom Moesia. This province has on the east the mouths of the Danube, on the south Macedonia, on the west Histria and on the north the Danube."[17] There is, however, no mention in his text of Thracia which never ruled Moesia. The latter was later named Dacia Aureliana and Dacia Ripensis by the Romans.

Fifteen hundred years later, the British historian Arnold J. Toynbee (1889-1975) defined Thrace as the southeastern portion of the Balkan Peninsula, home of "the Thracian-speaking people who once extended from Silesia to the Upper Tigris basin."[18] They seem to have expanded from Western Europe in the direction of Asia Minor rather than toward Eastern Europe. They certainly did not have any common heritage or genetic pool with the Daco-Getians, and were definitely not their original parent tribe.

Finally, Mircea Eliade (1906-1986), the great Romanian religious thinker, dedicated an entire chapter of his work to the Thracians, "great anonyms" of history; he alternates between discussing them and Daco-Getians. Since he was a product of the rigid Romanian school of history in which the words and ideas of professors were written in stone, he assumed that Thracians came to the Balkans from the Ukraine before the Bronze Age. That was the established theory at the time; it was also held that the Daco-Getians were part of the Thracian tribal family. Eliade was not interested in challenging this assumption.

Like other historians, he heavily relied on Herodotus, but was open enough to admit that around 335 B.C. Alexander the Great:

> ...crossed the Danube to conquer and subdue the Daco-Getians. The failure of his campaign allowed these Thracian tribes to remain independent and to improve their national organization. While the southern Thracians were defini-

tively integrated into the orbit of Hellenism, Dacia did not become a Roman province until A.D. 107. An equally unfortunate destiny seems to have pursued the religious creations of the Thracians and Daco-Getians.[19]

In a few words, Eliade made clear that the Daco-Getians lived across the Danube, and "these Thracian tribes" which were not part of Thracia remained free, while the real Thracians had been absorbed into Hellenism. Obviously Thracia and its people had lost their national identity, while Dacia (he neglected to specify that it was a fraction of this country) was occupied by Romans in A.D. 107. (He also neglected to take into account the fact that the occupation lasted only 165 years.) What Eliade did make clear was that Thracians and Daco-Getians had distinctive religions, a crucial criterion for establishing the separate identity of two breeds of people in ancient times.

So, historical evidence indicates that the Dacians and their tribal cousins, the Getians, lived in *Getarum Terra*, as Strabo named the vast geographic regions along the Danube. This land proved to be an inviting ground for the Celts, Greeks, Romans, Thracians, and numerous barbarian tribes migrating in search of resources to plunder and better living conditions. However, as noted, when they crossed certain boundaries, they all had to confront the Dacians—the only people powerful enough to block population movements through Eastern Europe.

As many historians recorded and as Strabo substantiated, the Scythians were the masters of Eastern Europe up to the second century B.C. when numerous Sarmatian tribes flooded the steppes between the Don and Bug rivers. The result was that the Dacians had to contend with new nomadic neighbors that kept pushing each other out, producing a ripple effect south along the coast of the Black Sea. In a short period of time, the two ethnic populations intermingled and joined in a common mission—repelling the advancing Roman armies.

Prior to this, the military power in ancient Europe since 400 B.C. was concentrated in the hands of the Celtic tribes (Keltoi/Celts) who eventually migrated to the regions now known as Austria, Belgium, France, Hungary, Spain, and southern Germany. They were the first farmers to use the plow and enrich their soil with fertilizer (from animal droppings); they also had a crop rotation system. Yet, despite the technological advances and their relatively high level of civilization, they left no written record of their culture. Still, they are known to have been the first Europeans to use horses in their wars, and the first to make horseshoes, the purpose of which was to help their horses endure longer marches and charge with greater speed on the battlefield.

The Celts were extremely proud of their horses and famous for the number and quality of their cavalry outfits. Fanatical fighters who shouted mightily as they charged, they were the most feared people in ancient Europe. They attacked and devastated Rome in 390 B.C. Their leader, Brennus, agreed to leave the city only after he received 500 kilograms/1,102 pounds of gold as tribute.[20] They may have left Rome to the Romans, but the Celts nevertheless controlled the Italian Peninsula for the next forty years; they then headed toward the Balkan Peninsula.

In 279 B.C. their invading tribes entered Illyria, defeated the Macedonians, dashed over Thrace, and settled in Greece. For the next one hundred years, this takeover proved to have been a mixed blessing. By entering Transylvania, the Celts had an enormous impact on Dacian life at social and economic levels. They reshaped the tribal nation by applying their mining skills, making weapons, and instituting new social rules. However, only so many Celts could settle in Dacia before its name would need to change to *Celtia*. Soon, the Dacian tribes asserted themselves and controlled the unwanted migration of Celts with firm combat.

Up to this point in time, the combined military force of the Dacian tribes continued to keep the migratory barbarian tribes at a respectful distance. The fluvial road of the Danube made it possible for the Dacians to remain in economic contact with the rest of Europe, and also helped them dominate the neighboring territories. It also served as a means of ingress for invaders who moved eastward following the winding route of the great river that split Europe in half.

The first major attempt to organize the tribes of all the Dacian territories was initiated in 170 B.C. by Rubobostes, who reigned in Wallachia and Dobrudja. Judging by his name, this king was a Celtic chieftain who became a Dacian leader; his nickname, "Glorious Tumult," further evidenced the powerful impact of the Celts in Dacia.

Since he was well aware of the benefits of uniting the many diverse tribes who could then defend the rich Carpathians, the king led his warriors into Transylvania. Through a combination of force and persuasive argument, Rubobostes convinced this population to cooperate for the common good and established the first major alliance of the Dacian tribes. It transformed the Dacian farmers and hunters into regimented archers and cavalry, and resulted in an army strong enough to prevent the Celts, Greeks, Macedonians, Thracians, and Romans from moving into Dacia. Rubobostes would soon raise Dacia to the level of a major European power. He fought the Bastarni and forced them towards the Prut River, but he accepted the Celtic Dardani and Scordici who guarded the Danubian line of Pannonia and eastern Moesia.

After his death at the end of the second century B.C., Dacia continued to be a power that garnered respect both north and south of the Danube River. When the Romans began their expansion into the Balkan Peninsula, conquering Greece, Macedonia, and Thracia by the middle of second century B.C., they began to gradually move along the Black Sea into the Dacian territories. In no time, they considered Moesia open for colonization and built military posts there in order to control the land. In 109 B.C., the Dacians raided the Roman settlements, and, defeating the cohorts of Minucius Rufus that had been sent to push them beyond the Danube.

Fifty years later, King Burebista (r. 70-44 B.C.) conquered the city of Histria, which by now was almost a "porto franco" state owned by rich Greek merchants and the remaining nobility of Lysimachus. Thus, Histria became permanently incorporated into Dacia. This conquest brought Roman retaliation, and, in 71 B.C., Marcus Terentius Varro (involved in the defeat of Spartacus' army) led a punitive expedition that recaptured the commercial cities of Apollonia, Callatis, Histria, and Tomis. The Dacians retaliated ten years later and defeated Antoninus Hybrida near Histria.

In 60 B.C., Burebista, who was determined to bring the entire western Black Sea shore under Dacian rule, carried out a speedy and bold campaign against Olbia/Olbiopolis, a wealthy commercial city dominated by Greek merchants. After a sweeping military strike, his troops occupied the 48 x 64 kilometer/30 x 40 mile heavily populated Olbian territory, thereby extending the Dacian borders to the west bank of the Bug River.

The Dacian warriors used their military might to control the fortified cities in Pannonia, including Zemplin and Zidovar among others, and attacked the Celtic tribes that had expanded their settlements in the lands toward the Black Sea. In a short time, the Dacians imposed their conditions on the Anarati, Boii, Eravisci, Pannoni, Scordisci, and other Celtic tribes who could no longer consider themselves the masters of the land. Branches of these super-tribes had previously settled in Western Dacia. Yet many tribes of Breuci and Sagestani close to the Illyrians remained defiant and sealed off access to the Adriatic Sea for the Dacians.

After defeating so many Celtic tribes, and after his military engagements culminated in his victory at Nezider Lake in today's Slovakia, Burebista annexed more territories in the direction of Moravia. Then he subdued his most competitive military foe—Upper Thracia. Thus, half of the length of the Danube and all of Moesia above the Haemus Mountains were under Dacian domination. Now, the dense Dacian population of the Pannonian flats and also Moesia were under the reign of Burebista. The melting pot of Dacia had come about on the battlefield.

Burebista's decisive victories attracted the attention of General Pompey, who sought refuge in Thracia and asked Rhescuporis, king of the Sapei tribes, to help him defeat Caesar. Once again, there is room for speculation regarding the role of General Varro, Pompey's supporter and adviser, in dealing with the Dacians. Varro had demonstrated his military power along the Danube line and had already convinced the Illyrians and other tribes to be allies of Rome. He probably had promised the Dacians that all the cities in Dobrudja, some of which were occupied by the Romans, would be returned to Burebista if the king joined the anti-Caesar coalition.

Meanwhile, the Thracians were courted by Marcus Antonius (Marc Antony), another example of the rivalry between the Dacians and Thracians. This could also be the reason why General Gaius Antonius Hybrida, Antony's uncle, led a punishing campaign against the Getians from Dobrudja. His army contained a sizable number of Thracians, to whom the Danubian territories were promised. But the general was defeated, and Burebista entered into an agreement with Pompey who refused to help the Thracians.

Burebista sent Acornion, an envoy of Greece living in Dacia, from Dionysopolis (Balchik in today's Bulgaria) to negotiate an armed alliance with Pompey, who had his military camp near Heraclea Lyncestis. It is likely that the proposals offered by the Dacian king were accepted by Pompey, and Burebista traveled with his court and warriors to meet the great Roman general, probably in the middle of Moesia. It was a shrewd but risky move for such a ruler, essentially a publicity stunt. He wined and dined the man he believed to be the future Roman emperor. The event would consolidate his leading position among all the Dacian tribes, provided that Pompey was indeed victorious.

In so far as he met with Pompey, Burebista also gained another ally against the Thracians and consolidated his status in the Balkan Peninsula. Regardless of the outcome of the battles between the Caesarian and Pompeian legions, the Dacians had no reason to worry that the power of Rome would affect them. Their more immediate worry was the movement of German tribes towards Dacia. They were coming from the Scandinavian Peninsula and Baltic and had already forced the Celts toward Britannia and central Europe.

In the second century B.C., Germany's population was comprised of countless tribes; records show that there were as many as forty in regions where the people spoke a proto-Germanic language. As this name indicates, they were a large ethnic family who stood out from the other barbarians because of their physical build and their ways of living and fighting. Jordanes wrote that "part of them who held the eastern region and whose king was Ostrogotha, were called Ostrogoths, that is, eastern Goths, either from his name or from the place. But the rest were called Visigoths, that is, the Goths of the western country."[21] More accurately, the Ostrogoths built a vast empire from the Don to the Dniester in what is today the Ukraine, and the Visigoths advanced towards the Danube River. But the true land of Germania was between the Vistula and Rhine rivers.

Soldiers by birth, the Germans worshipped their freedom and were ready to die to defend it. Slavery was unknown to them, and they did not impose it on others. Violent and predatory, but proud, honorable, and loyal, they were reliable fighters who soon set a high standard for bravery and dignity. These blond giants with their attitude of fierce determination frightened the smaller, dark, and agitated Italians when they met. The results of numerous battles confirmed this first impression.

The Germans did not exploit their iron resources, nor were they were skilled workers, hence their main weapons were the mace, the javelin, and the shield. Happy to die fighting, they did not consider withdrawing from the battlefield. Those who were forced to retreat or could not defend their leaders escaped disgrace by committing suicide, "to put an end to this infamy" as Tacitus (ca. 56-ca. 117) put it. Indeed, fighting in retreat was considered a full defeat, and the Germans killed their own families before killing themselves in order to not be taken prisoner.

War was their main job, as the names of their tribes indicated — Alemanni (all men), Cattani (armed men), Franks (freemen), Saxons (axmen), and so on. Tribes of Teutons and Cimbri could raise a military force of more than a million, and they did so, thereby destroying an entire Roman army at Arausio (Orange) in 105 B.C. Fifty years later, Caesar could not have defeated the Celts if he had not hired the German cavalry, and, in 71 B.C. he had to fight hard to push the invading Suebi Germans out of Gaul.

During peacetime, the men were hunters, drank beer, and produced charcoal that they sold at a large profit to the Romans. The Germans did not have buildings or well-built houses. They also did not have cities, fortified towns, strongholds, and forts. Their families lived in leather tents, log huts, or pit houses. They dressed in the skins of animals. German boys were raised to be warriors, and girls to become devoted wives and mothers. Polygamy was unknown in German society. Impressed by such virtue, Tacitus concluded that "marriage is considered as a strict and sacred institution"[22] and secured by rigid rules. For all their virtues and faults, the German tribes proved to be a formidable fighting force that no other European power wanted to challenge.

The kingdom of the Marcomanni, which gradually encompassed today's Bohemia and Moravia, was close to the Dacian border. As the name "marching men" indicated, these Germans, together with others, were always busy with new invasions. The Marcomanni eventually pushed the Celtic Boians/

Boii toward Dacia, where they settled. Tacitus described the tribe of the Cattani as the most robust and brave of people. They occupied the land from the Hercynian Forest adjoining Dacia and they proved to be friendly neighbors. Intermarriages between the Germans and Sarmatians who lived west of the Theiss (Tisza/Tisa) River created a distinctive tribe called the Venedians, who settled in Western Dacia. East of the Prut River, the German Bastarni/ Bastarnians occupied what is today eastern Bessarabia. And, still more German tribes found their way to prosperous Dacia, which made use of their military skill and power for defensive purposes.

As noted, intermarriages between the Celts and Germans produced the powerful tribe of the Bastarni. In the first half of the second century B.C., the Daco-Getian king Oroles (the Eagle) led an effective campaign to stop their westward invasion across the Prut River and the Danube Delta. His victory established the Dacian border beyond the Dniester.

All in all, many Celtic and Germanic tribes found good shelter in Dacia and became a solid component of its society and military establishment.

The assassination of Pompey by Caesar's supporters in Egypt ended the period in which Rome was positively disposed toward the Dacians. Varro, who was one of the most brilliant minds of his time (he authored more than six hundred books about history, science, agriculture, medicine, and music) was involved with the assassination; he was subsequently forgiven by Caesar who named him the head librarian of Rome. The Dacians and their king Burebista were now declared enemies of the Italic republic.

After seizing power, Caesar tripled the number of permanent professional soldiers in the Roman army to thirty-three legions. By doubling their payment to 225 dinari a year and offering them a share of the war booty, he gained their loyalty. He was determined to transform the Roman republic into an empire with a militarized government. To that end, he assumed a dictator-like role that allowed him to strengthen his powers of leadership both within and beyond its borders and to boost the Roman economy through successful military campaigns.

To extend his imperial influence into Eastern Europe, Caesar colonized the shore of the Black Sea. The mission of these colonists was to populate the cities which had been conquered by Rome and build new commercial outposts in grain-rich Getia and Scythia. In order to protect marine transports to Rome, he hunted pirates and crucified them. These commercial advances undoubtedly opened up a path for military expansion. In essence, Caesar intended to transform the Black Sea into a Roman lake. But his dream of a Pax Romana came up against the Dacians who were determined to pre-empt any possible invasion of their lands.

Burebista's Getian cavalry stormed and partially destroyed the Roman colonies of Harpis and Tyras. Much to Rome's surprise and indignation, the Roman and Greek trade from those regions continued to be strictly controlled and taxed by the Dacians. Such economic restrictions and military conflicts could not be overlooked by Rome. It clearly saw that Dacia was in competition with its imperial power and with its intention to dominate the Danube and Eastern Europe. These two military powers therefore quickly found themselves on a collision course.

When additional Celtic tribes invaded Transylvania in 60 B.C., thus threatening to take over its riches, they were crushed by Burebista who led an army of two hundred thousand men. Even if this number is another historic exaggeration and a product of legend, it is clear that the Dacian army was strong enough to chase the unwanted Celts out of what are today Hungary, Czechoslovakia, and part of Austria.

They destroyed all Celtic resistance along with their fortifications all the way to the foothills of the Alps and proceeded as far as the shore of Lake Constantza in Helvetia (Switzerland). This marked the end of the Celtic domination in southeast and Eastern Europe. For all these achievements, Acornion named Burebista "the first and the greatest of the Thracian [*sic*] kings." In order to be eligible for this title, Burebista probably also had to conquer parts of Thracia.

Given all of these victories in adjacent territories, he was able to create a mini-empire that was feared by Caesar. The Daco-Getian kingdom measured more than 2,000 kilometers/1,243 miles in circumference and extended from the Bug River to Vindobona (Vienna), from the Tisza River in the north to the Haemus Mountains in the south, and to the Black Sea.[23] The Dacians controlled or influenced the vast territories from the Hercynian forest of Bohemia to Apollonia in the south of Thrace (now the Bulgarian city of Sozopol), and from modern Lvov to Prague and Varna (Odessus). Because of its geographical size, Dacia was the second largest empire in Europe and the continent's third military power after the Romans and Germans.

Caesar, the ultimate conqueror of Gaul, saw the rise of the Dacian kingdom as an enemy that had to be destroyed before it became bigger and stronger. He had already made plans to invade Dacia and thereby extend Roman control beyond the Danube, which was then the border of the unknown barbarian world. His assassination stopped that military campaign in the making. Shortly thereafter Burebista was assassinated as well. This resulted in Dacia's being divided into many principalities. By the year A.D. 1 both of these adversarial powers were in a state of civil war and faced uncertain futures

One might think that by this point in time historians had a thorough knowledge of the lands and peoples of Eastern Europe. Yet Strabo, who wrote forty-three encyclopedic books and redesigned the world map, proved the contrary. In his *Geography* of eight volumes he described his adventurous trips beyond the familiar northern borders of Greece in the mythical manner of Homer, Herodotus, and others of his illustrious predecessors. From the start he hugely exaggerated, proclaiming, for example, that the Pontic (Black) Sea was "the largest of the seas in our part of the world" and even calling it a "Second Oceanus."[24]

He connected the "one-eye Cyclopes" with the history of Scythia which he placed above India to the east of the Mare Caspium (Caspian Sea). The latter he named Hyrcanian; he took it to be connected with a northern sea. In fact Scythia marked the end of Strabo's world. In one of his most complicated narrations, he placed the Maeotic people and the Sarmatians between the Hyrcanaian Sea and the Pontus as far east as the Caucasus. The countries of Scythians, Hyrcanians, Parthians, Bactrians Achaens, Zygians, and Heniochians were "beyond the Hyrcanian Sea." He listed names which are equally barbarian and exotic sounding, many of which never entered into any other historical records.

It is obvious that Strabo had a great deal of knowledge of the Greek and Roman world around the Mare Internum (Mediterranean). But once he crossed the Danube, he began to duplicate the errors of Herodotus and Thucydides, both of whom he greatly respected. Because of its geographical position, Dacia was not very accessible to Strabo; he inaccurately described numerous families of tribes and their movements around that land.

To his credit, the famous ancient geographer showed the rivers Tanais (Don), Borysthenes (Dnieper), and Ister (Danube) merging into the Palus Maeotis (Azov) and Pontus Euxinus seas and contoured their lines with reasonable accuracy. He placed Olbia City on the Borysthenes since he missed the real river, Hypanis. He called the Danube Delta "breasts," as the sailors did, and mentioned "the Scythian desert" in the same context.

Strabo generously made the Dnieper River a border of "the country of the northernmost Celts,"[25] when, in actuality, it was the land of Sarmatian Roxolani tribes whom he believed to be "the most remote of the known Scythians."[26] He called their cold and uninhabitable land a "Scythico-Celtic zone," even though one of these nations was in the east and the other in central Europe. Moreover, he called the Scythians by the name of "Saka" and believed Dacia to be their homeland. Strabo named the Sarmatians "Sauromati" and scarcely distinguished them from the Scythians. Despite his misconceptions, however, he did correctly understand that Eastern Europe was formed of a complex and diversified federation of tribes.

While Strabo rarely mentioned Dacia or the Dacians by name, following the trend of the Greeks who referred to them as the Getae/Getan, he correctly located them south of the Ister (Danube River). He was surprised that earlier geographers "were completely ignorant of Iberia and Celtica; and vastly more ignorant of Germany and Britain, and likewise of the countries of the Getans and the Bastarnians."[27] Overall, however, his *Geography* was a valuable source when it came to documenting the importance of the Celts, Getians, Germans, Sarmatians, and Scythians in the making of Eastern Europe.

Fifty years later, Pliny the Elder (A.D. 23-79), an admiral of the Roman navy and a prolific writer of history, took an interest in the Sarmatians, whom he believed to belong to the Scythian family. He had no doubt that the Getians were another Sarmatian tribe that lived in the Danube Delta and south of it.

Seventy-five years later, astronomer Ptolemy (the English name for Claudius Ptolemaeus, (A.D. 90-168) who lived in Alexandria, which was still the epicenter of the scientific community, decided to update and correct the map of the world. A brilliant mathematician and researcher, he created a geographical guide that lasted for the next thousand years and served as the ultimate authority in cartography. His famous world map was a sensation in A.D. 150. It showed distant lands and seas with unusual names. Moreover, his approximations of longitudes and latitudes framed Europe's nations, mountains, and rivers with a surprising near accuracy.

The name of Dacia had the distinction of being printed on this map with the largest letters, thereby marking for posterity the outstanding land of Eastern Europe. The Carpathian Mountains were not shown, but Dacia (after the Roman occupation) was correctly indicated as being bordered by the Mare Ponticum (Black Sea), the Danubius (Danube), the Tyrase (Dniester), and the Tibiscus (Timis) rivers. The names of other lands surrounding Dacia are clearly printed: Moesia Inferior and Superior to the south above Thracia and Macedonia; Dalmatia, Pannonia Inferior and Superior with the Iazygi as the western neighbors; and Eurasia to the northeast of Dacia. The map shows that the Romans possessed quite an accurate geographical awareness of the size and components of their empire. But, once again, the lands beyond its borders remained shrouded in a foggy approximation of myths and legends.

On Ptolemy's map, Eastern Europe began east of Germania, and the Vistula River is shown to flow perpendicularly into the Oceanus Germanicus (the Baltic Sea). Parallel and farther east above Dacia were the Carpatus (Carpathian Mountains) and Borysthenes (Dnieper River), meeting the Hypanis (Bug River), both flowing into the Black Sea next to the Taurica (Crimea) Peninsula. North of Dacia was Paludes Maeotides (Azov Sea) into which the Tanais River flowed. The river divided Sarmatia into two halves: the European and Asian portions. Ptolemy believed "European Sarmatia is terminated on the north by the Sarmatian Ocean."[28] North of Asian Sarmatia and the Hyrcanum (Caspium) Mare, he showed Scythia. It was at the end of the world as it was then known.

There is no doubt that after the Dacian wars against the Romans, Ptolemy knew exactly where Dacia was situated, but his *Geography* reflected what was known prior to A.D. 104. He stated precisely that the Tyras (Dniester River) separated parts of Dacia and Sarmatia, and "the Axiaces River (Tiligul) flows through Sarmatia not far above Dacia, and from the Carpathian Mountains."[29] He listed the tribes of the Ophlones, Osilici, and Tanaite, identifying them as living by the bend of the Tanis (Don) River, and the tribes of Amadoci, Carpiani, Chuni, and Navari, as located in Sarmatia near the Dacian border.

He went on to provide a startling demographic description of Dacia's eastern neighbors: "The greater Venedae races inhabit Sarmatia along the entire Venedicus bay; and above Dacia are the Peucini and the Bastarnae; and along the entire coast of Maeotis are the Iazygi and Roxolani; more toward the interior from these are the Amaxombi and the Scythian Alani."[30]

Actually, many of these tribal formations were long residents of Dacia, which was now beyond the geographic limits of Roman rule, and so they were free Dacians. In fact, the Peucini and Bastarnae/ Bastarni belonged to the same Germanic tribal family that had already been identified by Tacitus as living between the Carpathian Mountains and the Black Sea, below the Sarmatian border.

Also part of the Dacian federation were the Carpi/Carpiani, one of the original tribes, as well as the Sarmatian cousins, the Roxolani and Alani, none of whom were Scythians. Ultimately the great Ptolemy was nearly as confused as his predecessors over the ethnic diversity of the many overlapping names of Eastern European tribes. One thing was for sure: a large area around Dacia was inhabited by multi-ethnic tribes who maintained a close and submissive relationship with the powerful Dacians.

During Ptolemy's time, the Roman Empire had been extended across many lands and seas. Eastern Europe was targeted as the next vast region to be acquired. But, that was not going to happen. Barbarian hordes from Asia were stampeding toward Dacia and the Balkan Peninsula with alarming speed and power. And, above and beyond all those who would battle and conquer, there was the peaceful expansion of Christianity. It proved stronger than any form of military domination and shaped a new history for the Roman Empire and Europe.

NOTES

1. Arnold J. Toynbee and Edward D. Myers, *A Study of History*, vol. 11, *Historical Atlas and Gazetteer* (London: Oxford University Press, 1959), 122, map 24.

2. Herodotus, *The History*, trans. David Grene (Chicago: University of Chicago Press, 1987), map 294-295, 4.24.

3. Herodotus, *History*, 4:51-57.

4. Jordanes, *The Gothic History of Jordanes*, ed. and trans. Christopher Charles Mierow (Cambridge: Speculum Historiale, 1966), 61.

5. Jordanes, *Gothic History*, 62.

6. Jordanes, *Gothic History*, 30.

7. Jordanes, *Gothic History*, 63.

8. A cuneiform inscription from this period was discovered in modern Transylvania, thereby raising the question of whether Persians did indeed invade the Dacian territories. The prevailing view is that this clay table could have been brought there at a later date by a Roman officer who inherited it or that it was simply brought and left there as an antique souvenir from another place.

9. Jordanes, *Gothic History*, 65.

10. The irony was that Alexander was considered barbarian by the Greeks, who did not allow him to compete in the Olympic Games.

11. Strabo, *The Geography of Strabo*, trans. Horace Leonard Jones (London: William Heinemann; New York: G. P. Putnam's Sons, 1924), vol. 3, bk. 5, 107.

12. Strabo, *Geography*, trans. Jones, vol. 3, bk. 7, 287.

13. Strabo, *Geography*, trans. Jones, Fragments of Book 7, 107.

14. Strabo, *Geography*, trans. Jones, Fragments of Book 7, 349.

15. Strabo, *Geography*, trans. Jones, Fragments of Book 7, 373.

16. Strabo, *Geography*, trans. Jones, Fragments of Book 7, 349.

17. Jordanes, *Gothic History*, 60.

18. Toynbee and Myers, *Study of History*, 71.

19. Mircea Eliade, *A History of Religious Ideas from Gautama Buddha to the Triumph of Christianity*, trans. William R. Trask (Chicago: University of Chicago Press, 1982), 171.

20. Unfortunately, pillage by the Celts destroyed the archives in Rome, leaving only legends and oral history modified by the passage of time as a record of events in ancient Europe.

21. Jordanes, *Gothic History*, 82.

22. Tacitus, *The Germania of Tacitus*, vol. 5, *History*, The Latin Classics (New York: Vincent Parke & Company, 1909), 377.

23. A fortress with the Dacian name of Getidava can be found on the Vistula River in today's Poland.

24. Strabo, *The Geography of Strabo*, ed. G. P. Goold, trans. Horace Leonard Jones, Loeb Classical Library (1917), vol. 3, 77.

25. Strabo, *Geography*, ed. Goold, 277.

26. Strabo, *Geography*, ed. Goold, 441.

27. Strabo, *Geography*, ed. Goold, 357.

28. Ptolemy, *The Geography* (New York: New York Public Library, 1932), bk. 3, chap.5.

29. Ptolemy, *Geography*, bk. 3, chap. 5.

30. Ptolemy, *Geography*, bk. 3, chap. 5.

Chapter Three

The Making of Dacia and Its Leaders

There are no precise records of the ancient Eastern European history of any ethnic group, especially when it comes to tribal names. Sometimes the names of the conqueror and the conquered are interchanged. Tribes may have nicknames which derive from a particular location—a river or a mountain, for example. This can make tracing their origins difficult, particularly if that nickname changed repeatedly. To complicate matters further, over time many of these tribes were later identified under newer names inspired by the ethnic composition of the peoples, their spiritual beliefs, and so on.

When a tribe was invaded or absorbed into a stronger one, it formed a new coalition and the original tribal name was replaced or changed to reflect the new association. Hundreds of years later, the tribe might take back the original tribal name, but most probably a corrupted version of it. So, again written names were changed, mostly by Greeks and Romans, and these corrupted written names were then later copied by others, often erroneously. And of course, the English spelling of the same names make them almost unidentifiable.

The presence of homo sapiens in the Carpathian Mountains (named after the Carpi/Carps tribe—*karpe* meaning "rock") has been traced back thirty thousand years[1]. It has generally been assumed that the Dacian land was later populated by Indo-European migrants.

Many European tribes migrated to the land of India—perhaps because of the biblical floods or the Ice Age, but they never assimilated with the natives there. After 4000 B.C. these Aryans tried to find their way back to their ancestral lands in Europe. Bringing their culture with them, many settled between the Caspian and Black Seas. As was the case in the ancient world, only tribes that were related, shared the same physical characteristics, and had similar languages and religious rituals were accepted in ancestral tribal lands. For this reason, some of these Aryan tribes were welcomed in Dacian areas.

The Dacian lands were inhabited by a mix of ethnic groups that shared a common Carpatho-Danubian ancestry traceable to before the Iron Age of the ninth century B.C. While much remains uncertain about this, we do know that these tribes belonged to the Caucasian race until the Hunic invasion. A number of historians have speculated that the Dacians were a northern branch of the Thracian tribes from the south of Balkan Peninsula or Illyrian migrants from what are today Albania and Montenegro.

Whether there is merit to this or not, it is generally accepted that the original Dacians belonged to the same family of Celtic, Italic, and Germanic mammoth tribes who shared spiritual beliefs that included worship of the wolf and fear of the dragon. In fact, Strabo hinted that name Dacian came from *Dai*, a version of the Phrygian *daos* that meant "wolf." It is possible that their name meant "the wolf people" in the ancient world.

By 500 B.C. many clans and tribes that wandered into this area travelling from the Eurasian steppe toward the Danube were also absorbed into the Dacian population, which was numerous and powerful enough not to be subjugated or eliminated by intruders. The majority of these migrants came from the genetic stock of Iranian Sarmatians (Armed Horsemen), who were gradually pushed out of the Kuban steppes toward Eastern Europe by other invaders. In turn, the Sarmatians chased the Indo-European Scythians (Scythe Armed Men) toward the Crimea and Ukraine. The Scythians then settled between the Borysthenes (Dnieper) and the Hypanis (Bug) rivers in the vicinity of Dacia.

Some wandering Scythian sub-tribes moved along the Black Sea toward the Danube, and others roamed the west coast of the Black Sea and eventually mixed with the native Dacian population below the Danubian Delta.

The Sarmatians proved to be stronger and more numerous that the Scythians, and eventually overtook the Scythian military and economic power. Subsequently, a large number of Sarmatians migrated to Dacia. The Dacians took advantage of the vacuum created by the departing nomadic tribes and extended their control along the Black Sea beyond the Bug River. This takeover was favored by the friendly Sarmatian and Scythian tribes who much preferred lax Dacian control to Greek and Roman rule.

Due to the general inaccessibility of Eastern Europe and the vast distances between its settlements, Greek and Roman historians were able to develop only a vague idea of its geography and population mix. Disregarding what they knew about the ethnic diversity of the tribes and their various locations, historians grouped the Dacians, Getians, Sarmatians, Scythians, and southern

Balkan Thracians together and chose a name for all of them—barbarians, which the Greeks and Romans considered to be uncivilized foreigners.

To complicate things even further, the letter *D* was easily replaced with *Thr*, and in no time the Dacians became Thracians, and the Thracians became Dacians. The Scythians were also called Sacians, many times passing as Dacians. Another case in point is the mixing up of the name Sarmatians with Saurmatians and Suormatians; these were, in fact, three distinct tribes who lived in south Ukraine around the Sea of Azov and as far south as Mesopotamia (Iraq). The same was true for the Celts, who were also referred to as Keltoi, Celtians, Gauls, Galli, and Gaulois, and subdivided into Belgae, Galati, Irish, and so on, depending on the territory in which they lived and the language used to describe them. Apparently each version of their name meant "people in hiding," a term which was also applicable to the Dacians who lived in densely forested lands.

The Dacians, like the Cimmerians and Illyrians, were the aborigines of Eastern Europe; however, due to the inaccuracies in ancient documents and then later to translations which were only approximations of the original, they became a negotiable historical commodity. The Greek view of the name "Dacian" was easily deduced from their definition of the word "slave" as it was used in Athens. Indeed, in the sixth century B.C., Dacians, Thracians, and other members of the Balkan tribes were sold in the slave markets within Greece under the name of their land of origin. A Thracian was also known as a Thraex.

At the time when Greece was expanding northward, Scythian influence reached only as far as the mouth of the Danube and its tributary the Pyretus (Prut) River. Beginning in the second part of the sixth century B.C., many Scythian tribes settled west of the Prut, reaching the Hierasus (Siret) River. They also crossed the Danube into today's Dobrudja, where they some of them settled. This area was sometimes known as Scythia Minor.

The four successive migratory waves of Scythians (most likely the Masogetae from the Maeotian branch described by Herodotus) deeply influenced the genetic composition of the people living in Dacia and created a twin nation of Getae/Getians, who were often mentioned by Greeks traders on the shore of the Black Sea.

The Scythians brought with them advanced weapons like the bow and body armor made of metal. In Dacia, they found raw iron and precious metals, especially gold, upon which they became extremely dependent. Today, Scythian treasures discovered in the Romanian locales Bihor, Cioara (near Turnu Magurele), Craiova, Gorj, Medgidia, Ostrovul Mare, Popestipe Arges, and other locations, evidence the expansion of the Scythians across what was early Dacia.

After 300 B.C. many Sarmatian tribes crossed the Prut River and settled
in what are today the Romanian regions of Bucovina, Maramures, and Moldova, where they occupied the rich land. They were so numerous that in Latin
documents the Eastern Carpathian Mountains were named Montes Sarmatici.
Later, other Sarmatians, forced in from the west by movements of the Celtic
tribes and the Roman armies, migrated to the lower Danube area. Numerous
incoming waves of Sarmatians eventually dissolved the power of the Scythians who were in search of a national identity and so strengthened the genetic
make up of the Dacian people.

Thus many of the Sarmatian and Scythian tribes ended up being dominated
by the Dacians. Together they formed a solid tribal alliance that would evolve
into a national identity. Until the first century B.C. each major group of these
tribes had its own kings or elected leaders who ruled over the tribal chieftains.
These chieftains and kings often fought among themselves over domestic
and political issues and over desirable lands. However, they also functioned
collectively much like the Delian League, and when the Dacian territory was
attacked or invaded, they set aside their differences and united against the
common enemy.

Because it acquired large amounts of territory and came to possess great
military might during the hundreds of years of chaotic and bloody conflicts in
and around the Carpathian Mountains, Dacia became an important player in
the rich and complicated dynamic of ancient Eastern European history. Much
of the credit for this goes to the partial Roman conquest of Dacia in A.D. 106
and to the heroic battles that are documented on Trajan's Column in Rome.

Five main ethnic groups went to make up the Dacian nation: the Greater
Dacians, the Sarmatians, the Scythes, the Celts, and the Germans. A map by
Claudius Ptolemy, the geographer of the ancient world, shows at least twenty-
five major tribes living within the Dacian territory. He grouped them under
the names of Albocensi, Anarti, Arpi, Biephi, Britolagi, Buridensi, Cau-
coensi, Ciagisi, Contensi, Costoboci, Cistoboci, Cribici, Dardani, Dimensi,
Metanasti, Obulensi, Peucini, Piarensi, Picensi, Piephigi, Potulatensi, Pren-
davensi, Ratacensi, Saldensi, Sensi, Tensi, Teurisci, Tricorensi, Trogloditi,
and Iazygi/Iazyges. These tribal names can be found on later maps, but with
minor changes. More precisely, the prefix *es* was inserted in place of the letter
i. For example, Albocensi became Albocenses, or vice-versa. In time, some
tribes received the suffix *oi* that was common in the Dacian language, and
thus the Anarti were known as Anartoi, Costoboci became the Costoboi, and
Carpi were called Carpians.

The names of many other major tribes that also lived in the same area for a
long time can be added to the map of Greater Dacia, including the Ansamensi,

Carpi, Daesi, Geagisoi, Crobizi, Getians, Harpi, Roxolani, and, of course, the super tribe of Magni Daci (Greater Dacians) who occupied what today are Bukovina, Galicia and Maramures. Other early tribes were the Keiasigi, who lived in Central Dacia, and the Apuli, who gave their name to a later Transylvanian capital, Apulum (Alba Iulia). The Anarti, Biephi, and Teurisci tribes were situated in northern Transylvania. Given that Dacia was centered around Transylvania, kings Coson (who minted his own coins), Deceneus, Comiscus, Coryllus/Scorilo/Corylus, and Duras ensured unity, stability, and prosperity of their people around this central land they governed.

The most important and largest tribes of Northern Dacia were the Motsi/ Moetsi (Mo⬜) from the Apuseni Mountains who extended their territories to the Cris, Maramures, Galicia, and Upper Dniester region. A branch of the same tribe, Moesi/Moesians, settled south of the Danube in an area then known as Moesia, now Bulgaria.

Ptolemy clearly indicated a *Mysia superior* and a *Mysia inferior* on his map (well above Thracia), both of which were inhabited by the Moesians. Too often, these people were confused with the Mysians who lived in Mysia, east of Thracian Bosporus, outside of Europe in what is now northwestern Turkey. The Mysians had minimal impact, but the Moesian bloodline continues today in the Aromanians — the estranged Daco-Valachians/Vlahians who still live scattered throughout Albania, Bulgaria, Serbia, and other Balkan countries.

Many of these tribes can be located on earlier maps of Eastern Dacia in what is today the Bacau region; there they were often called Carpo-Dacians. Equally ancient were the Caleti, Rami, and Costoboci who lived in Moldova and southern Ukraine. The Calipizi controlled the land between the Dniester and Bug rivers. King Dicomes of the Getians used those tribes to extend Dacian rule to the line of the Dniester. The tribe of Tyragetae was a well recognized name in the ancient world. Herodotus located them by the River Tyras (Dniester) "that is the border between the Scythian and Neurian countries [the land toward the Belarus]. "At the mouth of it live those Greeks who are called Tyrite."[2] The Tyragetae most probably also spoke Greek because they manned an important commercial port in which Greek was the international language of trade. The likely origin of their abbreviated name, Tyrite, was used in casually spoken Greek. But their real name, Tyragetae, tells exactly who they were — Getians living on the Tyras River. They extended to the coastal land of Dobrudja as had their cousins, the Massagetae, before 500 B.C. In fact, Pliny the Elder mentioned the Tyragetae in his *Naturalis Historia*.

In the southern Dacian province of Dobrudja there lived the tribes of Crobobizi, original Getians. Their King Chranabon was mentioned by Sophocles (ca. 496-406 B.C.) in his play, *Triptolemos*. The Getians became famous because their tribes were the only ones to fight back against the Persian invasion led by Darius toward the Danube River. Herodotus met them and wrote that the Getae were "the bravest...of the Thracians."[3] They were known to have been ruled by capable kings, none of whom were Thracians as Herodotus wrongly assumed. Among these kings were Oroles, who kept the Romans at bay; Rhemaxos, who defeated the Thracian king Zoltes who raided Moesia in 200 B.C.; Zalmogeticus (meaning "Getian wolf"); and Zyraxes who fought the Romans.

In 300 B.C. another Getian King, Dromichetes/Dromichaetes/Dromichaites, defeated and captured Lysimachus (one of Alexander's generals) who was king of Thrace (northern Greece and today's European Turkey) and wanted to extend his land to the Danube. Strabo pointed out that Lysimachus "found the barbarian kind-hearted."[4] After Lysimachus gave up Moesia in favor of Dromichetes, the two former enemies became friends and in-laws, thus perpetuating the myth that Geto-Dacia was the same as Thracia. One hundred years later, rival Getian kings, Roles and Dapyx disputed their reign over Getae, and the Roman General Crassus took advantage of this fact.

The Dacian king, Cotiso (ca. 30 B.C.-ca. A.D. 14) ruled over the Danubian region and northern Thracia in the first century B.C. and A.D. He was so powerful that the king wanted to marry his daughter Julia to the Dacian king. He was often mistaken for Cotys, a Thracian king killed by his uncle Rhescuporis in A.D. 19. Because so many names have been interchanged, historians often assumed there was only one king who ruled over the northern part of the Balkan Peninsula. In reality, the Dacian King Duras (r. 68-87) fought the Romans and their Thracian ally to keep them out of Moesia.

Across north of the Danube in what are today Banat and Crisana there lived the homogenous tribes of Andori, Luggi, Luncani, Potulatenses, Predavensi, Ratacenses, and Seni. In Oltenia, the Suci tribe settled around their main center, Sucidava, near the mouth of the Alutus/Aluta/Olt and the Danube plain. West and east of them were the Saldensi and Ordensi.

Given all of this confusion over which tribes were which and where they were settled, it is easy to understand why researchers and authors, both past and present, are mistaken about many aspects of Dacian and Eastern European ethnic history. The most common mistake is to treat the Balkan and East European people as a single ethnic group.

In time, numerous tribes migrated from Eurasia toward Dacia, including many nomadic Iranian tribes who were attempting to avoid the Huns and other Mongol barbarians. The Sarmatian Alani/Alans (also spelled Alauni by Ptolemy) settled by the Sea of Azov in the third century B.C., only to be pushed west until they arrived in the plentiful area of today's Bessarabia. Their massive migration was promptly halted by the Dacians at the edge of the Prut River. When they found other Sarmatians there, such as the Roxolani, along with the elements required for a stable life, the Alani pledged their loyalty to the Dacians and settled there

This entire region, collectively known as Alania, was separated by the Prut which had been renamed Alanus Fluvius. The Alani proved to be reliable allies of the Dacians and later of the Goths, to such a degree that they came close to being identified as a Germanic tribe.

The Sarmatian Iazygi (tribal cousins of Roxolani), a mighty and numerous group of warriors who forcibly occupied large Dacian areas along the Tisza valley, created a very different set of conditions when they migrated to the area. They temporarily dislocated the native Dacians who had lived there for hundreds of years and thus created irreparable bad blood between the two peoples. Their takeover was brutally challenged and ultimately reversed by King Burebista who broke the fierce opposition of the Iazygi and repossessed the Dacian land. This was a territorial clash that was never forgotten by either of its participants, one that had enormous historical repercussions in later years.

The Sarmatians, who refused to be assimilated into the Dacian culture, settled north and west of the Vistula River in present day Poland in order to avoid another confrontation with the Germans. They became a sort of root that was then grafted onto the Slavic tribes of the later Polish and Belarus nations. The Scythian tribes who refused to become part of the Dacian federation went back to the Don and Volga rivers and became the original Ukrainians, while the Dacianized tribes of Berziti and Drogobeti ended up in what is today Slovenia.

Others, like the Roxolani, co-existed with the Dacians and proved to be their most enduring allies in the face of the ongoing invasions. Their closeness was reflected in the typical Dacian costume that consisted of long, tight pants with a shirt hanging over them like a miniskirt, a woolen mantle, and a long, round sheepskin mantle over the shoulders. The striking resemblance between the native costumes of the Dacians and the Sarmatians demonstrates the interaction of their tribes. Unlike the Dacians, though, the Sarmatian warrior's fish scale armor made of laminated horse hooves that covered their bodies and even their horses made them a distinct and legendary presence on any battlefield.

As previously noted, so many early Sarmatian nomads had been assimilated in Dacia that they dominated northern Moldova. They were also well represented in other parts of Dacia. A golden, ceremonial helmet found in a grave near Bucharest confirms their presence in the Baragan flatland of the Danube. The Dacians, Sarmatians, and Scythians would become immortalized as ancient relatives in sculptures, for they wore the same kind of lamb fur hat with a sharp point folded to one side or forward (similar to that of the Vedic god Mithra). The last king of Dacia, Decebalus (r. A.D. 87-106) is portrayed on the Column of Trajan as wearing such a hat.

The largest portion of the population in ancient Europe was Celtic, with some one hundred twenty-five major tribes that occupied the western section of the continent, mainly Gallia, Iberia, Illyricum, and along the Danube. They were distinguishable from other races by the fact that they were largely built and had reddish hair and light color eyes. There is evidence that their ancestors, known under the names of Daesi, Decies, and Tasi, inhabited a portion of the Tisza River area as early as the Bronze Age; this raises the question of whether Dacia was named after them. Likewise, Celtic tribes such as the Anarti are known to have populated Transylvania since time immemorial.

Always undeterred as warriors, the Celts had a repugnant reputation as headhunters. Their passion for war and conquest led them to storm Rome in 390 B.C., an act that made them the major military power in Europe. Some settled along the Danube, building settlements like Vindobona (Vienna), and many entered Dacia to farm or mine the fertile and metal rich land.

The Tribalii who lived in the Dacian land of Banat and southwest Oltenia (now both in Romania) made history when, led by Syrmos, they opposed Alexander the Great's march across the Danube in 336 B.C. Before confronting the Roman invaders, they sheltered their families on islands in the river. The always victorious Tribalians took a position on the south bank, planning to ambush the Macedonians in a dense forest. Ironically they themselves were ambushed, but there were no further consequences for the remainder of the Tribalii who decided to negotiate with the Macedonians. Their Celtic roots and name faded in time because they were assimilated into the Dacian culture.

The Galatians invaded the Balkans in the third century B.C. After they were forced out of Greece and Macedonia, most of them crossed into central Anatolia. Their offspring, the Caleti, settled south of the Danube River which they named Dunau; they consolidated the settlement of Galati, known today by the same name in Romania.

The diminished power of the Macedonian Empire in the Balkans encouraged the Celts to invade Thracia and Greece in 279 B.C. But their expansion into the Balkan Peninsula was derailed by the Dacians south of the Danube. Eventually, the Celts established a Gallic kingdom in the south. It endured only briefly, and twenty-five years later revolting Thracian tribes pushed them out of the land they had occupied.

Many uprooted Celts then fled to Dacia, which gladly sheltered any enemies of Thracia. Among them were the Scordisci, who took refuge in

Western Dacia along the Danube and founded Singidunum (Beograd/Belgrade). They attempted to forcibly take control of the Dacian territory, but were defeated in 135 B.C. and accepted the terms imposed by King Cosconis. Many Scordisci and Breuci settled in Dacia nevertheless and were eventually absorbed into the local population.

Among numerous Celtic tribes were the Dardani who cohabited with the Illyrians and expanded to form their own kingdom of Dardania; it encompassed parts of what are today Albania, Macedonia, and Serbia. Their offshoots, the Dani and Ardeni, settled in the Ardeal region they called Ardeuna, today's Transylvania.

The Osii, a branch of the Ausci tribe, founded the city of Iasi; the Andori tribesmen founded Hunedoara; the Luggi, the city of Lugoves/Lugos; and the Trinovantes built Tarnova while the Turoni established Turnu, all of which exist today. The name of the Trascau Mountains, derived from the Tevrisci and Tricasses settlers, has persisted as well. The tribe of Branovices founded the Bran (Raven) settlement, which also still exists in Romania. Other Celtic tribes and sub-tribes, such as the Catini/Kotinoi, later settled in the areas rich in malleable metals and became industrious miners.

Under the firm rule of King Burebista, many large Celtic tribes were subdued and became integrated into Dacian culture, among them the Boii (Cattle Owners), who were forced out of Bohemia (Home of the Boii) by the German Cimbri and Teutons. The Boii drifted along the Danube rather than try to return to their homeland. When they tried to claim Dacian land in 40 B.C., they were defeated by Burebista, and they settled in what is today Austria. He also defeated some of the Scordisci tribes and took over the lands south the Drava and Sava rivers in today's Croatia, Dalmatia, and Serbia. The Scordisci, most of them already Dacianized, proved to be most reliable allies.

The eight years of Caesar's destructive campaign in Gaul forced numerous Celtic tribes to find shelter in the Dacian land, out of the reach of Roman occupation. Later, in 9 B.C., other Celtic tribes were displaced from Bavaria, first by the German Marcomani and then by Roman legions led by Drusus the Elder. They, too, safely escaped to Dacia.

By A.D. 1 Dacia contained more than 150 Celtic settlements, many of them located near iron and precious metal mines. While the Apuseni Mountains and the regions of Cris, Mures, and Orastie remained densely populated with the Daci Magni and not with Celts, the Celts left an enduring legacy elsewhere in Dacia. The Celtic Avereni founded Havrina, which is today's Suceava, while a branch of the Carnutes built Cornute, or present-day Cornea.

When the Dacians would not agree to a Celtic takeover, territorial conflicts erupted into battles in fertile areas including Apahida, Aradu Nou, and Ciumesti. Two thousand years later, weapons, shields, and other battle remains were discovered, thereby providing concrete evidence of the armed confrontations between Dacians and Celtic invaders.

A modern excavation in Ciumesti, Romania, revealed a superb helmet with outstretched eagle wings mounted on top of it; it likely belonged to a rich nobleman of the third century B.C. At that time, noblemen and chieftains had golden body armor while that of the soldiers was metallic armor; both types were beautifully ornamented. Around their necks they wore torques, of braided gold or silver. Beautiful inlays of gold and precious stones made their weapons so valuable that warriors would die rather than surrender and hand them over to the enemy.

Despite their reputation as ferocious fighters, the Celts were known to have a mild character. Few territorial conflicts developed within Dacia primarily because the Dacians were busy with salt extraction while the Celts were mining metals, iron ore, but mainly copper. Later the Celts worked the gold and silver mines as well, but mining in general remained under the control of the Dacians.

A segment of the oldest Celtic tribes in Eastern Europe, the Velky (of Belgae origin), mixed with the native Dacian population. Their offspring later became known as Vlahi, Valachi, Valahians, or Wallachians. They extended their territories into the Balkan Peninsula and as far as Bohemia. All in all, the Celtic influence on Dacian life was enormously productive and beneficial to the rest of population.

The Gallo-Germanic invasions of Dacia created a stronger breed of people and capable leaders than might otherwise have developed among the earlier Dacians. Fifty years after these invasions, King Decebalus bore a name that may come from two Celtic words meaning "the legal leader." He became a most able leader and never hesitated to make clear to the Romans and the Thracians who was in charge of the last thousand miles of the Danube and the lands of Moesia. He also had an excellent relationship with the German tribes, and maintained a powerful command over the first Gothic tribe that had arrived in east Dacia. Decebalus used their military striking power to repel many Roman expeditions aimed at the Dacian border. Over a period of twenty years, he waged three wars against the Romans, refusing to accept their imperial domination. And upon losing the last war, he committed an "honorable" suicide, an event that put the Dacians on the map of Europe.

By the beginning of the Christian Era, Dacian history was similar to that of the Germans: both people had proud and unbeatable warriors, and both dominated territories rich in minerals and grains. Likewise, both territories were situated at the northern end of the Roman Empire, delineated by the great Rhine and Danube rivers whose sources were in almost the same geographic location. This natural border provided a vital barrier between the Romans and the barbarians.[5]

Germany's population consisted of countless tribes, forty of which were mentioned in historical records as being in regions where people spoke a proto-Germanic language. Their enormous population could easily provide an army of one million warriors, a military force that gained much respect in Europe. In time and much like the Celts, because of their many territorial disputes, internal strife, and military confrontations with other invaders, many of the Germanic tribes were uprooted and relocated to Eastern Europe.

Prior to the first century B.C., some Germanic tribes had already arrived in the flat fields of Pannonia (Upper Hungary) and entered Western Dacia. Their raids also covered part of Dobrudja and Moesia. Many of these tribes were related by blood to other Germanic tribes already established in Dacia. One of them was the Cauci/Chauci, so large and powerful a group that, for a period of time, some of the Carpathian Mountains were named the Caucaland.

Most probably these people were a branch of the Chaucians, whom Tacitus described in his *Germania* as "the most respectable...and wanting no extension of territory, free from avarice and ambition, remote and happy, they provoke no wars, and never seek to enrich themselves by rapine and depredation."[6] No wonder they were so well received by the Dacians. Later arrivals included a splinter group of the numerous Suevi/Suebi tribes who moved along the Danube and settled in the Banat region and adjacent area of Pannonia.

The Dacians also welcomed the Gothinians for the reason cited by Tacitus—"they submit to the drudgery of digging iron mines."[7] He described them as coming from Gaul and speaking in the Gallic tongue—clearly they were a tribe that was distant from the Germanic Goths who were still in the Ukraine. They were so numerous that the Roman name for the Getians was Gots/Goths, a fact which may prove that their heritage was at least partly Germanic. Most likely, the strong and hard working migrants found immediate employment in Dacia.

While many tribes from central Europe entered the Balkans, the most important of them were the German Bastarni whose invasion from the western Ukraine toward Transylvania was promptly rebuffed by Dacian King Oroles. Around 150 B.C., they eventually settled east of the Siret River, pushing the Celtic Costoboci toward Bukovina and the Sarmatian Roxolani north of the Danube Delta.

Bastarni (spelled Basternae by Ptolemy who placed them "near Dacia") assimilated so well that they became the stable population of Moldova and

Dobrudja, both of which were so often mistakenly identified as being part of Scythia. They proved to be loyal to the Dacian efforts to keep Getia free.

Defeated by the Romans in 30 B.C., the Bastarni were forced to withdraw to an area north of the Danube where they joined the Peucinians (whom some call the Bastarni). They safely lived in the Danubian Peuce region of Dacia toward the end of the last century B.C. and were quickly absorbed into the Roxolani population. Their land above the Danube Delta was called Bastarnia and later became part of Bessarabia, which was frequently misnamed Sarmatia. Their land of Moldau was, in time, renamed Moldova.

Two more German tribes that also settled in Southern Dacia were the Quadzi/Quadians (coming from what is today Bohemia) and the Buri. Eventually the intermarriage between Quadzi and the Celtic Launi resulted in the united tribe of Cataluni. And due to intermarriages between the Germans and Sarmatians who lived west the Tisza, a distinctive tribe called the Venedians settled in Western Dacia.

The Buri founded Buridava (Stolniceni) on the Aluta (Olt) River, a tributary of the Danube. Their rich and powerful settlements became important Danube trading posts and thus part of the Dacian heartland. The Buri had the distinction of providing Dacia with one of its most powerful kings, the previously mentioned Burebista. He probably came from the Buridensi/Buridavensi tribe of the same geographic area, and the translation of his Gothic name was "Brave Heart." He certainly lived up to his name since he created the first Dacian Empire.

The many diverse Dacian tribes were united for the first time by King Burebista who initially ruled over most of what are today Transylvania and Wallachia. He was also feared by Caesar. Until he was assassinated, Burebista labored to extend the borders of Dacia to their maximum length either through negotiations or military campaigns. The Greeks were so impressed with his achievements that they named him "the first and the greatest of the kings of Thracia." Once again, the name of Thracia was substituted for Dacia, ironically because, at that time, Burebista ruled over most of Moesia, some of which was arbitrarily considered part of Thracia.

Strabo, who spelled the king's name as "Boerebistas", provided a glowing description of him as:

> ...a Getan [who], on setting himself in authority over the tribe, restored the people, who had been reduced to an evil plight by numerous wars, and raised them to such a height through training, sobriety, and obedience to his command that within only a few years he had established a great empire and subordinated to the Getae most of the neighboring peoples. And he began to be formidable even to the Romans, because he would cross the Ister [Danube] with impunity and plunder Thrace as far as Macedonia and Illyrian country.[8]

From this brief but credible description, we can draw two conclusions: 1) The Getae, or, as the Romans named them, the Daco-Getians, were not Thracians whose country was pillaged, and 2) Burebista's raiders were allowed easy access through Moesia, which was populated by the Dacians.

Strabo acknowledged that the Celts who united with the Thracians and Illyrians were subdued in the same manner by Burebista as were the Pannoni, Taurisci, Triconeses and the Boii (also known as "milk people"); the latter were pushed eastward by Germans out of what is today the Czech Republic. Tacitus named the Dacians "Boians" and noted they had Critasiros as king.[9]

The list of tribes annihilated by Burebista evidences the fact that they opposed his efforts at unification of Dacia under one ruler. He did not brook any competition, and he controlled at least eighty fortified cities throughout his kingdom. Historical testimonies indicate that Burebista led large and powerful formations of warriors — some sources estimated his army at two hundred thousand, although Strabo cited "an army of forty thousand men,"[10] still an impressive military force.

Burebista conducted raids as far northeast as Olbia in the heart of Eastern Europe and subdued the bellicose Bastarni as well as many Sarmatians and Scythian tribes. He also swept south of the Danube, bringing all of Moesia under his control. This was an easy task since the population was Daco-Getian and did not want to be ruled by the Greeks, Romans, and Thracians.

These things having been said, it is now necessary to discuss at greater length the difference between Dacians and Thracians, two groups who were erroneously and almost universally believed to be the same people. The Dacians and Thracians were never "eternal brothers," as they have often been described by historians. Some historians have even classified the tribes of Dacians, Getians, and Thracians under the single name of "Pelasgi/Pelasgians," who inhabited the Aegean regions before the Hellens, an obvious misnomer because there was never a Pelasgic Empire in the Balkans. Also, the Dacians and Getians were most certainly not Greeks who came from Ahei, Eolieni, Dorien, and Ionieni.

If the colloquial Latin word for "Goths" was *Getae*, then Getians could have been a Dacianized branch of an ancient Germanic tribe. The tall, blue-eyed, and blond-haired Getians certainly fit that genetic background. The Dacians came from the same Aryan background as the Celts, while the Thracians had dark-olive skin and more closely resembled Semitic peoples.

Indeed, the Thracian kingdom was well known during Herodotus's time. As he erroneously and exaggeratedly described it: "This nation of the Thracians is the biggest of all mankind, except for the Indians."[11] Herodotus does, however, make particularly informative remarks regarding the difference between Daco-Getians and the Thracians: "They have many names, each in his own territory, but they all use the same customs in everything—all, that is, except the Getae, the Trausi, and those who live above the Crestonaeans."[12]

He further differentiated between them when he praised the Getians as far braver than the Thracians, and described the habits of the non-Getians (rituals of birth and death, polygamy, skin tattoos) which differed from those of the Dacians. He wrote: "Who are the inhabitants to the north of this country (Thracia), no one can exactly say, but beyond the river Ister [Danube] the country seems desolate and limitless."[13] He then continued, "According to the Thracians, bees possess the entire country the other side of the Ister, and it is because of the bees that none can travel further than this."[14] In other words, he had no knowledge of the Carpathian tribes. To him, Sarmatians, Scythians, Tribalii, and Getians—and in fact all the peoples residing north of Greece, including the Dacians—were Thracians.

Four hundred years later Ovid, who was exiled from Rome to Tomis (Constantza in today's Romania) and lived in the midst of the Getian people, perpetuated the same confusion when it came to distinguishing the ethnic tribes around him. The bitter poet believed he was surrounded by Sarmatians, Scythians, Bessi, Celts, even Slavs, and that he lived "among the savage Goths."[15] But he knew he was not living in Thracia which he marginally mentioned only a few times in his poems.

Ovid made sure to complain that he was "almost a Getic bard" since "I blush to admit it, I've even composed in the Getic language",[16] evidence of the fact that ethnically, the city of Tomis was Getian, already part of the Dacian population. Yet, the Dacians were not mentioned by the distressed Latin poet who was forced to learn a Dacian language. Most ironically, as Ovid himself notes, he was considered a barbarian by the Getians.

But Strabo was prepared to clarify the issues of Dacians and Thracians in Moesia, even after he made clear that "Now the Greeks used to suppose that the Getae were Thracians; and the Getae lived on either side of the Ister, as did also the Mysi, these also being Thracians and identical with the people who are called Moesi."[17] The key word here is "suppose"; it was thus that Strabo disclaimed what he had learned from the Greeks about the mixed identity of Getians and Thracians. However, he knew precisely that Getians were "the ones who lie to Pont and to East"—a long way from the Thracians. Strabo seemed to support this claim when he wrote:

From these Mysi sprang also the Mysi who now live between the Lydians, Phrygians and Trojans. And the Phrygians themselves are Brigians, a Thracian tribe; as are also the Mygdonians, the Bebricians, the Medobithynians, the Bythynians, and the Thynians, and, I think, also the Mariandynians. These people, to be sure, have all utterly quitted Europe, but the Mysi have remained there.[18]

Again, the expression of import here is "quitted Europe," since Mysi and the above listed Thracian tribes lived in Asia Minor in what is today Asiatic Turkey. It is possible that a half century after Burebista's rule, a fraction of Mysi remained in Moesia, but again, Strabo clearly stated that Thracian Chersonesus connected Europe with Asia "by the strait, seven stadia wide."[19] However it is viewed, the land of Thrace was more than two hundred miles south of the Danube. In the ancient times, that was a very long distance, and it can only nullify the theory that Dacians were "North Thracians."

According to Strabo, the Thracians/Trakes who "as a whole consists of twenty-two tribes"[20] settled south of the Haemus (Balkan) range of Stara Planina in what is now Bulgaria. These high mountains were the border between lower Moesia and Thrace, with the Struma River as its western border. At that time, Thrace/Trakia/Thracia/Tracia was situated in today's southern Bulgaria and Turkey. Its most important tribes were the Abantes, Apsinti, Asti, Bessi, Bistoni, Cicones, Edeonians, Odrisi, Mysians, Samei, Sapei, Thyni, Tirizi, Tonzusi, and others, none of which were to be found near Dacia.

From this it can be concluded that Thracians entered Europe from Asia Minor, while at least some of the Dacians originally came from the Eastern Europe. Moreover, Thracia was part of the Hellenic world and never part of Eastern Europe. The contrary was the case for the Dacians since they were deeply rooted in the Carpatho-Danubian lands.

As Herodotus mentioned, the Getians and the Thracians spoke different languages and they had different living habits. Their distinctive territory was marked by the Getic Sea, another name for the Black Sea, and by the far away Thracian Sea/Thrakikos Pelagos, as part of the Aegean Sea was known. Thus, we can generalize that the Dacian tribal formation belonged to Eastern Europe, and the Thracians belonged to Asia Minor. The Thracians were strong tribes of Asiatic origin, with many claims on European territory, mostly parts of the southern Balkan Peninsula. The Dacians forced them out of Moesia, and this fertile region continued to be much disputed by many other Balkanic powers.

The Dacians must have won most of these battles since they succeeded in colonizing the northern part of today's Bulgaria and Yugoslavia. As previously noted, the tribes of the Picenses, Tricorneses, and especially the Moesi were closely related to the Dacians. Future historical events would confirm the veracity of the above conclusion. All in all, the ancient world of Dacia was complex and far from harmonious, but Daco-Getian unity was never in question.

Once again, after describing how Burebista's empire was divided into five parts after his assassination, Strabo accurately noted: "Daci, whereas others are called Getae-Getae, those who incline towards the Pontus and the east, and Daci, those who incline in the opposite direction towards Germany and the sources of the Ister. The Daci, I think were called Daï in early times."[21] He went to explain that certain slaves called "Geta and Daii" were Scythians, also called "Daee". Indeed, as explained before, Getians were genetically based in early Scythian tribes that settled in the present Dobrudja, often referred to as named Little Scythia, or Scythia Minor. None of these areas were Thracian.

Historical lack of clarity about the origins of the Dacian people and the details of their civilization was most evident almost two thousand years after this initial stage of their development. For example, M. Rostovtzeff's *Iranians & Greeks in South Russia,* published in 1922, is richly documented, yet it also grossly overestimates the role of the Thracians. Obviously influenced by Herodotus, Rostovtzeff went so far as to place the Thracians at various locations across the Balkan and Crimean Peninsulas and the Ukraine; he also made them responsible for majority of the Sarmatian and Scythian exploits. He mentioned the Dacians only a few times. Ironically, however, when commenting on the significance of Trajan's column, he substituted the name of the Dacians with the Sarmatians and Thracians. From his chronology, one might think that Trajan's legions attacked Thracia in 101, when in fact Thracia had become a Roman province more than fifty years earlier.

Rostovtzeff also noted that Getians held Dobrudja during the Persian, Macedonian, and Roman expansions in the northern Balkans because they were "strongly influenced by the Thracian population." However, a few lines later, he stated that the enemy of the Thracian kingdom "were not Scythians but Getians."[22] The historical reality was that the Thracians could not help themselves against powerful invaders, let alone save the Getians who were located far from Thracia. Logically, the Getians could have obtained help only from their patrons, the close neighbors of the Dacians.

Rostovtzeff reiterated "that the Thracians were always the bitter enemies of the Scythians." He wondered why other historians had made "the substitution of Scythians for Cimmerians in the south Russian steppes" after he complained the Cimmerians were mistaken for Massagetians "whose name recalls that of the Getians, a Thracian [*sic*] people"[23] He was obviously aware of the mistakes of the previous historians, yet he persisted in associating Dacians with Thracians, and this despite the obvious genetic and territorial distance between them.

Defining who was a Dacian, however, proved to be no easy task. It was as difficult as deciding who was a Roman. Probably the Italics (who included the large tribes of Latins, Ligurians, Umbrians, Sabinies, Samnities, and Veneti) were considered Romans, as were the many tribes living within the well established Dacian federation. For sure, the Dacian population was a mixture of many tribal groups who were forced into submission after being defeated by the powerful original Greater Dacians.

In Rome, the Dacians, Getians, Moesians, Sarmatians, and any other tribes who lived in Dacia were known as "Bracati," because the men wore tight pants and *bracinar*, a shepherd's wide belt.[24] A Dacian tribe of Racati could be found in southern Slovakia. Their common national costume illustrates their connection to Dacia.

Further, light may be shed on the question of who the main Dacians were if one interprets the name of their capital Sarmizegethusa, the center that united the Sarmatians and the Getians. The difference between them is chiseled in the marble of Trajan's Column: the Sarmatians kept their hair tight in a topknot on their heads, while the Getians combed their long hair over their heads. The Dacians were strong looking people with blond hair cut across their foreheads, trimmed on the sides; they had trimmed beards as well. Clearly, the newly arising empire of Dacian people presented a real danger for the Romans who soon would clash with them over conjointly claimed Balkan territories.

The Roman historian Cassius Dio described General Marcus Crassus's campaign in Moesia as "war with the Dacians and Bastarne." Considering the level of confusion of that prevailed among other ancient historians, he made a surprisingly accurate observation about "Dacians on both sides of the Ister," adding that "the Triballi are reckoned in with the district of Moesia and are called Moesians, except by those living in the immediate neighborhood, while those on the other side [north of the Danube] are called Dacians and are either a branch of the Getae are Thracians belonging to the Dacian race that once inhabited Rhodope."[25]

The last two lines of his definition of the Dacians reveal the fact that he, too, struggled with the many names that identified the same "race" and also with his own belief that Getae (Getians) were Thracians who, in their turn, were Dacians who once inhibited the Rhodope Mountains.

Dio may have added to the historical confusion, but he did correctly point out that at one time the Thracians lived in the mountains that today are between Bulgaria and Greece. He made a vital connection between Dacians and

Getians and clearly stated that, in his time, the Thracians were no longer to be found as a nation. A closer inspection of the rest of his text reveals puzzling, yet precious little information about the Dacians.

A key point here is Dio's assumption that the Bastarnae were "properly classed as Scythians" and that they easily "crossed the Ister and subdued the part of Moesia opposite them, and afterwards subdued the Triballi who adjoin this district and the Dardani who inhabit the Triballian country."[26] What Dio did not understand was that all these tribes had been Dacianized for hundreds of years and the Bastarnae (initially a mixture of Celts and Germans) did not "subdue" the others, but took them along as allies against the common enemy, the Thracians, who were aligned with Rome. That is, for them to cross Moesia, which also belonged to the Dacians, was not a problem.

In fact, two lines later, Dio acknowledged that Bastarnae with others "crossed Haemus and overran the part of Thrace belonging to Dentheleti [a Thracian tribe], which was under treaty with the Romans."[27] Needless to say, General Marcus Crassus had to repel the invasion. Dio was obviously aware of the bellicose event and tried to shed light on the complicated ethnic issue underlying it. He admitted:

> In ancient times, it is true, Moesians and Getae occupied all the land between Haemus and the Ister; but as time went on some of them changed their names and since then there have been included under the name of Moesia all the tribes living above Dalmatia, Macedonia, and Thrace, and separated from Pannonia by the Savus, a tributary of the Ister.[28]

He was certain that "two of the many tribes found among them are those formerly called the Triballi, and the Dardani, who still retain their old name."[29] Dio was not aware that these two tribes were also part of the Dacian confederation. Nevertheless, he did press the question of whether or not Thracia was a parent tribe of the Dacians and almost succeeded in demonstrating this was not the case. What these two nations did have in common was the Balkan Peninsula—they lived at opposite ends of it.

The Dacians had the rare historical distinction of not appearing on any map of the migratory peoples of Europe. Yet, they were well settled due to the richness of their soil and were protected by the natural barriers offered by the Danube, Tisza, and Dniester rivers, as well as by the Carpathian Mountains. Unlike the Thracians whose land was occupied by the Greeks, Persians, Macedonians and Romans, the Dacians remained free. They defied any avaricious imperial powers to co-opt them and repelled all barbarian invasions.

In that spirit, the Dacians made numerous pre-emptive military expeditions to neighboring lands and relied on them to serve as buffer zones. These raids were eventually stopped by the Germanic tribes of Cimbri and Teutons. Because the Dacians preferred to extend to the west, their tendency was to belong to the Occidental world and not to the Oriental one, the latter being the desire to the Thracians. Located on the borderland that separated Europe from the barbarian world, the Dacians seemed destined to live in isolation between the two worlds.

Moreover, the Dacians could not have been Thracians simply because Dacia was not Thracia geographically speaking. Thracia and its people were occupied by the Romans long before they planned to invade Dacia. In A.D. 100, with a surface area of almost a half million square kilometers and a population of two million, Dacia was the second largest empire in Europe and the third military power on the continent.

After part of Dacia was occupied by the Romans from the years 106 to 275, new colonists poured across the Danube attracted by the rich opportunities of the new land. When the Romans left, wave after wave of invaders, most of them Germans, entered Dacia. All of which had obvious impacts on its population. After the Aurelian era (270-275), Dacia became a Gothic land due to successive invasions of Visigoths, Ostrogoths, Avars, and other Germanic tribes. In fact, at the court of Honorius, all these invaders were known under the Latin name of Getae, probably because the Getian pastures were a sort of rest stop for the barbarian armies which were underway to various points in the Roman Empire.

Later, historian Jordanes entitled his book *Gettica* in the belief that the Daco-Getians were Goths. Even though this theory does not hold water, it cannot be denied that a good part of the Dacian population had Germanic blood in their veins, and the Ostrogoths, Vandals, Visigoths and other German invaders of the Balkan Peninsula found a friendlier shelter in Dacia than they did elsewhere.

Other invaders, such as the Huns with their millions of horses, did not care for the Carpathian Mountains and took over the Pannonian vast pastures; they left almost no traces of their presence in Dacia. Centuries later, the Magyars and Slavs also avoided Central Dacia for the same reasons, and the Bulgarians settled in Moesia where they depended on the local Dacian population, who were and still are called Vlachs/Wallachians, or Aromanians.

Over time, and often as a result of intense geopolitical conflicts the Dacians persisted in being the only nation who spoke a Romance language in Balkan and Eastern Europe. As for Thracia and the Thracians, they vanished from the records of history after the Bulgarian and Serbian invasions of sixth and seventh century A.D. while Dacia and its people who never left their lands survived and became what is now Romania.

NOTES

1. The *New York Times*, September 30, 2003, reported that a Homo sapiens jaw-bone, with five large molars, thought to be 34,000-36,000 old, was discovered in a cave in the Carpathian Mountains of Romania.

2. Herodotus, *The History*, trans. David Grene (Chicago: University of Chicago Press, 1987), 4.51.

3. Herodotus, *History*, 4.93.

4. Strabo, *The Geography of Strabo*, trans. Horace Leonard Jones (London: William Heinemann; New York: G. P. Putnam's Sons, 1924), vol. 3, bk. 7, 217.

5. British historian, Edward Gibbon, hinted that Dacia had once been part of Germania/Germany. Others speculated that the name *Dacii* (Dacians) came from the German for "Dutch."

6. Tacitus, *The Germania of Tacitus*, vol. 5 of *History* (The Latin Classics, New York: Vincent Parke & Company, 1909), 403.

7. Tacitus, *Germania*, 415.

8. Strabo, *Geography*, trans. Jones, vol. 3, 211.

9. Dacian national costumes are worn by today's people in the mountain region of Matra and Tatra. A large Wallachian region still exists between Moravia and the Mala Fatra Mountains in the eastern Czech Republic.

10. Strabo, *Geography*, trans. Jones, vol. 3, 213.

11. Herodotus, *History*, 5.3.

12. Herodotus, *History*, 5.3.

13. Herodotus, *History*, 5.9.

14. Herodotus, *History*, 5.10.

15. Ovid, *The Poems of Exile*, trans. Peter Green (Berkeley: University of California Press, 2005), bk. 3, 9.33

16. Ovid, *The Poems of Exile: Tristia* and the *Black Sea Letters*, trans. Peter Green (Berkeley: University of California Press, 2005), bk. IV, 13.18-19

17. Strabo, *Geography*, trans. Jones, vol. 3, 175.

18. Strabo, *Geography*, trans. Jones, vol. 3, 175-177.

19. Strabo, *Geography*, trans. Jones, Fragments of Book 7, 373.

20. Strabo, *Geography*, trans. Jones, vol. 3, 371.

21. Strabo, *Geography*, trans. Jones, vol. 3, 213.

22. Michael Ivanovitch Rostovtzeff, *Iranians & Greeks in South Russia* (Oxford: Clarendon Press, 1922), 87.

23. Rostovtzeff, *Iranians & Greeks*, 41.

24. The Latin term *bracatus* means "wearing breeches or trousers"; it signaled that an individual was a foreigner. In modern Romanian, the verb *a imbraca* means "to dress" or "to wear".

25. Cassius Dio, *Roman History* (Loeb Classical Library: 1917), vol. 6, bk. 51, http://penelope.uchicago.edu/Thayer/E/Roman/Texts/Cassius_Dio/51*.html (17 Feb. 2008), 22.6-7.

26. Dio, *Roman History*, vol. 6, bk. 51, 23.2-3.
27. Dio, *Roman History*, vol. 6, bk. 51, 23.4.
28. Dio, *Roman History*, vol. 6, bk. 51, 27.2-3.
29. Dio, *Roman History*, vol. 6, bk. 51, 27.2-3.

Chapter Four

Transylvania, Religious Center of Dacia

Archaeological discoveries attest to the existence of human settlements in the Dacian territories long before the Bible was written. During the reign of Alexander the Great, the Bible was translated into Greek at the famous library of Alexandria, Egypt. Because Dacia was so distant from the Holy Land, it was never mentioned in these texts; it was therefore not part of early religious history. The Dacians were monotheistic just like the Jews, but no Hebrew influence was to be found there.

The Paleolithic Dacian tribes who lived in the Carpathian Mountains were invaded by migrating Aryans who returned to Europe from India before 1000 B.C. Many of these Aryans settled in and around hospitable Transylvania and along the Danube. Although they were not Indians, Mongols, or Semites, they brought with them aspects of the Vedic culture and religion they had absorbed after hundreds of years of life in the northwest section of modern-day India.

This Hindu influence was eventually seen in the religion of the indigenous Dacians who inhabited the Carpathian and Danubian lands; it is also reflected in the names of many natural phenomena and geographic locations in Dacia. Examples include the rivers Somes (the god Soma), Olt (altar), and Crisana (Lord Krishna). The latter is also the name of one of the longest rivers in India.

The Moksha spirituality and language were prevalent enough in Dacia that the suffix *deva*, which in Sanskrit means the "shining one" in the sense of "god-like", was attached as *dava* to the names of many Dacian settlements that contained shrines or ritual altars. In the past, more than fifty cities in Romania incorporated the suffix *dava* into their names; there is still a city with the name of Deva.

The fact that the Dacians used the word *deva* or *dava* did not mean that they believed in Hindu dogma and gods, but their spiritual rituals did include chanting the Sanskrit sacred word *aum/om*. This word was preserved in the Romanian language as *om* (person), with the same meaning as *homo* and *homme* in Latin and French, respectively. Varful Omul, the Om Peak of the Bucegi Mountains, was probably named for its famous solitary sphinx—a large boulder in the shape of a human head.

Herodotus shed light on Dacian religious beliefs when he wrote about the spirituality of the Getians, who were a tribal mixture of Dacians and Scythians: "To the strength and fierceness of the barbarians, they added a contempt for life, which was derived from a war persuasion of the immortality and transmigration of the soul." He briefly added: "Before he came to the Ister, Darius subjugated the Getae who believe they were immortal."[1]

Herodotus also described one of their rituals: "These are the very Thracians who also threaten the god, shooting their arrows into the sky at a moment of thunder and lightning. They do not think that there is any god except their own."[2]

The Daco-Getians believed that the clear sky reflected the benevolence of the Creator and provided protection. They considered clouds to be the adverse agents of gods spying on them—bad omens, and lightning and thunder, signs of anger. They would stop fighting during thunderstorms because they believed that the sky was ordering them not to continue. Shooting stars and eclipses were taken as messages to be interpreted by their priests.

The great traveler and historian Strabo wrote that, when Alexander the Great led his phalanges to the shore of the Danube, he encountered people he believed to be Celtic warriors. Indeed, originally they had been Celtic Tribalii, but they had been Dacianized long before Alexander discovered them. Their ambassadors approached the Macedonian king with presents, and when they were asked what they feared the most "they replied they feared no one, unless it were that Heaven might fall on them."[3] They shared the beliefs of the Getians, who would shoot arrows at the "evil" clouds they believed were damaging the sunny, protective sky. Records show that, five hundred years later, in 101 during a Romans siege of the fortress Tapae in Transylvania, a storm suddenly began and the defenders quit fighting, in incident which reveals a certain continuity with the Dacian belief in anger from the skies.

A brief review of the spiritual landscape of the Eastern European tribes can be an aid in understanding how the Dacian religion differed from that of their neighbors. Let us begin by taking a look at the spiritual beliefs of the Scythians, Sarmatians, Celts, and Germans, all of whom shared the ancient land around Dacia. We will also examine the influence of other religions on the

Daco-Getians, and note the defining differences between the Dacians' beliefs and those of the Thracians.

The greater majority of the Scythians who galloped over the endless steppes of southern Ukraine represented their nomadic religion with a sword whose tip was driven into the ground.[4] Herodotus, who traveled to Scythia, describes this as a sort of instant altar, one that was adorned with the blood of a sacrificed prisoner whose head had been cut off with the same sword. Their wise men were revered prophets who could predict the future by casting willow rods or braiding and unbraiding tree bark with their fingers. Prophets whose predictions proved false were burned to death atop a bonfire.

Herodotus also described the Scythian religious rituals, including human sacrifice and the drinking of blood from an enemy skull; in addition, he documented their methods of choosing prophets, and their use of steam to release hemp's hallucinatory properties. Many of the Scythian tribes of Eastern Europe worshipped the Great Goddess, chief deity whom they adopted from the Iranians along with god of the moon, of healing and elements of Mithraism.

Those Scythians living around the Black Sea came into close contact with Greek merchants and were influenced by Hellenic spirituality. According to Herodotus they worshipped "Hestia [the goddess of earth] in special and then Zeus and Earth. Earth they regarded as Zeus's wife. After these, they worship Apollo, the Heavenly Aphrodite, Heracles, and Ares."[5] Herodotus further noted that the Scythian name for Hestia was Tabiti, that Zeus was called Papaeus, and Earth was known as Api. Most probably the natives adopted some Hellenic gods worshipped by the Greek colonists in the Thracian cities.

The Sarmatians were fire and water worshippers; water was scarce and fire was a precious commodity in the flat and deserted lands of the southern Ukraine. Like the Scythians, they believed in a pantheon of gods, one of whom was Dumuzi (of Summerian origin), who unleashed lightning and supervised fertility. Many other gods of earth, sky, home and, of course, gods of war, were held in high regard. Their society was matriarchal, and priestesses were the main healers and prophets. Sacrificing human beings to the gods was a common practice among them and one that may have been adopted from the Celts. They buried their dead in shallow graves and then burned fires above them in a purification ceremony. When an important chieftain died, his servants and wives joined him in a common grave.

The Celts worshipped almost two hundred *dias/deos* (gods).[6] There was a god for just about every aspect of life, including the god of theft. The goddess of fertility was Macha, whose name has been retained in the Romanian language as *moasha* (midwife). Their priests were named druids who performed spiritual and social tasks, from being prophets to serve as judges and other vital roles for the Celtic tribes. They believed in the immortality of the soul, and for them the other world was a druidic version of Nirvana. Their burials included spectacular ceremonies and festive public feasts. The rich Celtic mythology was not assimilated into the non-Celtic cultures, since druids performed rituals only among their own people.

The Germans were also polytheists. Their main god was Wodan/Odin, who oversaw wisdom, war, and death. To soldiers who fell in battle he promised a place in Valhalla, the temporary paradisiacal military camp in the sky, built to reward the heroes with all the pleasures they deserved until they were called to fight the next war.

The influence of Greek religion was perceptible only in a limited area along the shore of the Black Sea and into Getia/Getae. The ruins of a temple dedicated to Zeus, like the one in Histria, still exist today on the shore of the Romanian portion of the Black Sea. There are, however, no other signs of Greek influence in Transylvania or elsewhere in Dacia.

In contrast to the other tribes with which they shared their land, the Dacians were monotheistic. They had been contending with religious wars since the migratory Celts and Germans had entered their land. But most of the religious disputes originated with the neighboring Thracians who had earlier adopted the Greek gods under different names. In spite of all this, the Dacians did not succumb to any outside religious influence and stood fast in their belief in their own god, a deity who gave them a unique and unmistakable identity—Zamolxis/Zalmoxis—and who was thought to have lived among them as a messenger, prophet, and teacher for a lengthy period of time.

In the fifth century B.C., Herodotus mentioned "a man Salmoxis or this is some local daimon among the Getae"[7] and wrote of the belief that King Scyles of the Scythians had received a thunderbolt from God after which he lived in a cave for three years, only to "vanish from the presence of the Thracians" and subsequently return to them as a prophet. He would have been accurate when he commented, "but I do think that Salmoxis lived many years before Pythagoras."[8]

The same god Zamolxis was described by both Plato and Strabo. Plato wrote that he learned from a military physician about Zamolxis[9], who was a Thracian king and "also a god" and so skillful that he can even give immortality. Apparently, in Plato's view, as well as in Herodotus's, all of the barbarians from the Pontic (Black Sea) shores were to be lumped together regardless of their names or tribal origins. Furthermore, Zamolxis performed miracles and could heal not only an eye or a headache, but the entire body and soul as well, in the manner of Egyptian or Hindu medical practices. Most important to this was the fact that this divine treatment had to be administered with a certain charm, meaning in good faith and joyfully.

Strabo devoted one of his longest statements (twenty-four lines) to a description of Zamolxis and the religious rites of the Getae/Getians. An abbreviated version is as follows:

> In fact, it is said that a certain man of the Getae, Zamolxis by name, had been a slave to Pythagoras and had learned some things about the heavenly bodies from him, as also certain other things from the Egyptians, for in his wanderings he had gone even as far as Egypt; and when he came on back to his home-land he was eagerly courted by the rulers and the people of the tribe, because he could make predictions from the celestial signs...

Strabo continued this passage by describing Zamolxis as a priest and a messenger of god, a partner of the king, and living in "a certain cavernous place" meeting only the king and his own attendants. He was highly respected by the rest of people and "called god among the Getae."[10] By all accounts, then, he was probably neither an impostor nor an ordinary shaman.

Parenthetically, it is necessary to point out that the legend of Zamolxis was very much associated with the equally legendary life of Pythagoras (ca. 569-ca. 475 B.C.). The renowned Greek philosopher and scientist had many followers, among them Zamolxis, who was more like his personal servant. It was in this role that he traveled with Pythagoras to Egypt where he studied with high priests from Theres. There the Persian army took the master and his pupil prisoners, and they spent a few years in Babylon where Zamolxis learned about Zarathustra and monotheism. They returned to the island of Samos, Pythagoras's birthplace, toured the Greek sacred sites, and settled in Italy.

In Croton, Pythagoras launched his mathematical career (he never used "0", but only whole numbers) while formulating his ideas about religion. He believed in a divine plan and a supreme God who ruled above the other gods of the sun, moon, and stars, including earth. He thought that any god could be approached through conversation, prayer, philosophy, and mathematics. He practiced purification of the body and soul through music, self discipline, vegetarianism, and even some rituals that attracted the enmity of the Croton people.

Because he became involved in politics and advocated autocratic rule, Pythagoras enraged his fellow citizens; at one point, he evidently barely escaped capture by them with two of his followers when his meeting place was set afire. Very likely, Zamolxis was with him then; it was at that point that he decided to return home and apply his mentor's teachings to the Dacian people. Having seen social humiliation first hand, he did not copy the flamboyant style of his master. To the contrary, Zamolxis decided to take refuge in a cave in a Transylvanian mountain.

The Daco-Getians then learned about a wise man of incredible erudition who spoke their language and had messages from mysterious lands. Some people visited Zamolxis in his cave and confirmed rumors about the living saint who had a divine plan for the Dacians.

Zamolxis was to the Dacians what Zarathustra was to the Persians. He had hypnotic powers, performed grand magic, he could heal the sick, predict drought and famine, and convey people's messages to god. He identified blessed locations as sites for *davas* (temples) and named their high priests who dressed in togas. He was the king's primary adviser, and, by invoking mysterious forces, he helped the Dacians win wars.

He immersed himself in contemplation and meditation for three years and hid in a Carpathian cave, most likely Cioclovina near Gradistea. When he again appeared before his believers, the crowd's reaction was similar to that induced later by the resurrection of Jesus.

Eventually Zamolxis disappeared altogether and his worshippers declared him a Supreme Deity. His spirit was said to reside in a cave in Kogaionon Mountain, a mythical location that was subsequently declared sacred. When there were problems to be solved, the Dacians contacted his spirit by sending messengers there.

Zamolxis's performance of sophisticated shamanistic works caused him to be identified as a religious reformer, prophet, and eventually the god of the Daco-Getians who dedicated themselves to a monotheistic tradition. He preached that fighting the enemy was the sacred duty of everyone, including women, and that by dying heroically the Daco-Getians would go directly to his heaven. Through this commitment to sacrifice in battle, he created a legacy of fanatic warriors. After he was proclaimed god, the Dacians fiercely competed with each other to determine who would be given the honor of sacrificing his life and becoming a messenger of this deity. Every five years, one warrior had to be thrown on top of sharp standing lances. If he died immediately, he had been received by Zamolxis. If he survived, he lived in shame for the rest of his life.

Zamolxis introduced a moral code which was based on the Pythagorean guidelines for living, including vegetarianism. He also advocated abstinence from alcohol (the vineyards were to be set afire) and urged compassion for one's fellow man. Most importantly, by unifying the culture's religious beliefs he created the monolithic Dacian nation. He left no carvings or paintings of his image—only many followers. One of these followers was his namesake, Zalmodedikos/Zalmodegikos (approximately 250 B.C.), a Getian king and religious authority.

Because the Dacians settled permanently on their lands, their religion was solidly anchored in their *dava/deva* divine sites. Religious life was well organized in Dacia; as noted, it was centered in Transylvania, mainly the area of Hateg. Thus the *kapnobatai* (also known as ktistai or learned men/priests), "the ones who walk on the clouds of smoke," lived on the highest terrace so as to be close to Zamolxis. There they practiced astronomy and other sciences; they created an urano-solar symbolism based on an advanced calendar. The sacred temples of Costesti and Sarmizegethusa are evidence of this. Unlike the Hebrews and Romans who considered the stars to be glued to the sky, the Dacians believed that their trajectories had meanings and these meanings could be deciphered.

Dacian priests were celibate and lived an ascetic life. They officiated at services in honor of Zamolxis and performed many other religious rituals, one of them being chasing away the *strigoi* (evil ghosts of the dead) from cursed individuals. This was a form of exorcism that combined prayer with the use of the smoke incense and holy water sprinkled on the suffering person and the "haunted" house. Archeological discoveries produced a common object of worship that most likely existed in each Dacian home, a pyramid shaped lamp that also existed in temples. It served to spread light and sacred scent. In so far as they performed such shamanistic rituals the Dacian priests were spiritual and physical healers.

The Jewish historian Flavius Josephus (ca. 36 -ca. 100) noted the presence of Getian priests who served Zamolxis. They lived in *skiste* (caves) and were named *sihastri* (hermits).[11] One of them was the prophet Deceneus, also known as Decaeneus or Dekaineous. His name was formed from two Celtic elements "the wise righteous."

Strabo was interested in how the Dacians (whom he called Getians) lived, how they practiced their religion, and what sort of leaders they had. He described Deceneus as "a wizard, a man who not only had wandered through Egypt, but also had thoroughly learned certain prognostics through which he would pretend to tell the divine will; and within a short time he was set up as god." The Getians listened to him so much that they were willing "to cut down their vineyards and to live without drinking wine!"[12]

Around the year 451, Jordanes made a vague reference to Zamolxis as "a man of remarkable learning in philosophy," but obviously the old god was only a memory. The historian mentioned another similar man named Zeuta and Dicineus (Deceneus), and noted as well that "priests were appointed... called first Tarabostesei and then Pilleati. Moreover so highly were the Getae praised that Mars, whom the fables of poets called the god of war, was reputed to have been born among them."[13] Unlike other historians, Jordanes thought very highly of Deceneus whom he believed to be a Gothic priest given almost royal power by the king he named Buruista.

Jordanes was a great storyteller, but not always accurate. He used the names of Gets/Getae and Goths interchangeably and credited them with having the same religion, which was not the case. But, at least he was aware of Zamolxis and understood him to be someone who offered a spiritual identity and a new faith to a large segment of the population of Eastern Europe.

What Strabo and Jordanes did not mention was that Deceneus was also great teacher of astrology, astronomy, cosmology, ethics, logic, philosophy, physics, and military leadership. Whether he was Celtic or Dacian, a wise man or a shaman, he was obviously a disciple of Zamolxis. And, when it came to claiming to know divine will, his authority was unquestioned.

Deceneus not only had the attributes of a high priest, but was also entrusted with supreme ruling powers. Second in command after the king, he was responsible for many religious and social reforms. His order created a caste of respected priests and, ultimately, a sober and united tribal society. In this capacity, Deceneus advised the young king Burebista on how to impose a rule of abstinence on the Dacians, one modeled after the example of the Essenes. He ultimately ruled as a king on his own rights. At least two of his successors, Comosicus and Scorilo/Coryllus/Scoricus, became high priests and eventually Dacian kings.

The area of the Orastie Hills in Transylvania, part of the Sureanu Mountains, was the economical, political and spiritual center of Dacia. Cogaionon/Kogaion, most likely a sacred mountain, was identified by some historians and archeologists as the Hill of Gradistea; it was 1200 meters/3600 feet high. Deceneus built a new religious sanctuary nearby at Sarmizegethusa.

Unlike other capitals in the ancient world, Sarmizegethusa Regia (royal site) was not a military fortress, nor was it of political importance; rather, it was a sacred area that covered more than 161 square kilometers/62 square miles in the Orastie region. Each sacred shrine was so designed that its multi-layered terraces ensured good visibility of the ceremonial altars and the officiating priests. These places were marked by round temples some 30 meters/98 feet in diameter and also contained quadrangular courts enclosed by long buildings. Instead of the wood, limestone, or clay bricks used in other fortresses, the ramparts of Sarmizegethusa and other sanctuaries were made of *dacite* (andesite), an extremely hard volcanic rock. In many walls every seventh piece of stone was larger than the previous one, a design which may have had religious significance according to astronomical calculations. A vast and elaborate underground tunnel and sanctuary completed the sacred establishment.

The Dacian religious complex was a meeting ground for pilgrims who came to visit the place at which their god Zamolxis had once lived. It was also a sort of civic center where priests acted in the capacity of advisors and judges. Astronomical research was done at Sarmizegethusa, research which led to the creation of a complex solar calendar that predicted solar eclipses. Inside the solar sanctuary was an impressive calendar made of stones which helped the high priests calculate an eighty-four year cycle based on a 360-day year. It is believed that for practical reasons the Dacian calendar consisted of thirteen months with twenty-eight days in each month, resulting in a 364 days a year with four equal seasons of thirteen weeks each. This was an advance over the Roman calendar, which was based on phases of the moon and numbered the days of the year at 355 days, with variation in the month of February.

The "profane" area of this region—where the general population and the soldiers lived—is easily discerned from the "sacred" area where the temples and high priests were located. That the city's religious rituals were sophisticated is clear from its andesite sundial that points north, as well as from its quadrilateral sanctuaries; the latter have survived to this day.

The Dacians considered Godeanu to be another sacred mountain, and they populated it with round temples they called *stane* (in modern Romanian this means either a shepherd's camp or a stone statue). Such revered locations were established across the land, including in Batca Doamnei, Costesti, Piatra Craivi, and other areas. In them, the priests (named *ktistai* by Strabo) officiated at religious services, made offerings to god, and carried out human sacrifices. In times of war, they became military leaders.

Among the high priests was Diurpaneus, a most powerful military leader of the Dacians who in the year 85 defeated the Roman cohorts led by Oppius Sabinus, governor of Moesia, and killed the Roman leader. It is believed that he changed his name to Decebalus, the king who would defend Dacia in two major wars against Emperor Trajan and his legions.

Dacian religious beliefs bore some similarities to those of the Celts. Both believed in the immortality of the soul. The Celts thought that their dead warriors went to a hall of the brave, very much like the one that the Dacians envisioned as the eternal realm of Zamolxis. This shared belief made the warriors of the two tribal nations willing to perform the same supreme sacrifice while fighting enemies. The Celtic knots with their weaving of "fate lines" represented the labyrinth of truth, a symbol which came to be used by the Dacians as religious and artistic decoration but without their assigning it any further spiritual value. Later, the Romanian Orthodox church adopted these as well.

In most ways, however, Dacian religious beliefs diverged greatly from those of the nomadic Celts, Germans, Scythians, Sarmatians, and especially the Thracians. While some Thracians in Moesia shared the god Zamolxis with the Dacians, most Thracians were polytheists. And because they lived in the southern Balkans near the Greeks, they could not help but be influenced by Hellenic gods and mythology. According to Herodotus, the Thracians worshipped Ares, Artemis, and Heracles (Hercules), who later took the shape of a heroic Thracian horseman. Thracian nobility was inclined liked to worship Hermes, the son and messenger of Zeus.

The Greek gods Orpheus and Dionysus were also popular with the Thracians. Orpheus was a bard who lived prior to Homer; inspired by the Egyptian mysteries, he created a religious cult that became a part of the Hellenic mythological system. A pacifist and healer, he believed in moderation, vegetarianism, and abstinence from alcohol. He was a skillful player of the seven-stringed lyre, and known to charm any audience, including wild beasts. Orpheus was an earlier Thracian version of the great Pindar, the Greek father of lyrical poetry. His shamanic powers were legendary, and he was credited with traveling through the Underworld and discovering the secrets of Inner Nature that led to the Inner God.

Dionysus was known by the Romans as Bacchus and by the Thracians as Sabadiosa/Sabariosa, or Sabos/Sabazius. Before he was mythologized as the god of wine and celebration he spent time in India and other distant lands. He was thought to play the flute and promote divine ecstasy through hallucinogenic alcohol and wild sexuality. In his limitless love for his fellow men, he introduced pederasty to the Thracians. King Lycurgus ordered his arrest as part of an effort to punish the orgiastic cult members, and Dionysus escaped to Sabazius, his birthplace. A Dionysiac temple was built in Maroneia near the Ismaros Mountain in Hellenic land. No such temple was to be found in Dacia.

Neither of these "two antagonistic gods"[14] were adopted by the Daco-Getians since they were relatively disconnected from both Hellenic philosophy and Greek spirituality. The Thracian god Gebeleizis was probably a corrupt Thracian name for Zeus, and identified by Herodotus as Zamolxis, but not a Dacian deity. In fact, after the time of Herodotus, he was never mentioned again.[15]

Thracian death rites were very different from those of the Dacians, even though both groups believed in an afterlife. The Thracians, like the Sarmatians, burned their dead, a ritual not found in the Dacian religion. Thracians built impressive graves with expensive stonework and engraved dedications in the style of the Greeks and Romans. The Dacians, on the other hand, did not believe in idols or statues, and their cemeteries went unnoticed because their graves had no headstones. The Dacian dead were buried with their faces up and their heads to the east; the bodies were fully clothed, the men armed with weaponry and the women adorned with jewelry.

There were other notable differences between the Thracians and the Dacians as well. Herodotus described the Thracians as "being tattooed," a custom the Dacians did not follow. Strabo also wrote about the Getian women as the chief founders of religion, and noted that it is the women who provoke the men to the more attentive worship of gods[16] He added that because the "zeal for religion is strong in this tribe, and...because of their reverence for the gods, the people abstain from eating any living thing."[17] Indeed, many historical sources indicate that Dacian priests urged ascetism, vegetarianism, and abstinence from alcohol—none of which constituted religious norms for the Thracians.

Ironically, while the Thracian practices were acceptable to the Greeks and Romans, the Daco-Getians who neither worshipped the same gods, nor honored the same customs were considered "pagans."

The Dacians, like many of the peoples of the Balkan and Italic peninsulas, honored the "spirit-wolf." The Greek Lycaeon, the wolfish Zeus, and the Roman Apollo Lyceaus, along with the Goddess Feronia (the Mother of Wolves), were all part of a long-established worship of the wolf. In Greece, philosophic gymnasia were dedicated to Lukeios (wolf god), hence the term "lyceum." The Romans, as is well known, believed the infants Romulus and Remus were raised by *lupa* (a she-wolf). One of the most celebrated Roman holidays was Lupercalia (wolf day).

The Dacians likewise glorified the wolf, but at a higher spiritual level. According to Strabo, the name Dacia came from *Daii* and *Daus*, both of which are very close to the Celtic/Gallic word *Daoi*, meaning wolf people. Legends and traditions claimed that the Dacoi/Dacians were nicknamed "wolf people" and so their land came to be referred to as Dacia. They considered the wolf to be the lord of animals. In their religious beliefs, the wolf was the only effective power against evil, so it was also regarded as a guardian warrior. Because wolves lived in packs and took good care of their offspring, the animals were models of family dynamics. Dacians considered the relationship between man and wolf so close that they believed in the transformation of man into werewolf.

The military symbols of antiquity were often animals that inspired either horror or admiration. The Egyptians were proud of their cobra; the Greeks had the Minotaur, half man and half bull; the Celts loved the boar and the Romans sported the eagle on their standards. The wolf was the standard for Dacians.[18]

Dacians considered themselves to be "wolf warriors" and adopted a battle flag that was named *drago/draco*. It was the demonic representation of a portable deity with three meanings: the wolf's head symbolized the conquest of the earth's surface, the snake body signified underwater domination, and the wings represented the vibration of life. The elongated part could represent the tail of a comet, since the Dacians strongly believed that any luminous, celestial display would destroy their enemies.

The Daco-Getian flag looked terrifying to their enemies because it projected the image of something undefeatable. It was carried on the tip of a lance and the open jaws of the wolf produced an eerie sound when the wind passed through it. It was, in essence, a flying deity, believed to have the power to keep away evil spirits and protect its bearers from harm.

A flying dragon unearthed at an archaeological site in Prahova in modern Romania provides evidence that Dacians used this symbol since the fourth century B.C. More than ten versions of this standard were chiseled five centuries later on the Column of Trajan in Rome. Most likely each tribe had its own variation on the design. Two hundred years after the Roman-Dacian wars were commemorated on the Column, many Cohors Dacorum (Dacian Cohorts) serving in the Roman army still proudly bore the wolf-dragon standard in their travels throughout different parts of the world. It could be seen on the tombstones in a cemetery in Chesters, Britannia, where it marked the graves of the Dacian warriors who had served there.

The spiritual life of the Dacians was active and sophisticated. Their superstitions were connected with the surrounding environment. They worshipped the sky and possessed a solar cult. A shooting star across the sky at night was considered to be a warning of misfortune, drought, war, and so on. Dacians burned large piles of wood, as Romanians do today during many of their festivals. Their purpose in doing so was to implore the god for more light and warmth, especially during the winter season.

The Dacians also used the magic of song and dance to tame the sky. Their songs were of gratitude, love, marriage, sadness, departure, grief, and war. They had specific ritual dances for young people, men, women, elderly people, weddings, and so on. Most of the dances also involved singing and/or shouting, and the rhythm was marked by whistling and the stomping of feet as they moved in intricate steps. Their fast-paced choreography can be traced to the tradition of walking on the embers of sacred fires in an effort to bring vigor, fertility, and health.

They also believed in the magic power of plants and animals, including birds. Basil was regarded the plant of purity, and it was considered to be the only ingredient in holy water that would keep *strigoi* (evil spirits) away. Marjoram was thought to invoke feelings of love; shamrock was a symbol of good luck; pine was believed to attract eternal life and happiness. Braches of pine were mounted on the roofs of houses which were under construction and around gates and pillars at weddings; people carried them in funeral processions as well. Dacian myrrh was the perfumed smoke of burning pine incense nuggets. Tea made from tilia (linden) and nettle leaves was thought to be a healing medicine, as were raw garlic and perfumed honey, both of which were applied to bleeding wounds. Lovage was the herb used to attract a mate.

As noted, the Dacians buried their dead. Those who died unmarried were buried in wedding clothes. The souls of the dead were believed to repose in the sky, and their departure from earth was marked by mournful songs filled with love and messages of loss and regret. The lives of the departed were celebrated and honored with a *pomana* (funeral feast). This Vedic tradition of showing kindness and sorrow to the departed was also observed by the Scythians and Sarmatians.

Another Dacian custom was the *parasta* (memorial feast). It was repeated after a number of weeks, months, and even years after the death of a loved one. A special ritual dish of *coliva,* a pilaf made of boiled wheat kernels and honey, was served to mourners. It represented the resurrection and restoration of life, just as grains are renewed and replenished when planted. All of these traditions are still kept by Romanians today.

The song of the cuckoo bird and the owl near the house was a warning for disaster and death in the family, while the stork and the sparrow nesting on or under a roof were a sign of good luck and happiness. The immensity of the sky was called *vazduh* (the seen spirit), a religious word still used in the Romanian language.

All of these spiritual traditions puzzled the Roman poet Ovid who was exiled at Tomis (Constantza). Even though he was surrounded by Roman colonists and most probably classic Roman temples, the sad bard who once defied the gods with his sexual revolution was mortified at the idea that, after his death, his noble spirit might mingle with the local pagans. The concerns he recorded are further evidence of the fact that the Getians, like the Dacians, did not worship Roman gods.

When the Roman legions introduced Mithraism to all of Europe, the Persian god Sol Invictus (Unconquered Sun) became the protector of the Roman soldiers. The hymn of Legio XXX (Ulpia Victrix) was dedicated to Mithra, now the Soldier God. It told of the expiration of the great Roman world and its religion.

In time, the religions around Dacia changed as well. Ares, the only son of Zeus, became Mars, the Roman god of war. He was followed by Mithra, the god of light from the East, easily accepted by the Dacians whose clothes were similar to the Mithraic costume, including a cap with the conic end folded forward. It is not clear to what extent the introduction of the god Mithra interfered with Dacian belief in Zamolxis, but the Column of Trajan accurately showed the Dacian noblemen and priests wearing the Phrygian cap.

That the god Mithra was important to the Dacians is indicated by the fact that names such as Mitra, Mitrea, Mircea, Mitru, Mitu, Mitrus, Mitrita, Mitrache, Dumitru, Dumitrache, Dumitrescu, Dumitra, Dumitreasca, etc. (*Dum*, an abbreviation of *Domn*, stands for "Lord.") have persisted in the Romanian language today Mithraism and the period of Mithraic religious culture was strongly challenged in far away Palestine where, in A.D. 33, a group of legionaries crucified a spiritual rebel accused of plotting to overthrow Roman authority and introduce a new religion.

Jesus was not a military or a political leader, and never had an army or the wealth necessary to impose his will. But his message of peace and the brotherhood of mankind proved to be stronger than a war, revolution, or any law. His revolutionary teachings were embraced by the foreign legions who preferred to adopt a new religion rather than worship traditional Roman gods.

Unfortunately, "love your enemy" was a message which conflicted directly with the militaristic policy and the ideology of racial dominance promoted by Rome founded on slavery. But the resurrection of the dead and the notion of a last judgment were concepts that were too complicated for the diehard Romans. They preferred to believe in the well-defined purity, simplicity, and power of each of their generally benevolent gods. Since they were eager to please their citizens, the emperors rejected the Christian faith and proceeded to persecute the peaceful, yet revolutionary Christians.

The resurrection of Jesus made the invisible God a believable reality. But it took the fanatical dedication of Peter/Petre and Paul/Pavel to actually found the Christian church and make Christianity an organized religion. One verse from Paul's epistle to the Romans stated, "For I am persuaded that neither death nor life, nor angels nor principalities nor powers, nor things present nor things to come, nor height nor depth, nor any other created thing, shall be able to separate us from the love of God which is in Christ Jesus our Lord."[19] Within the space of a few years, Christians had succeeded in transforming the tortuous symbol of the cross into a sacred and beloved symbol of brotherhood, love, forgiveness, and peace. The two perpendicular lines of the cross also symbolized the extension of the new religion to all four cardinal points of the globe.

Even as Nero's persecution resulted in the beheading of Paul and the inverted crucifixion of Peter (both of whom would be named saints in the new Christian church), the new religion had began to have an impact on the history of the Roman Empire. Desiring to be affiliated with a religion of hope, forgiveness and everlasting life, more and more people came to call themselves Christians.

During this period, a massive plague killed huge numbers of Romans and legionaries—more than had been taken by any other natural calamity or war. One of its victims was the Emperor Titus himself, who had destroyed the temples in Jerusalem (renamed Aelia Capitolina) and caused the Jews to disperse throughout the world. Some fifty thousand Jewish families settled in Rome, transported there by this emperor who wanted the city of Jerusalem emptied of Jews. They were blamed for spreading Christianity and many were executed, as were Christian legionaries.

When entire Roman military units converted to Christianity, they were forcibly relocated to remote corners of the empire so as to ensure that they would to contaminate the remainder of the troops. After the occupation of Dacia in 106, many Christian cohorts of the Roman army ended up in Transylvania where their marriage with the local women produced the Christian children of Dacia. This process of "religious osmosis" worked both ways, however, and the Romans also adopting some of the Dacian beliefs. For the monotheistic Dacians, shifting from belief in Zamolxis to belief in Jesus, both of whom promised a happy life after death, was an easy transition.

Two hundred years later, during his campaign to conquer Rome, Emperor Constantine (ca. 280-337) dreamed of a cross displaying the words, *In hoc signo vinces* (With this sign you will be victorious). The next morning he ordered the cross to be painted on each legionary's shield. Although he was heavily outnumbered, he won the battle of Milvian Bridge and entered Rome in triumph. Soon, the symbol of Jesus was present everywhere in the Eternal city. At that time, the Roman Empire had fifty-six million inhabitants, fifteen million of whom where Christians, and three million, Jews.

Constantine the Great (born in the Dacian land of Moesia Superior) declared the cross to be the symbol of Christianity and proceeded to unite the divided Roman Empire under it in A.D. 324. The treasures of pagan temples were confiscated. Not only was the Church thereby protected and helped, but it itself eventually became the stabilizing factor in uniting the multi-national population of the empire. Its bishops (as opposed to Roman senators or generals) became the most important officials of the empire. One year later, the emperor ordered the Old and New Testaments to be combined into a single book.

Having established Christianity as the official religion of the empire, Constantine decided to replace the most celebrated pagan holiday, December 25 (the end of Saturnalia), the festival of winter solstice, with Christmas day.[20] Indeed, December 25th was *Dies Natalis Invicti* (the Birth of the Unconquered), or Mithra, the Persian god who defeated darkness. A similar day was celebrated by the Dacians at the end of December—the Holiday of Renewed Sun. In Sarmizegethusa there was a "High Room of Sun" dedicated to that holiday. The Romanian Orthodox Church still uses sun symbols, carried on standards during gospel proclamations and incorporated into mural paintings in the form the ever watchful eye of God.

Thus Mithra-the-Pagan was replaced with Christ-the-Righteous. Christ's birthday was celebrated not only by the men but also by women and especially by children. As the imperial decree proved extremely successful, Christianity grew stronger, and Byzantium, renamed Constantinople, became the New Rome.

The Goths and the Gepidaes/Gepides brought a large number of captured Romans into Dacia. Among them were many Christian priests who immediately began their ardent missionary work. Because the New Testament had already been translated into the Gothic language, it was probably also translated into the Dacian language, thereby making their conversion easier. The newly adopted religion provided a forceful spiritual motivation to unite and cement the young Daco-Roman nation.

The Christian Saint Andrew is known to have been a missionary in Dacia, and Saint Sava was martyred on the Buzau River, also in Dacia. Their spiritual work was facilitated by the presence of Dacian priests who, while they had worshipped Zamolxis, were used to a saintly life and amenable to the concepts of Christianity. A certain Dacius, Saint of Durostor/Durostorum (currently the city of Silitra in Dobrudja), had deep roots in the Dacian heritage. Bishop Niceta of the Dacians (335-414) lived in Remesiana (Romatiana, now Bela Palanka in Serbia) in Dacia Mediterranea, whose capital was Serdica (Sofia, Bulgaria), where he wrote six books on Christian baptism.

The heritage of Saint John Cassian is well documented. He was born in 360 in the Roman province of Scythia Minor, today's Dobrudja. In addition to the Dacian language, he spoke Greek and Latin. His numerous trips to Constantinople, Egypt, Jerusalem, and Rome ultimately led him to Marseille. There he was ordained as a priest, and established two monasteries that observed strict monastic rules.

He wrote twelve religious books in which he preached about fighting against sin, the importance of prayer, the quest for spiritual perfection, the Reincarnation of the Lord, and the Virgin Mary, mother of God. He also wrote about the "ancient heritage of our forefathers," describing the land of Dobrudja, its beauty, and its traditions. He died in France in 435, where his Christian legacy later brought him sainthood.

The only conflict that developed between Dacia and the early Christian church was controversy around the Dacian support of Arius. (Arius, a priest from Alexandria, had decreed that Jesus was created by the eternal God, and was therefore not himself divine.) This conviction was shared by the Goths, Germans, and Vandals, all of whom believed in one God but not in a family of saints connected with Jesus Christ.[21]

By the year 400, as the righteous Christians of the Eastern Empire were separated from those of the Western Empire, the Dacians became part of Eastern Orthodoxy—the Correct Believers of the Church of Constantinople. The enormous influence wielded by Roman Christians is evidenced in their dictionary description of Dacian Christians: Their *Dumnezeu* 'God' came from *dominus deus*; *crestin* 'christian' from *christianus*; *cruce* 'cross' from *crux*; *sfant* 'saint' from *sanctus*; *a boteza* 'to baptize' from *baptiserium*; *bierica* 'church' from basilica; *popa* 'priest' from popa; and so on. The Slavic influence would once again rewrite the church dictionary of the Romanian people who retained their Latin heritage and continued to regard it as the source of their Christianity. To this very day, many martyred saints like Saint George are shown as armed with weapons and dressed in legionary uniforms on the icons and painted walls of Romanian churches.

Another item of note is the fact that Catholic churches inherited much of their content from Roman temples, e.g. statuary; however, the Romanian Orthodox Church uses Byzantium's iconography and mural painting to depict its saints.

Once again Trajan's Column provides a literal illustration of history and sheds light on what would become the religion of Dacians and their neighbors. It was during Trajan's reign that the Gospel of Saint John was written down in Greek by one of the apostle's followers. Thus, the monumental column also reflects scenes of the Dacian wars that established a new religious nation in Transylvania. The engravings show how the legionaries entered Dacia by force of arms, only to end up as family men and peaceful Christian colonists. Overall, the Roman invasion influenced many aspects of Dacian culture, not the least of which was its religion.

The majestic column survived the collapse of the Roman Empire that was brought on by the barbarian invasions and the advance of Christianity.[22] The testimonial column with its images of Dacia and its people has survived earthquakes and wars and still towers over the Vatican. It may withstand many other demographic and religious changes as well.

NOTES

1. Herodotus, *The History*, trans. David Grene (Chicago: University of Chicago Press, 1987), 4.93.

2. Herodotus, *History*, 4.94.

3. Strabo, *The Geography of Strabo*, trans. Horace Leonard Jones (London: William Heinemann; New York: G.P. Putnam's Sons, 1924), vol. 3, 203.

4. This Scythian ritual has survived even to our present day. Both European and American soldiers sometimes stick a bayoneted rifle into the ground to show respect for a fallen comrade.

5. Herodotus, *History*, 4.59.

6. The names of the Celtic gods usually began with prefix *dues* or *deo*, meaning "forever", indicating a connection between Deus and Zeus. As noted, later the Dacians took up the name of *Dumnezeu* (the Final God), still used today by the Romanians.

7. Herodotus, *History*, 4.96.

8. Herodotus, *History*, 4.96.

9. The name had many versions and was thought to be derived from many sources: *Zalmoxis* 'the Enlightened', *Zalmoksha* 'a Nirvana visitor', *zal-moxis* 'the Old Prophet'.

10. Strabo, *Geography of Strabo*, trans. Jones, vol. 3, 185-187.

11. To this day, ascetic *sihastri* live in Romania *in skituri* (isolated convents).

12. *Strabo, Geography*, trans. Jones, vol. 3, 211.

13. *Jordanes, The Gothic History of Jordanes*, ed. and trans. Charles Christopher Mierow (Cambridge: Speculum Historiale, 1966), 39-40.

14. Mircea Eliade, *A History of Religious Ideas from Gautama Buddha to the Triumph of Christianity*, trans. William R. Trask (Chicago: University of Chicago Press, 1982), 184.

15. Eliade was inclined to believe that Orpheus and Dionysus fulfilled the spiritual needs of the Greek spirit after the decline of Homeric religion. Certainly, the Daco-Getians did not worship these two gods, since they would have been quite distant from their own culture.

16. Strabo, *Geography*, trans. Jones, vol. 5, 185.

17. Strabo, *Geography*, trans. Jones, vol. 5, 185.

18. Because the wolf was also revered by the Germans, it is possible that the word for "wolf" (der Wolf) became the word "V*olk*" (a people). Since the Dacians were known as Vlaks or Valachs/Wallachians, they were therefore also "the wolf people".

19. *The Holy Bible*, New King James Version (Nashville: Thomas Nelson Publishers, 1982), Romans 8:38-39.

20. The word "Christmas" derives from "Christ's Mass," meaning the Celebration of Christ.

21. By the end of the sixth century A.D, the church of Constantinople had eliminated the teachings of Arius, and the authority of the Eastern Orthodox Church remained unchallenged.

22. The statue of Emperor Trajan, who was considered a pagan because he persecuted Christians, was removed in 1588 from the top of the column and replaced with a figure of Saint Peter. The latter still adorns it.

Chapter Five

Language and Culture

The lack of a written Dacian alphabet has prohibited historians and linguists from doing anything other than speculating about the languages spoken in that Carpatho-Danubian region of ancient Eastern Europe. There is no doubt that a common language was a vital necessity in a tribal federation of two million people with a Dacian centralized leadership. In this case, that language would have belonged to the Indo-European group brought by the "Aryan returners" from India. Also, it probably had much in common with many other languages spoken around Dacia.

Herodotus, the curious Ionian Greek traveler, ventured along the shore of the Black Sea between 400-430 B.C., where he met the Sarmatian tribes (whom he called Sauromatians). They spoke a language similar to that of the Scythians, a dialect of the Tokharian language which was of Indo-Iranian derivation. The Sarmatians and the Scythians were in close contact with the eastern Dacians, who included the Getians. It was likely that many understood a dialect of Greek or Latin since Herodotus did not claim to have a language problem. It might therefore be reasonable to think that the Dacians spoke a Centum language related to the Celtic, German, and Latin dialects.

There is also some speculation that spoken Dacian was a distant dialect of the Illyrian (Albanian) language, the only one not connected with any of the semantic roots of area's other language families. Another unlikely theory is that the Daco-Thracian language was the dominant tongue of the Balkan Peninsula and similar to the Greco-Aryan spoken by Greeks. But eyewitnesses to that ancient period who heard both languages testified that Dacians and Thracians spoke differently. As for a Sarmatian and Scythian influence on the Dacian lexicon, these giant tribes also spoke an Indo-European language; however, they gradually lost territory, power, and population and ultimately became dependent on Dacian benevolence. This included the surrender of their language.

It is likely that the Dacian language was spoken in Moesia as far south as the Haemus Mountains, while Thracian was spoken from Rhodes to Thessaly, the land of the Bessorum and home of the Bessi tribe. For sure their city names ended mostly with *para* and *bria* and not in Dacian *dava*. While the Dacians clearly pronounced the consonants *b, d, g, k, p,* and *t,* the Thracians pronounced *bh, dh, gh, kh, ph,* and *th*—different sounds and intonation. The eastern Thracian tribes spoke the tongue of the Mysians of Western Anatolia in Asia Minor, who belonged to the Satem language group.

The Greek historian Strabo wrote that "the language of the Daci [Dacians] is the same as that of the Getae [Getians]," indicating the unity of these two major populations of Dacia.[1] From this we can deduce—and in fact it is confirmed by Roman historian Cassius Dio—that the people of Moesia, who were closely related to the Dacians and Getians, also spoke the same language as the Dacians. It is, however, important not to confuse the European Moesians with the Asiatic Mysians.

So, if the initial Dacian language belonged to the Centum group and was probably rooted in the Sarmatian and Scythian dialects, over time a kind of reversal occurred in the same way that the Celtic/Irish language ended up being dominated by English. This fact ensured effective communication throughout the vast areas of ancient Eastern Europe and most of the Balkan Peninsula.

We can therefore safely conclude that Dacian-speaking regions would have included parts of Alania and Bessarabia, Banat, Bukovina and Maramures, Crisana, Dobrudja, Galicia, Moesia (Bulgaria and Serbia), Moldova, Oas, Pannonia (Austria and Hungary), Transylvania, and Vallachia (what is now the major part of Romania). The Dacian language would have been similar to today's Russian, which shares enough by way of cognates and sentence structure with other Slavic languages that it can be understood by those living in Bulgaria, Serbia, Ukraine, and Poland.

As for the Greeks and Thracians, their language might have been be related, but it differed from that of their neighbor, the Macedonians. We know for a fact that King Philip did not speak Greek, and his Macedonian infantry could not understand the Thracian cavalry. His son Alexander the Great learned Greek from his tutor, the eminent philosopher, Aristotle.

Greek was the dominant language of the ancient world. It served as a vehicle for dissemination of the Bible as well as a vast array of arts, literature, sciences, and philosophy. It was also the commercial language of sailors and travelers, and was used in many trading posts along the western coast of the Black Sea. The Greeks traded heavily with Daco-Getians, but as is often the case, foreigners ended up having to speak the local tongue, and so the Dacian language prevailed in Dacian lands. This also was the situation when Celtic and Germanic immigrants settled in Dacia—they, too, found themselves having to learn the host language. This is not to say that Dacians were not receptive to other languages, and in fact, as is often the case, words and phrases from the other languages would have found their way into the Dacian vocabulary.

Latin presented a different set of problems for Dacia. Due to the many Roman conquests of European and Mediterranean lands, it became the standard for international communication among the major western European tribes and nations. But the language that was thus transmitted was not the pure Latin spoken in Rome by the orators, patricians, writers, and politicians; instead, it was rough, convoluted in its pronunciation and strongly contaminated by barbarian words—a kind of Esperanto of ancient Europe.

This Latin vulgaris was commonly used by the foreign legionaries and auxiliaries of the Roman army, as well as in communications between local peoples and provincial administrators and in international commercial transactions. Since it was a multi-purpose language, it was understood by Celts and Germans, and also by the Dacians. It was surely the language that "navigated" around the Mediterranean Sea and along the main European river, the Danube, half of which flowed through Dacia.

It is not clear how many Latin words were absorbed into the Dacian language before the Roman conquest of Transylvania, or how many Dacians could speak it; it is, however, known that people there spoke a form of corrupted Latin with important foreigners and in commercial transactions as necessary. It was so popular that many speculated that Dacians spoke a proto-Latin language. Certainly Trajan's Column shows the Dacian emissaries and prisoners talking to the Romans without any interpreter.

There is obviously much that we do not know about the Dacian language. Nevertheless we can speculate with some assurance that the Dacians were not isolated linguistically and that their tongue was a major language of Eastern Europe. The subject of the Latin language will be revisited below as will that of its use in Dacia and the lands surrounding it.

The name of a nation usually derives from a word related to a clan, a location, or an epithet that reflects an important image or symbol, and/or is connected to a craft or an occupation. Ultimately, a name is a verbal symbol. The Dacians most probably took theirs from *Dasyave Vrka*, Sanskrit for "wolf to the *Dasyu*" (heroic warrior). The Phrygian word *Daos* and the Indo-European word *Dhawos*, both meaning wolf, are pronounced similarly. Thus, as noted above, the name for the Dacians meant the "wolf people"; it also clearly reveals that they had some affiliation with other European languages. Thus the Greeks named them Dakos and Dakoi, and the Germans knew them as Daoi and Dauos, while the Romans called them Dacus and Daci, using the word *dacigena* for a Dacian-born person.

The Dacians and Germans shared the same cult of "wolf brotherhood," and Valhalla was the hall of the Valks/wolf warriors. This leaves room for speculation that the words *Vlach* (Dacian mountain men) and *Volk* (German commoners) may have the same origin. Many tribes worshiped the wolf and adopted the word as their name in one form or another—Luvians, Luceres, Lykians, Hirpini, Hyrcani, to name a few. If the wolf was locally called *walus/valus*, then some Dacians likely changed their names to Wallachs or Vlachs, meaning "the people of wolves" or "wolf-worshipping people." As previously noted, the Dacian flag displayed a flying wolf, thereby confirming the identity between the people and the beloved beast of the Carpathians.

It has also been speculated that the Dacians received their name from the appellation "Dutch," a Germanic denomination of tribes near the North Sea. Or, that Denmark was initially named Dacia or vice-versa. Somehow the Dutch *boer* and the German *bauer* persisted in the Romanian language as *boier/boyard*, meaning a farmer or landowner.

The "returning Aryans" most likely enriched the language originally spoken in Dacia. The Vedic influence was further reflected in place names that recalled sacred sites and deities in India. For example, in present-day Romania one can find towns with the names Brasov (Brasiva), Crisana, Deva, Somes, Timis, and Vedea. The name of the Bihor region could be a slightly modified version of the name Bihar, a state in India. Many words from the Indo-Germanic tongue have persisted to the present day in the Romanian language. Examples include: *om/aum* 'person', *mudra/mutra* 'mark of identity', *apa/apha* 'water', *ziua/diaus* 'day', *dumbrava/dumbraba* 'grove', *casa/kasha* 'house', *poteca/pathaka* 'path', *rai/rai* 'heaven', and *stapan/sthapana* 'master'.

Many Dacian words are also preserved in modern Romanian, among them: *abur* 'steam', *amurg* 'down', *balaur* 'serpent', *baiat* 'boy', *barba* 'beard', *barbat* 'a real man', *batal* 'ram', *barza* 'stork', *bordei* 'hovel', *brad* 'pin', *branza* 'cheese', *brau* 'belt', *burta* 'belly', *buza* 'lip', *carlig* 'hook', *catun* 'village', *cioban* 'shepherd', *ciomag* 'club', *codru* 'forest', *copac* 'tree', *copil* 'child', *gard* 'fence', *gata* 'ready', *groapa* 'hole', *grui* 'hill', *grumaz* 'nape', *mamaliga* 'polenta', *manz* 'colt', *matura* 'broom', *nai* 'panflute', *obraz* 'cheek', *parau* 'brook', *parleaz* 'stile', *ridica* 'lift', *sambure* 'seed', *stapan* 'boss', *stana* 'sheepfold', *stejar* 'oak', *strugure* 'grape', *tare* 'hard', *traista* 'shoulder bag', *varza* 'cabbage', *vatra* 'hearth', *viscol* 'blizzard', *vodza* 'leader', *zimbru* 'bison', *zana* 'angel', and others.

It is known that a dictionary of medicinal herbs was compiled by Pedanius Dioscorides in first century A.D. It listed some 500 healing plants, many of which have Dacian names with Greek and Latin translations. One of them is unmistakably called *dakina* 'wolf's head' (equivalent to garden valerian), and another one was *dracontos*, which is the rosemary shrub.

It is interesting to note that Transylvania's original inhabitants were the Motsi who, like the Illyrians, spoke an original European language. Often referred to as "the Greater Dacians," the Motsi migrated south of Danube into Moesia which came to be named after them. Names of purely Dacian origin were attached to rivers, such as Aluta/Olt, Marisia/Maris/Mures, Porata/Pyretus (Prut), and Samus/Somes; and to the Tisia/Tisza settlements, including Abrutum (Abrud) and Petrodava (city of stone), known today as Piatra Neamtz.

The name of the Dacian capital, Sarmizegethusa, most probably combined the Sarmatian and Getian words *sar* 'horse' and *gethusa/sageta* 'arrow', which also indicated the *gethate/cetate,* a center where the horse-mounted archers met. On another interpretation, *sar* means 'mountain'; *mize,* 'center'; *geth*, 'water'; and *usa/dava*, 'shrine'. Loosely translated, it meant the Holy Mountain Center by the Water, referring to the Sargetia River that was located nearby. It became famous because King Decebalus buried his treasure beneath it after he lost the war with the Romans in the year 106. It is believed to be the contemporary Strei River.

The word *vale* 'valley' may have come from Valah/Vlach, meaning the man from the valley and referring to the sheep herders in the mountains. Part of Central Romania is still named Vlachia/Valachia/Wallachia, the 'shepherds' country'. The ancient city of Valcea in the heart of that hill-and-valley area may be the origin of the name for the entire area. As noted, the terms Valach/Vlach/Wallach may resemble ancient words of Celtic or German origin meaning roughly 'shepherd of the valley'[2], a term that complements the previously notion of a "people of wolves."

Magyars and other later arrivals in Eastern Europe named the Dacians "Vlachs," meaning people who spoke Latin—or a very similar language. This would seem to validate the theory that they belonged to a group of Latin speaking Europeans. The Vlachs/Wallachs were probably very numerous and formed a well defended group of tribes that left a lasting legacy. No doubt, their language was the foundation of modern Romanian.[3]

The Celts, some of the first immigrants to Transylvania, spoke a sort of Latin slang, a fact which facilitated the fusion between them and the Dacians. They were the most likely the ones who introduced Latin vulgaris into Dacia; after all besides Greek, it was the international language of ancient Europe. There is also evidence that the host's language came to be enriched with Celtic words, a fact which further demonstrates the active role the Celts played in Dacian life. Words such *bard* 'poet', *bulgar* 'chunk', *clan* 'group', *dura* 'round', *scut* 'scuttum', *lan* 'the crop of land', *boii* 'oxen'; personal names like Drosida, Gelu, and Vlad; city names like Bran (raven), Severin, and Galatzi; names of mountains such as Godeanu and Pelaga; the name for the entire land of Moldau/Moldova/Moldavia; and the name for the river Dunare/Danube (from *danu* 'to flow') with its Noviodunum (new fort), are some of the elements of the Celtic legacy as it is evidenced in modern Romanian.

It is possible that the ancient Celtic plural suffix *iceni* was incorporated into location names such as Falticeni, Urziceni, etc. This suffix did not, however, supplant the Dacian suffix *dava* 'divine', which appears in the names of the majority of such important settlements as Argedava, Sucidava, etc. Moreover, the center of Celtic culture in Dacia was called Ramidava (Rupea), and a large part of the Dacian population was named *comati* 'men with long hair'. (Caesar named the people *Galia Comata*, meaning long haired Gauls/ Celts.) The name of Decebalus, an important king (whose original name was Diurpaneus), was an epithet derived from the Dacians' spoken Latin *decie* 'ten times' and an abbreviation of *barbatus* 'bearded man', alluding to his power. This may have the same symbolic value as if it came from the Greek *dikefalos*, a wise person so wise it's as if he had two heads.

The German tribes that immigrated to Dacia also had an influence on the language as well. They left names like *catana* 'recruit', most likely originating with the tribe of Catani. The Buri of the Buridavensi tribe had a tremendous power and built their Buridava capital in what is today the county of Valcea (land of Vlachs), a city second to Sarmizegethusa. This tribe produced the first powerful Dacian king, Burebista, whose name (close to *du bist Bur*) is an anagram that indicated he belonged to the tribe of Buri. His name could mean "the wise leader," derived from archaic English *beorn* 'nobleman' and *wis* 'wise.'

During the Roman war against the Germans, the secretary of the future emperor Tiberius wrote (most probably in A.D. 15 when Tiberius tried to fuse Moesia Inferior and Thracia into a single Roman province) that the Dacians spoke their own Latin vulgaris. This validates the claim that the Dacians were neighbors of the Germans and that they were able to communicate with each other.

The Goths, who invaded Dacia in huge numbers, had at least a twenty-four letter alphabet borrowed from Latin and Greek, sufficient to translate the Bible and spread its teachings in Dacia. It is believed that the Dacians used the Roman capital letters as their written alphabet from the first century A.D. onward, and there is evidence to indicate that Trajan's personal physician, Criton, wrote about the similarity of the Latin and the Dacian languages.

Probably the situation was close to what later was the British experience in India, where a type of English is still in use.

The works of Roman poet Ovid provide a number of clues as to the similarity between the Latin and Dacian languages. Publius Ovidius Naso (43 B.C.-A.D. 17) was trained as a lawyer, but instead devoted himself to life as a flamboyant socialite. He wrote the scandalous *Ars Amatoria (Art of Love)* and other books that triggered a feminist revolution in Rome. His love affair with Julia, Emperor Augustus's nymphomaniac daughter, resulted in his banishment in the year 8 to the Getian shore at Tomis (today the Black Sea port of Constantza, Romania). This proved to be a cultural shock for the exiled poet who continued to write letters saturated with self-pity to Rome, hoping to change Augustus's mind and be recalled. Complaining about the "barbarians" he was condemned to live with, he wrote: "Only a few retain some trace of the Greek language . . . and there's not a single person in the population who speaks Latin."[4]

The unhappy poet repeatedly lamented about the private and literary misfortune he experienced, especially since he heard around him "Thracian and Scythian voices [that] chatter away." But he then provided still more precious information: "I think I could write verse in Getic. Believe me, I fear you may find my Latin diluted with Black Sea usage, local terms infecting my work."[5]

At this point one must stop and think about the manically depressed Ovid who obviously had no idea where he lived and about the fact that he saw "Thracians" around him who were in fact the routinely misnamed Getians and Dacians. The reader of his works must use caution in weighing the likely reality of life in Tomis against Ovid's desperate attempts to prove himself a victim at any cost.

The city was the metropolis of Eastern Europe, highly populated with Romans who oversaw the administration of Moesia under governor Pompeius Flaccus. The non-Romans in Tomis probably spoke a very accessible *lingua franca* of Celtic-Greek-Latin and Dacian mix, one that even Ovid understood because it was "overlaid by Getic." In fact, he admitted: "Already, I feel, I've forgotten how to speak my own language through learning the local lingo instead."[6] It is likely that Ovid learned the new dialect so quickly because it was the trade and diplomatic language.

This exiled poet continued to complain about the lack of an audience in Tomis, yet he recited a poem dedicated to Augustus in the Getic language, which he obviously understood. It was probably roughly equivalent to the Latin vulgaris (provincial Latin), mentioned previously.[7] By asking, "Will the Sarmatians or Getae read my work?"[8] Ovid unwillingly admitted that the locals could enjoy his poems. Moreover, half amused by the entire experience with barbarian language he wrote to his agent in Rome that "I blush to admit it, I've even composed in the Getic language," and confesses he might be considered "almost a Getic bard."[9]

When Augustus died (in A.D. 14), Ovid recited his *laudatio* written in Getic to the local audience. The great poet had re-invented himself in the land of Dacian speaking people. In spite of his endless complaints about how the "savage" natives destroyed his talent and corrupted his pure Latin, Ovid wrote close to 7,400 lines of poetry in exile, more than he had written in Rome.

The Roman victory of A.D. 106 against the Dacians brought two legions of more than twenty thousand soldiers and auxiliaries, administration personnel, and some two hundred thousand colonists into Transylvania. All these newcomers spoke Latin, and their impact was first felt in the language of Dacia Felix. Because Latin was the official language of the Roman Empire, all the imperial announcements, rules, records, and reports concerning Dacia were written in that language. Understanding Roman speech and writing was necessary for the welfare of the occupied Dacians. There were other equally important reasons for them to understand Latin.

Many Christian legionaries were banished to Dacia where they married the local women, thus producing an early Christian nation. In the newly mixed society, a child's first name was Roman while the family name remained Dacian. Suddenly baby boys were named Anton (from Antonius), Aurelian, Julian, Ovidiu (from Ovid), Marcu (from Marcus), Silviu (the one from the forest), and Traian (from Trajan). Common names for girls were Emilia (adulated), Gloria (glorious), Julia (young), Silvia (she who belongs to the woods), Victoria (victorious), and Virginia (unstained).

Even though the legionaries were not officially permitted to marry barbarian girls and so could not pass their family names onto their Dacian children, Rome tolerated this "illegality" since it produced future soldiers. Because of these mixed marriages, the military forts extended little by little into *canabae* (civilian settlements) for legionaries and their families;[10] a third society was thereby created in occupied Dacia.

Latin speaking husbands were forced to compromise and learn some Dacian as well, while their children learned both languages and passed both of them on to the next generation. This proto Latin had a tremendous impact on the native language. The addition of the suffixes *esc* and *esti*, with the plural ending in *i*, remain to this day in Romanian. Even though the new language was superimposed over at least two layers of linguistic combinations of Celtic and Sarmatian, another still more complex historic melding would occur: The

Dacianized Latin words and Latinized Dacian verbiage would combine to become the later Romanian language.

Yet, in spite of the Latinization of the Dacian language required by the presence of the Roman administration, only a few locations in Dacia bore the name of a Roman emperor. In the cemeteries around the twelve colonies built by the conquerors, less than half of the headstones bore pure Roman names. Some 20 percent of the deceased there were non-Roman colonists, and the rest were of Dacian heritage. In the occupied territory, the Dacians outnumbered the newcomers. While in Free Dacia the Roman presence was virtually negligible, it was still perceptible because the Latin language flourished there. For Dacians, it was a means of contact with the Western world.

Although the Dacian peasants had limited access to the official language of the Romans, they apparently understood it, too. After all, any document concerning their livelihood was written in Latin. However, the farther Latin migrated from Rome, the more it lost its elegance, precision, and even meaning. The character of the Latin letters was also drastically modified by local stonecutters, many of whom were aliens who chose lines because they were easier to chisel on the memorials and city walls. Conveniently, the Dacians used only the straight lines of Roman capital letters.

Over the course of 165 years of Roman occupation, the language of the occupiers had a huge cultural and social impact on the indigenous population, and that population, in turn, put its own imprint on it. Thus in Dacia, the Latin *aqua* became *apa* 'water', *arare/ara* 'to plow', *aurum/aur* 'gold', *bene/bine* 'good', *basilica/biserica* 'church', *caepa/ceapae* 'onion', *farina/faina* 'flour', *ferrum/fier* 'iron', *granum/grau* 'grains', *lingua/limba* 'languages', *lucrum/lucru* 'labor', *multus/mult* 'much', *nova/noua* 'new', *poma/poama* 'fruit', *populus/popor* 'people', *rota/roata* 'wheel', *sors/soarta* 'fate', *venator/vanator* 'hunter', etc. Other words replaced the Dacian names, like *manus/mana* 'hand', *mare/mare* 'big/wide' (same in Romanian), *musica/musica* 'music', *natura/natura* 'nature', *palma/palma* 'palm', and *taurus/taur* 'bull'.

Roman military terms produced many Romanian words, like *centura* 'belt', which came from centurion—a commander strapped with a large decorated belt, a distinguished sign of his authority over one hundred soldiers. The word *militar* 'military' came from *miliarium*, a unit of one thousand men. *Spada* 'sword' came from *spatha*, the standard broadsword for the Roman cavalry. The name of *gladiola/gladiolus* flower came from little *gladius*, a short stabbing sword used by legionaries. The Dacian knife was named *daca* in Latin vulgaris and later became *dagger*.

Administrative terms in modern Romanian, such as *taxe, notar, procuror, municipiu, prefect, moneta* 'coin', all have their roots in Latin, as do words ending with *patria* 'country'. Many names retained a dual meaning, such as the Dacian *cioban* and the Latin *pastor*, both meaning shepherd.

Latin words were adopted by the Dacians in the same manner as were those from the Celtic, Greek, Sarmatian, Scythian, and German languages. Still, the impact of Latin in the Dacian language proved lasting. Before the year 450 historian Piscus Panites traveled with Maximin, the ambassador of Emperor Theodosius II (the Young) to Attila's court in central Pannonia (most likely where Budapest is today). He crossed part of Dacia and noticed that the people of Banat spoke a "Romana Rustica," a sort of peasant Latin, proof in itself that one of the effects of the Romanization of Transylvania was the acquisition of the new language that stands today as the foundation of Romanian.

In the rest of Free Dacia, more ancient names remained unchanged, as they do today. In the Maramures region of Romania, the ancient villages are still Apsa, Botiza, Barsana, Ieud, etc. The rivers still bear the names of Barjava, Iza, Izes, Repedea, and Teceu. Dacian family names, like Babota, Borca, Codrea, Osan, Roba, and countless others, persist as well. Once more, all of this demonstrates the historic continuity between the Dacian people and later Romanians.

"Romansch," which is spoken in Eastern Switzerland by some fifty thousand people, poses an interesting case. Some scholars take it to be an archaic Roman dialect. In fact, it is not an Italic language, but an ancient Indo-European one, perhaps the remains of the Istro-Dacian branch of the society. Given that at the peak of its development the Dacian Empire extended into parts of Switzerland, it is possible that groups of Dacians never had a chance to return home and remained in these areas. Over time, they may have become what are now the few pockets of Romansch-speaking people. Their peasant architecture supports this theory, since it is very similar to that of the Maramures region.

As for the Dacian language, it became defunct between the sixth and tenth centuries A.D. when the already modified Latin lexicon was powerfully flooded with new words from waves of invaders into the Balkan Peninsula, mainly of Slavic extraction. Still, Romanians inside and outside of the former Dacian borders retained the Latin roots of their words just as the French, Italian, Portuguese, and Spanish languages do to the present day. Their Daco-Romano heritage is what ensured that they are the only Eastern Europeans to speak a Romance language, a fact which is reflected even in the heavily Slavonized liturgy that did not affect the Lord's Prayer of pure Latin roots. The poet Ovid would have been proud of his linguistic contribution to contemporary Romanian life.

Danubian cultural artifacts include the work of agrarian Dacians who left painted pots and other artistic-utilitarian objects. They have been found at Cernavoda (the former Axiopolis) and along the Danube River, a stream which connected many if not most of the European civilizations. Other archeological discoveries of ancient arts and crafts have been dated to approximately 4000 B.C., a time period which preceded the advanced settlements that produce the so-called cultures of Boian (in Vallachia), Dudesti (in area of Bucharest), and Costisa (in Moldova), among others.

The nomadic culture of the Sarmatians brought the Sacian civilization into the Dacian land, where the Scythian artistic influence was equally strong. Their Iranian artistic trademarks were also imprinted upon the Daco-Getian culture.

The Greek influence in Dacia was significant as well. The vast number of imported iron objects for everyday use, such as amphoras and arts and crafts items extant throughout Romania, testify to their presence.

The La Tene culture was brought to Dacia by the migratory Celtic tribes when they engaged in mining and proved to be excellent metal workers. Bronze and iron weaponry, decorated glassware, necklaces, bracelets, clasps, and other objects of obviously Celtic origin were found in impressive quantities all over Romania, again providing concrete evidence of their presence there.[11] The Celts brought the numerical system based on twelve/a dozen, which the Dacians adopted as dividing the day in twenty-four hours, the year in twelve months, and so on.

Transylvania proved to be the cultural cradle of the Dacians, as the archeological findings of the Cotofeni, Cucuteni, and Petresti sites, among others, attest. These sites featured ceramics painted in Dacian colors that continue to be seen today in Romanian folk costumes. The Romanian tricolor of blue, yellow, and red is still the national flag.

The Dacian civilization thrived from the Bronze Age onward, when the Italics introduced their ancient Latin language there via trade routes. The large variety of lamps, buckets, fibulas, ornaments, and helmets of Italic design found in present-day Romania, together with the Latin roots of the Romanian language, are all evidence that this early culture existed on the fringes of Dacia.

The Dacians did not have a desire to impress the world, so they did not build temples, palaces, and civic buildings for posterity (even though they could have built in gold and silver everything that the Romans built in marble!). Strictly pragmatic and tending toward the ascetic, their art was meant to please only themselves, and focused on rural themes and the natural world that surrounded the villages. Dacian civilization is probably best known for its woodworking—Dacians perfected the skill of cutting and chiseling complicated ornaments into massive pillars and gates. The most common of the patterns used were floral, birds (especially the rooster), animals, including what it is called "wolf's teeth," and cosmological motifs of the sun and stars. The Dacian flying dragon was often the centerpiece of the carvings.[12]

The Motsi of Transylvania made everyday objects from wood and excelled in producing barrels, buckets, troughs, spoons, and other useful implements, as they do today. Architecture which used materials other than wood was also simple and practical. The capital of Sarmizegethusa was defended by a cordon of military fortifications similar to the one on top of Blidaru Hill. The bunkers' massive ruins shed light on its important and powerful past.[13] All of these strongholds were made from straight-cut stone, dry brick, and timber of a strictly functional design, without ornamentation. They were encircled with walls of excavated dirt, especially in the flat land, in order to provide wide and deep defensive ditches filled with water. Celtic architecture, which used a combination of wood and stone, represented another more complicated level of design.

The musical tradition of the Dacians was close to the Indian/Iranian style of melodies and interpretation thereof. The Dacian musical instruments included the *nai* 'pan flute', *kobza* 'short bulky guitar', and the *dramba* 'mouth harp'. The short shepherd's flute was always handy, and the long, heavy *bucium/das Alpenhorn* horn was used for its tuba-like sound and for signaling over long distances.

But the most important musical influence came from the highly musical Celts. They were probably the only ancient warriors who paraded and attacked to the sound of music produced by long trumpets and other wind instruments. The Celts introduced the bagpipe to Dacia, and it remained a traditional Romanian instrument. Today, the Celtic influence is clearly detected in the Romanian *ballada* 'ballad' and *doina* 'sad love song'. Without a doubt, it was not Thracian music, about which Strabo was writing when he said, "From its melody and rhythm and instruments, all Thracian music has been considered to be Asiatic."[14]

Dacian dancers seemed to impress foreigner visitors, among them the Greek historian Xenophon (ca. 431-355 B.C.) who described a dance with an agricultural theme. Aristotle also mentioned a dance that had a war theme. Many such theme dances still survive, the best known being *Calusari* (*Horse Riders*). This military dance shows the recruiting and training drill of the fighters, who respond with wild shouts, earth-shaking footwork, deafening whistling, and club handling to the commands given by their leader. The leader carries a standard embellished with ribbons and flowers for luck, the centerpiece of the dance.

The dancers are equipped with bells and garlic attached to their ankles and knees to keep the evil spirits away and to impress the enemy. The change of formations, the athletics of movements and rhythms, are choreographed with a high level of complexity. The dance was obviously a reflection of the undying Dacian fighting spirit. Dances of a fast pace, like *Batuta, Brau Ciuleandra,* and *Sarba,* were unmistakable Celtic line tap dances; they are still part of Romanian folklore today.

The influence of the Vedic civilization was also perceptible in ancient Dacia, most obviously in the way people dressed. Men wore large white shirts over long, tight white pants, with black vests or coats. Women wore long colorful *fote/dhoti* (wrap skirts) and long white *marama* (veils) around their heads and shoulders. Men's clothing was embroidered with simple geometrical designs, stitched in black and white. Women added different shades of red to richly flowered designs. Silver jewelry was dominant, for silver symbolized purity and chastity.

As for the former lawyer-turned-poet Publius Ovidius, who ignited a fashionable sexual revolution in Rome with his books *Remedia Amores (Cures for Love)*, he kept sending heartbreaking *Epistulae ex Ponto (Letters from the Black Sea)* to Rome, comparing himself to a ship which had been wrecked in a sea of barbarians. Why barbarians? Because Romans divided the entire world's population into those who were *civilis* 'modern' who spoke pure Latin, wore sandals, and believed in Roman gods, and *barbarus,* who were savage *paganus,* did not grow olive trees or have tile roofs, and had only one name. (The Roman citizens had a praenomen, nomen, and cognomen, such as Gaius Julius Caesar.) The awkward noise, *bara-bara-bara,* emitted by non-Romans produced an unpleasant animal-like sound. It was synonymous with the meaning of people who produced "non-sense", good-for-nothings who acted like animals, and therefore had to be identified as a lesser race of humans. They were people who hunted and lived hand-to-mouth. Probably the word *barbatus* 'bearded' was applied to the Dacians as well, since they sported trimmed beards.

However, the Daco-Getians belonged to a different classification of people. They were far from being barbarians. Three hundred years before Christ, Alexander the Great was utterly impressed by the way they carried themselves, and Trajan's Column portrayed them with a most civilized attitude. They may have learned Latin and some Roman ways of life, but their culture remained unchanged. As for Ovid, he created his best poems in Tomis, so evidently life among the Dacians did not stifle his talent.

Ironically, history dictated that the elegant Latin of Ovid would become a dead language, while the barbarian-contaminated Vulgar Latin is still spoken in Italy today in the form of Italian. From this later language, the family of the Romance languages developed, of which Romanian is one.[15]

Time and the apocalyptic events that changed the Eastern European civilization had less impact on the life of the Dacians than they did on others. Unlike their neighbors, the Daco-Romans maintained close relationships with the Latinized world in spite of the Slavic and Balkan culture and the historic process of "Balkanization."

NOTES

1. Strabo, *The Geography of Strabo*, trans. Horace Leonard Jones (London: William Heinemann; New York: G. P. Putnam's Sons, 1924), vol. 3, 215.

2. An ancient tribe named Volcae was part of the Celtic invasion of the Balkan Peninsula, but they vanished from history. Records mentioned its members as Wolcoi/Volcoi, who could have crossed the Danube River into Dacia and settled in what is today Vallachia. A location and entire area named Vlasca still occupies a large area north of the Danube River, below Bucharest. A Black Vallachia was often cited in early Medieval history, referring to the Vlachs living by the Black Sea, in the Dacian lands of Eastern Moesia and Moldova.

3. The Valahi/Vlachs are found throughout the Middle Ages not only in Romania but also south of the Danube throughout the entire Balkan Peninsula. At that time, just as today, they were the only Balkan people with a language whose roots were Latin. The Crusaders fought against them but found it wiser to have the Vlachs as reliable allies. Today they are the estranged Romanian people know as Aromanians or Macedo-Romanians, Megleno-Romanians and Istro-Romanians, all speaking Daco-Roman dialects, proving to be descendants of what was once the Greater Dacia.

4. Ovid. *The Poems of Exile: Tristia* and the *Black Sea Letters*, trans. Peter Green (Berkeley: University of California Press, 2005), bk. 5, 7.51-54.

5. Ovid, *Poems*, bk. 3, 14.47-51.

6. Ovid, *Poems*, bk. 5, 12.57-58.

7. It is interesting to note that the Gauls from Galatia in Asia Minor spoke the same language as the Cimbri and Teutons, the Celtic and German tribes of Central Europe respectively. It was therefore not difficult for Paul of Tarsus, who spoke Latin, to communicate with the Galitians and convert them to Christianity forty years after Ovid's death.

8. Ovid, *Poems*, bk. 4, 1.94.

9. Ovid, *Poems*, bk. 4, 13.17-19.

10. The Romanian language retained *cabane* as a word for isolated wooden houses.

11. In today's Romania, remnants of Celtic culture can be found in Fagaras and Muscel, remarkably preserved because of a millennia of isolation. Numerous Celtic art objects still beautify Romanian architecture, especially the Orthodox churches

which feature Celtic crosslets with no break lines and spiral knot panels with open lacework; the latter represent infinite life, good luck, and hope.

12. Today in the Maramures region wooden churches of incredible architecture and breathtaking beauty stand over 50 meters/164 feet high, a testament to the Dacian tradition of woodworking.

13. Similar strongholds with equally impressive walls were located at Banita, Bud, Capalna, Costesti, Covasan, Cugir, Fetele Albe, Piatra Rosie, Saratel, Tilisca, Zetea, and many other locales, all of which are now in ruins.

14. Strabo, *Geography*, trans. Jones, p.107.

15. Modern Romanian language has a lexical similarity with Latin of greater than 75 percent. The Aromanian language is spoken by pockets of the Vallachian population from modern Albania and Epir to Tessalia (Grecia) and Bitolia (Macedonia), Bulgaria, Hungary, Serbia, and other parts of Eastern Europe, as the legacy of the Daco-Romanians. It retained more Latin roots than all of the other Romanian dialects.

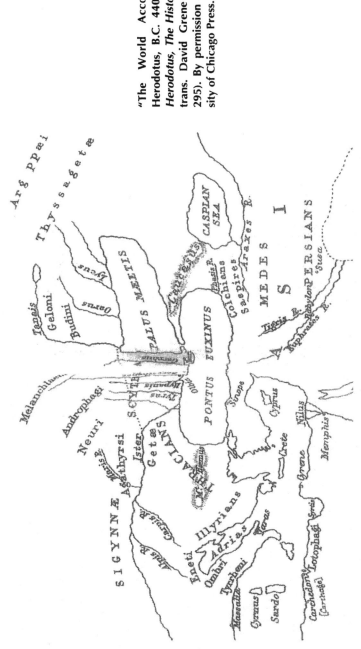

"The World According to Herodotus, B.C. 440." Source: *Herodotus, The History* (1987), trans. David Grene (pp 294-295). By permission of University of Chicago Press.

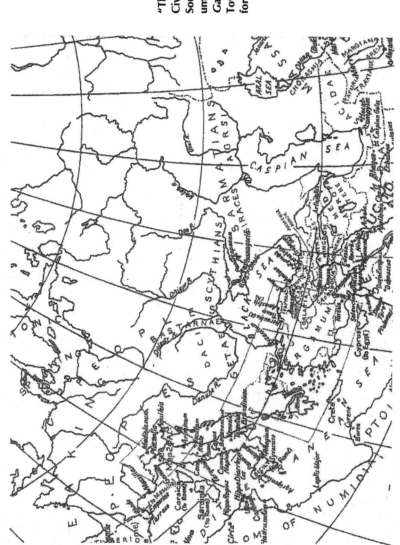

"The Extension of the Hellenic Civilization Overland 171 B.C." Source: *A Study of History*, Volume XI: *Historical Atlas and Gazeteer* (1959) by Arnold J. Toynbee. By permission of Oxford University Press.

Ptolemy's map of Europe. Source: *Cosmographia* by Ptolemy (Rome: Petrus de Turre, 1490)

Ptolemy's map showing Dacian tribes. Source: *Geographia* by Ptolemy (Basileæ: apvd H. Petrvm, 1540)

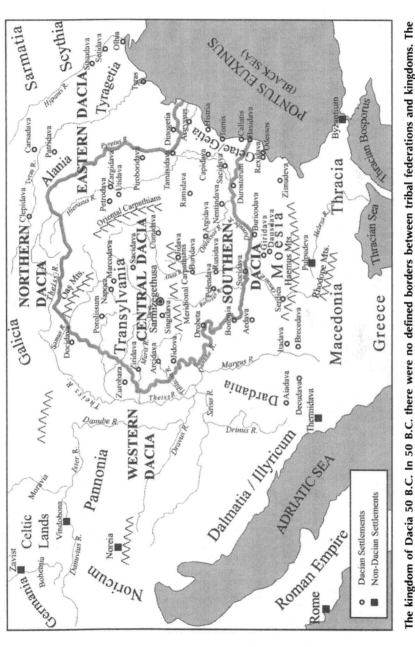

The kingdom of Dacia 50 B.C. In 50 B.C. there were no defined borders between tribal federations and kingdoms. The shaded border is that of today's Romania. Source: Map created by author.

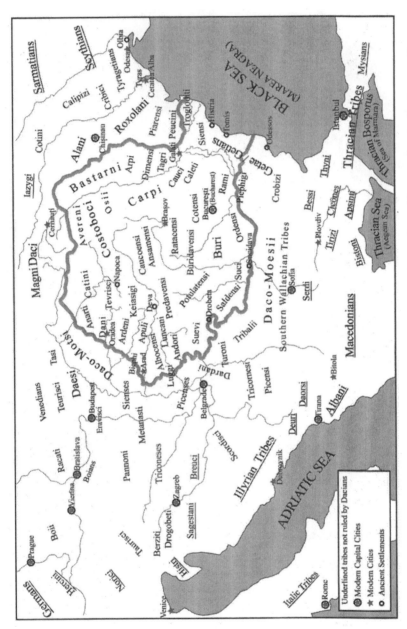

The main tribes of ancient Dacia and eastern Europe. This map includes modern cities as a frame of reference. Source: Map created by author.

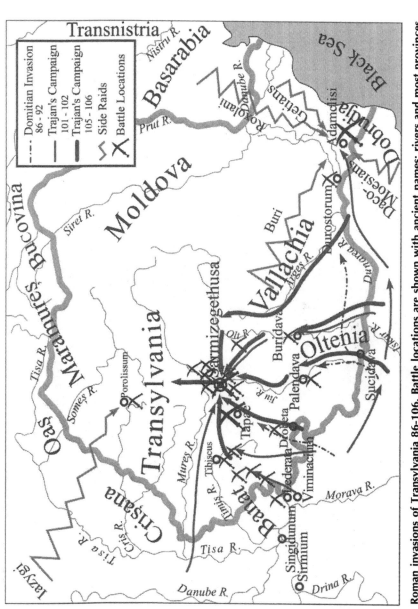

Roman invasions of Transylvania 86-106. Battle locations are shown with ancient names; rivers and most provinces with modern names. Source: Map created by author.

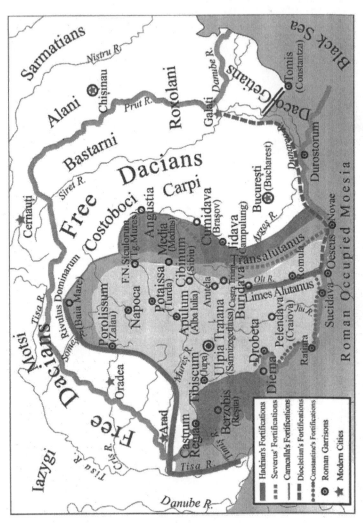

Dacia Felix and its Roman fortifications. This map shows the partial Roman occupation of Transylvania and the location of the main free Dacian tribes and other Eastern European tribes around Dacia Felix. Rivers and some cities are shown with Dacian, Roman, and Romanian names. Shaded areas show the gradual increase of Roman occupation. Source: Map created by author.

The Roman invasion of Transylvania in A.D. 101; Emperor Trajan, his Praetorian Guard and troops crossing the Danube at Lederata. Source: *The Column of Trajan* (2000) by Filippo Coarelli. By permission of Colombo Duemila, S.p.A. (Rome)

The surprise attack by Dacians, Buri, and Roxolani (on horses with fish-scale armor) at Tropeum Traiana (today's Adamclisi) in the winter of 101-102. Source: *The Column of Trajan* (2000) by Filippo Coarelli. By permission of Colombo Duemila, S.p.A. (Rome)

Dacians ram a fortress wall and Getians shoot arrows at the Roman defenders. Source: *The Column of Trajan* (2000) by Filippo Coarelli. By permission of Colombo Duemila, S.p.A. (Rome)

The Roman auxiliaries charge and a fallen Dacian tries to pull out an arrow while Dacian civilians carrying children evacuate. Source: *The Column of Trajan* (2000) by Filippo Coarelli. By permission of Colombo Duemila, S.p.A. (Rome)

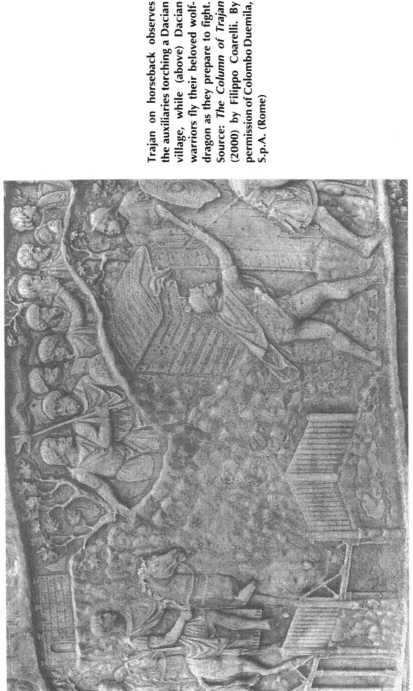

Trajan on horseback observes the auxiliaries torching a Dacian village, while (above) Dacian warriors fly their beloved wolf-dragon as they prepare to fight. Source: *The Column of Trajan* (2000) by Filippo Coarelli. By permission of Colombo Duemila, S.p.A. (Rome)

A full, ferocious combat scene shows Dacians using their curved scimitars and small shields, the ground littered with the dead and wounded--none of whom are Romans. Source: *The Column of Trajan* (2000) by Filippo Coarelli. By permission of Colombo Duemila, S.p.A. (Rome)

The Dacian leaders surrender to Trajan, overseen by King Decebalus with his arms extended; two Dacian flying dragon standards are displayed. Source: *The Column of Trajan* (2000) by Filippo Coarelli. By permission of Colombo Duemila, S.p.A. (Rome)

The second war in A.D. 105-106 is represented by this brutal scene of fallen Dacians still holding their curved swords, while Trajan watches from above. Source: *The Column of Trajan* (2000) by Filippo Coarelli. By permission of Colombo Duemila, S.p.A. (Rome)

It is a fight to the end, with besieged Dacians repelling each attack. An auxiliary holds a severed Dacian head whose body is still on the parapet. Source: *The Column of Trajan* (2000) by Filippo Coarelli. By permission of Colombo Duemila, S.p.A. (Rome)

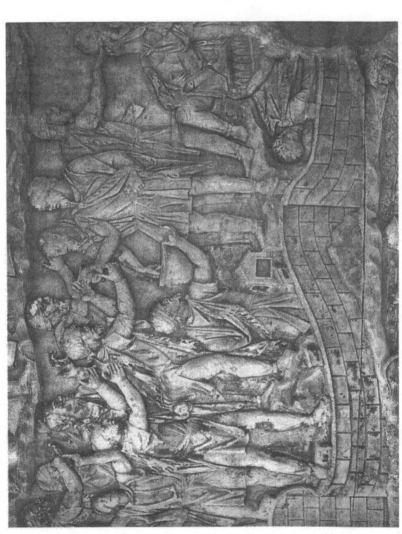

Dacian commanders and their soldiers share the last drops of water in the encircled Sarmizegethusa. It is often speculated that they drank poison instead of surrendering. Source: *The Column of Trajan* (2000) by Filippo Coarelli. By permission of Colombo Duemila, S.p.A. (Rome)

King Decebalus, between the trees, conducts a surprise counter-attack on a Roman garrison, but the war was lost for the Dacians. Source: *The Column of Trajan* (2000) by Filippo Coarelli. By permission of Colombo Duemila, S.p.A. (Rome)

Tiberius Maximus, a cavalry officer, tries to stop the Dacian king from committing honorable suicide. Source: *The Column of Trajan* (2000) by Filippo Coarelli. By permission of Colombo Duemila, S.p.A. (Rome)

Monument at Tropeum Traina (Adamclisi). Source: Source: *The Column of Trajan* (2000) by Filippo Coarelli. By permission of Colombo Duemila, S.p.A. (Rome)

A plaque from the Trophy of Trajan at Tropeum Traiana (Adamclisi) showing a Roman on the left, a Dacian on the right holding a curved sword, and a wounded Sarmatian holding a two-hand long sword. Source: *The Column of Trajan* (2000) by Filippo Coarelli. By permission of Colombo Duemila, S.p.A. (Rome)

Trajan's Column pierces the sky of Rome. Source: Private Collection

Ruins of Trajan's Forum around the Column. Source: Private Collection

Author at the base of Trajan's Column in 2005. Source: Private Collection

Rome's Arch of Constantine, featuring the statues of Dacians. Source: Private Collection

Statue of Ovid in Constantza (ancient Tomis), Romania. Source: Private Collection

This 1936 Romanian wedding picture in Valea Mare Pravat—a Muscel village—shows an unmistakable Dacian heritage. The author's mother, dressed in the Romanian national costume (first row, center), sits in front of the bride, her sister. Two traditional *plocads* (shaggy quilts), wedding gifts, are displayed on the balcony. The pine branches are a symbol of long life and prosperity. Source: Private Collection.

Chapter Six

Social, Economic, and Military Life

The population of ancient Eastern Europe where Dacia was situated consisted of a multitude of people in search of a safer and easier life. During the Stone Age, the immense forests sheltered packs of fifty to a hundred hunters and their families, who lived on fruits and plants. Related by blood or by common need, many of these packs united to become tribes with a population ten times larger.

The interaction of groups of people has been characterized throughout history in terms of elements such as alliance, avoidance, breeding, and conflict. Ancient tribes that spoke the same language as their forefathers considered themselves related to each other, but this did not stop them from periodically engaging in bloody fights incited by domineering chieftains or conflicting territorial claims. These fights eventually led to the conquest of populations and the annexation of patches of land, and they often marked the birth of tribal unions: one tribe came to subjugate to another and both were thereby redefined.

For obvious reasons, the hunting tribes conquered the sheep herding or farming tribes; the latter often had better and richer shelters than the hunters. Through such conquests tribal "herds" developed. They were well controlled by local chieftains who respected a leader with a great war record or a man with reputed wisdom, someone who was venerated by everyone. The warriors of these tribes were heroes who were adulated by youngsters since they also shared their enthusiasm for tough combat.

The warriors' status as defenders of their families and their domesticated animals was a supreme and vital necessity for the society. To stop an enemy from entering the camp and to protect it from plunder, rape, and murder were their main tasks. To kill before being killed was the only rule of survival, and the only male sport was training for war—the ultimate form of justice in the land. The population's main defensive strategy was to move constantly in order to avoid its attackers.

The organization and administration of these migratory populations—groups that had neither precise language nor borders—was a mystery for the Greeks and Romans who named them *barbarians.* "Barbaricum" was the land beyond the civilized world, an unknown abyss that induced equal amounts of both contempt and fear. Even though Dacia was classified as such an area on their maps, the Dacian tribes were not migratory and certainly not plundering barbarians. They had their own land with its center in Transylvania, and they formed a monolithic society. But they were one of the many peoples that made up ancient Eastern Europe.

In their continuous migration from Asia, vast numbers of Sarmatians and Scythians settled north of Dacia, and, during his travels through Eastern Europe, Herodotus discovered their societies. His documentation of this was highly influenced by his preconceived ideas and by the myths of his time, the legend of the Amazons being a case in point. While his descriptions are often highly imaginative, they still contain many valuable clues about the social and military life of those ancient Eastern Europeans.

Herodotus recognized the matriarchal character of the Sarmatian culture. He admired the Sarmatian women who wore men's clothes, hunted while riding at full speed, and fought elbow to elbow with their men. His records show that a virgin could marry only after she killed an enemy of her tribe. The main weapons used by this group were the bow, dagger, and battle ax. Their arrows had bronze heads, an advanced technical achievement for that time. The Sarmatians were some of the first warriors in antiquity who wore body armor, ingeniously made. They sliced the hooves of dead horses into the shape of fish scales and sewed them on their coats and trousers. This original design has been preserved in sculptures; it is one that distinguished them throughout their history.

The historian noted that the Thracians were polygamous, with "many wives" whom they buy "from their parents at large prices." The men had the right of life or death over their wives and children and "sell their children for export. As far as young maidens are concerned, they keep no watch over them but let them couple with whom they will."[1]

By contrast, the Dacians were monogamous. Like Sarmatians, Celts, and Scythians, they lived in a matriarchal society, and women played a leading role as the head of families and even in the military. A woman was able to choose a husband and marry at will; she was not his property, and she had the right to ask for a divorce, which meant that she could keep both her original inheritance and her maiden name. A husband had no right to decide on the life and death of his family members. The name and the origin of a Dacian newborn was given by the mother, and this in spite of the fact that during his reign Burebista attempted to institutionalize patriarchal power, including having the name and inheritance of a newborn come from the father. Dacian women are superbly featured on the Trajan's Column with beautiful faces, a distinctive hair style, and elegant dress, and they display a rare dignity.

Unlike the Dacians who did not use tattoos for any reason, the Thracians considered them to be "a mark of high birth"; the absence of a tattoo was a sort of stigma, an indication of inferior breeding. Herodotus described the Thracians as lazy, since "being a worker of the land [was] most dishonorable. Noblest of all is living from war and plunder."[2] Once again, the Dacians were obviously not Thracians.

Like the Sarmatian elite, the *tarabostes* of Dacia were proud to identify themselves as unique. The Dacian aristocracy was composed of the society's top ranking military families and the well-to-do families of the tribal chieftains. Their ranking in the social order was after the priests, who were the closest to the king. They dressed in toga-like shirts and wore Mithraic conical caps made of felt or lamb fur with a top that flopped forward. These hats, clearly and accurately depicted on Trajan's Column, made them instantly recognizable as *pileati* (the capped ones—Dacian nobility).

The Dacians also borrowed from the Sarmatians a mark or indication of noble blood: family monograms called *tagmas*. Colorful blazons, created with a polychrome technique that was surprisingly advanced for the times, were pinned as jewelry on their clothes or inlaid on their weapons and shields so as to indicate each person's rank. Dacian noblemen also adopted these distinctive marks of superiority in the form of round clasps for their hats. Tarabostes who were large land owners and lived in castle-like dwellings were the ones who proudly displayed the *tagmas*, which later became coats of arms.

The common men were called *comati* (long hair heads) or *capilati* (heads full of hair); they were the working class—artisans, farmers, shepherds, hunters, and others. Men wore long, tight woolen pants with linen shirts hanging over them halfway to the knee, a *chimir* (studded leather belt with pockets), a vest, and a *sarica* (long shepherd's sheepskin coat). Men and women wore the same *opinci* (leather moccasins) with *nojite* (laces that wrapped around their calves). Hemp, wool, and linen were the main fabrics they used; they were artistically stitched in three distinctive colors: yellow, red, and blue. At the lowest level of society were the foreigners and prisoners, who performed unwanted and dangerous jobs.

Initially, Dacia was ruled as a tribal democracy in which each member (men and women) had voting power. As the leadership became centralized, the society became a tribal monarchy led by chieftains, one of whom ultimately became a king in his own right. The many assassinations suffered by the Dacian kings proved they were not above or safe from assault by other members of society. Their dictatorial powers were extremely limited. Even the great Burebista who succeeded in creating a Dacian empire was not immune from capital punishment.

The empiric Dacian state was not founded on slavery or plunder, but on the labor of free men who created an advanced society. The Dacians are known to have freed prisoners of war and slaves who had escaped to their land and also to have hired skilled foreign craftsmen. They gave all newcomers the same rights as the natives. Few peoples in the ancient world displayed such humane treatment of foreigners. This fact alone clearly distinguishes the Dacians from the truly barbarian and slave-oriented societies of this period.

Although other cultures constructed their villages in river valleys, the Dacians considered these tempting locations to be dangerous. Attack by a foreign power was all too easy under such conditions. Indeed, invaders generally took advantage of the easy access to villages that was provided by a road running alongside a river. The Dacians therefore built most of their villages behind high hills and in the mountains, making their settlements difficult to locate and to access. This gave them the distinct advantage of having time to prepare to fight or escape.

The Dacians preferred hilltop settlements with large round sheds but, for obvious defensive reasons their *oppida* were surrounded by tall and thick wood beams called "palisades" with interior platforms from which they could fight. In the flatland areas, the villages were located in the middle of grain fields and fertile pastures for the same defensive reason—to put sufficient distance between them and any invaders to allow the people time to escape. A typical *sat* (village) covered a surface of 1-2 hectares (up to 5 acres) and contained fewer than one hundred log houses with conic shingle roofs called *sure*. Its villagers generally numbered fewer than five hundred. Rich settlements around the salt mines, such as the Rona village in Maramures, were populated by more than one thousand people.

Village properties such as pastures, forests, mountains, roads, bridges, waters, fountains were held collectively and a *şura mare* (central building) was constructed for meetings, festivities, dancing, and collective work. Individual properties consisted of a main hut, *grajd* (stable), *coşar* (barn), *coteţ* (bird or small animal shelter), and *tarla* (land enclosure) divided into an *ograda* (animal partition) and *gradina* (cultivated garden). For insulation and storage, the huts were built halfway into the ground and constructed of wood, mud and straw brick (baked by sun), stones, and beams covered with wooden shingles, straw, or a thatch roof. The Dacian architectural style was minimal, the design focusing on maximizing living space.

On average, a house had two rooms: the *tinda* (storage for immediate food supply and tools) and the *hodaia* (bedroom), with the *vatra* (fireplace hearth) and furniture fixed in the dirt floor and walls. Under or near the house was a *pivniţa* (cellar) for storing food supplies. High, strong timber fences and *zid* (walls) of excavated dirt reshaped into a fortified curtain encircled the villages. Each household was surrounded by twig fences with a large-roofed gate resting on large ornamented pillars, which made a proud statement for each family.

The Dacians worshipped the wolf and copied the wolf pack's strict family and social order. That is, they lived in close communities in which cooperation, from hunting to defense, was required for survival. Children were a treasure of the entire community and they were closely watched over. They were also treated with love, as depicted on Trajan's Column which shows the Dacians as protective and tender parents. Girls were raised to be skillful wives and loving mothers; young men were trained to become warriors, hunters, or shepherds. The elderly were venerated and attended to by the entire family and society. Kissing someone's hand was the sign of veneration for that person.

Religion played an important role in shaping the Dacian society, as was also the case in other tribal societies. Dacian religion was led mainly by the society's priests. The historian Jordanes is known to have held one of them in particularly high esteem. When explaining why Dicineus (Deceneus) was as important to the Goths as he was to the Daco-Getians, he wrote: "He taught them logic and made them skilled in reasoning beyond all other races; he showed them practical knowledge and so persuaded them to abound in good works."[3]

Deceneus, Jordanes added, "ruled not only the common men but their kings. He chose from among them those that were at that time of noblest birth and superior wisdom and taught them theology, bidding them worship certain divinities and holy places."[4] Very likely Deceneus was familiar with the Essene way of life and wanted to apply their concept of asceticism to Dacian society to keep people healthy and militarily strong. More than that, Deceneus understood that Dacian rural society needed faith in their god Zamolxis in order to survive the influence of other gods introduced by the immigrating tribes and by the Hellenistic religious contamination. Thus, by enforcing the Dacian religious codes, Deceneus helped maintain national identity and firmly unified the *dava*-ruled society.

Like the Druids, the Dacian high priests and elite tarabostes, both wearing conic fur hats with the top rolled forward, ruled the tribes and provided them with centralized leadership. They meted out justice, while the chieftains and warlords were empowered to respond to any emergencies. The Dacian kings were elected on the basis of their military valor and not in keeping with dynastical rules. The Dacian philosophy of life was stoic and commanded patience for everything. In a nutshell, it came down to the saying, *"Apa trece, pietrele raman"* ("Water flows away, stones remain"). And, the people themselves were living proof of this wisdom, as their society remained untouched by time and waves of migrating peoples.

The Greeks and Romans had virtually no knowledge of ancient Eastern Europe, except that it was a source of food and a place of mysterious legends. The only information about it came from Herodotus who noted in his historical narratives that the land of Scythia was rich in pastures, but had no forts or cities, and that the nomadic tribes lived from hunting, raising animals, and farming the vast grain fields. This was evidenced by the name of Scythia, a term which is related to the scythe/sickle, a reaping hook is still used to harvest grain in the Republic of Moldova and the Southern Ukraine.

Long before Herodotus traveled to Scythia in the fifth century B.C., the ever enterprising ancient Greeks extended their trade routes along the west coast of the Black Sea, which they initially named Pontos Axeinos (Dark/Inhospitable Sea). Above the Dacian shore they founded the cities of Tyras, Olbiopolis/Olbia, and other safe estuaries for the merchant fleets of Hellas. The chain of the Greek commercial ports transformed over time into cities that continued north from Olbia (near today Odessa) into the Crimean Peninsula, with Theodosia, Trebizond, and Chersonesus (Sevastopol). Their trading posts extended along the Sea of Azov with the settlements of Panticapaeum (Kerch), Phanagoria (Taman Peninsula), Tanais (in the Don River delta), and others.

Scythia was the breadbasket for the poorer Hellenic cities. Heavy wagons filled with grain and pulled by oxen would travel to the ports where they unloaded their contents into the Greek ships. Other wagons carried furs, smoked meat, and cheeses to these ships. Greek commercial agents used a barter system, so the Scythians traded their goods for much needed iron tools, horse harnesses, pottery, weapons, art objects, jewelry, perfume, fine textiles, and amphorae filled with olive oil.

But a long journey was required in order to reach Scythia, and the Black Sea was filled with networks of pirates and troubled by storms. Long before Herodotus had traveled there, the practical Greeks built intermediate ports midway on the Dacian shores for shelter. Other ports evolved into rich settlements on the Danube River, such as Aegyssus (Tulcea), Axiopolis (Cernavoda), Troesmis (Turcoaia), and Carsium (Harsova). They were destined to transport the interior trade of Transylvania and the Carpathians, facilitated by the Tibiscus (Timis), Aluta (Olt), Naparis (Ialomitsa), and Pyretus (Prut) rivers that flowed into the lower Danube, the commercial jugular vein of central Europe.

On the Chilia arm of the Danubian Delta there were trading posts as well, among them Aliobrix (Ismail) and Pardina (near Tulcea), which controlled the exit to the Black Sea. At the Black Sea, the Greeks built the fortified cities Odessus (Varna), Callatis (Mangalia), Tomis (Constantza), and Histria. In Callatis they minted coins, and in Histria they constructed a temple dedicated to Zeus, the remains of which can still be seen today. The Greeks were commercial agents, so their dealing did not create form of any vassalage over the Dacian tribes who remained the undisputed owners of the land.

In 500 B.C., Scythian horsemen stormed and sacked the prosperous city of Histria and settled around its fertile lands, mixing in with the Dacian natives and forming the population of Getia (Getae). These immigrants brought with them their advanced skill at grain cultivation and tremendously increased the importance of the Getian ports. The latter were able to offer the benefits of cheaper grains and journeys of shorter duration for the Greek and Roman commercial vessels.

The economic situation in Eastern Europe changed after Scythia was invaded by the Sarmatian tribes, which were comprised mainly of shepherds who previously dominated the vast steppes beyond the Caspian Sea which extended east of the Volga River. Forced by other migrating Asiatic tribes behind the western Don line, they found themselves in the territory of today's Ukraine. Like the Scythians, they used their commercial power and controlled the Greek jewelry trade. And, they influenced the Hellenic goldsmiths by demanding brilliantly colored items to match their colorful taste.

The Scythians left behind many rich treasures lavishly decorated with gold that had likely been mined in Transylvania and sold to the Greeks. Thus Dacia became the main gold supplier of the Balkans and Eastern Europe, an enviable title that attracted numerous marauding expeditions

Before the second century B.C., the Sarmatians nearly took control of Scythia, and their wild horsemen also controlled trade in eastern Black Sea area. The result was that many commercial cities in the area were sacked. Refugees migrated south to Getia where they joined their relatives who were thriving under Dacian rule. During the reign of King Burebista, the Dacians extended their rule northeastward and assumed control over the trading posts in Sarmatia and Scythia. Because they were not navigators, their conquest was on land with Getian cavalry and Dacian foot soldiers.

The Daco-Getians pushed the Sarmatians away from the Black Sea coast and raided defiant Olbia (which refused to pay commercial taxes to Burebista) and its vicinity. The ruined city never recovered. By 50 B.C., the border of Dacia reached the Dnieper River and the Dacians were in full military and economic control of the western Black Sea shore. They had eliminated their competition as far as grains were concerned and taken over the Greek commercial ports. Suddenly, these cities lost their porto franco status, and the Greeks had to pay taxes to the Dacian king. Some historians have erroneously described this as a Thraco-Cimmerian takeover, another blunder in documentation—substituting Thracians (who were confined to the southern tip of the Balkan Peninsula) for Dacians.

While the Sarmatian tribes looked for gold and objects made of metal during their raids, the Dacians already had those commodities at hand. Thousands of years earlier, when wandering tribes all over the world looked for the remains of meteorites from which they collected the metal needed for weapons and tools, the Dacians were already extracting copper and iron from Transylvanian mines. The Metal Mountains, the location of Chalcis in what are today the Baia de Arama and other copper rich areas, were named because of their ore content. In very early times, this area attracted immigrant workers.

After the Dacians claimed parts of Sarmatia, some tribes (mainly the Roxolani and Iazygi) migrated southwestward, seeking a more hospitable place to live in mainland Dacia. Like many others before them, they came to the impenetrable Danube Delta and were prevented by the Dacians from crossing the Prut River. Since they had no particular skills with which to bargain, they became the poor distant relatives of the Dacians. They took full advantage of the military vigor of these groups by enlisting their help in raiding and plundering the Roman-fortified cities south of the Danube. Eventually the Roxolani were happy to be accepted in the Dacian land, while the rebellious Iazygi kept claiming a land of their own outside Dacia.

Unlike the Sarmatians, the Celtic tribes who settled in Dacia made a significant contribution to the economic and spiritual life of the native population. The Celts were mine diggers, master blacksmiths, excellent forgers, and bronze casters. They monopolized the metallurgical works and paid the Dacians for the privilege with weapons, tools, jewelry, and other valuable objects. They also manufactured utilitarian objects such as axes, knives, plows, and furniture. The Celts produced iron rimmed hoops for wooden wheels, round metal straps for barrels, and they provided iron shoes for horses. This was an industrial achievement that gave the Dacians a tremendous economic boost.

The Celts excelled at working with copper, from which they created a rich variety of objects including cups, dishes, pots, and spoons. They introduced the pottery wheel, the spinning wheel, and sieves made of horse hair into Dacian culture. They were experts at creating colorful glass and also excelled at the sophisticated art of jewelry making, something much admired by all Eastern Europeans.

Most importantly, the newcomers found a Dacian market hungry for their weapons. The typical Celtic weapons were a three foot long sword of superior quality and a round shield, both of which were adopted and modified by the Dacians. The sword was made into a falax/*palosh*, a long dagger with a bent tip, probably so it could serve as a sickle as well as a weapon.[5] A later and final version was the curved *scimitar*, much depicted on Trajan's Column. A shorter version was called *sica*. The oval wooden shield, inlaid with beautiful copper ornamentations, was reduced in size as well. The Dacians did not, however, have a use for the Celtic war chariot (the equivalent of the modern tank), the metallic chest armor, or the iron pot helmet.

Masters of construction, the Celts combined brick and stone with wooden beams in vertical lines that were connected at the corners to create the *oppida*, a fortified location. Later on, Roman architectural trademarks such as the arch, brick work, mortar and the tile roof were adopted. In a short time, numerous Dacian strongholds took shape in strategic locations, locations that took full advantage of the natural fortress provided by the Carpathians that towered over the many river valleys. Building these fortified lines became an industry that was concomitant with defending the wealth of Dacia.

The wealth of Dacia was concentrated primarily in Transylvania where, in addition to mining its plentiful metals, smelting became a lucrative industry. A most useful trade was *vulchanos* (blacksmithing). It was a profession which was in high demand and done at many locations; even a mountain was named after this trade: *Vulcan*. Equally popular were the names *faurar* (smith), *cioban* (shepherd), *morar* (miller), *olar* (potmaker), and those for other industrial skills.

The extraction of rock salt was a booming industry as well. In ancient times, salt was second in value only to gold—it was called "white gold." The Dacian name for salt was *sare*, a word that was incorporated into the names of the Dacian settlements that benefited from the work in the *salinae* (salt pits). The most important and the oldest of these were Buridava (Ocnele Mari), which became an economic and military center along with Ocnita in what is now the Valcea region, and Pottaisa (Turda), whose salt mines were unmatched in the ancient world.[6]

Many of these Dacian cities and villages which developed around salt/ sare mining still exist today: Salina, Salnita, Saliste, Saratei, Slatina (salty spring water), Slatiori, Slatioara, Ocnele (salt mines), Ocnele Mari (large salt mines), Ocnele Mici (small salt mines), Ocnita, La Ocne, Ocnele Bacaului, Ocna Muresului, Targul Ocna, Ramnicul Sarat, and Salinele Turdei. Such "salty/sare" names were also adopted by families whose last names were, and still are, common in Romania: Ocnaru, Sararu, Sartu, Sararoiu, Saratean, Sarateanu, Sarasau, Slatinean, Slatineanu, and others. A certain tribe named Saldensioi drew its name from *salda* (salt), meaning people who worked in and lived by salt mines.

The salt mines made a significant contribution to the stability of Dacia. Because they were so important, they were guarded and managed well, with the ancillary effect that the Dacians became a stable power with a population that did not roam or migrate from their land. They preserved their own ham and fish with salt, thus their winter food provisions lasted a long time and could feed the entire settled population. Salt was needed not only for curing their meat rations but also as an antiseptic; it was also a vital element of the diet for their sheep, oxen, and other domesticated animals. Plentiful salty foods encouraged Dacian warriors to venture long distances and gave them stamina—in their own land they were able to outlast long sieges.

Salt was a basic preservative and one of the most precious commodities in the ancient world. While the European nations, armies, and tribes engaged in wars over salt resources, the Dacians lived quite literally above immeasurable sources of it. They were able to make full use of it and also turn it into a profitable business. Furthermore, while the Celts, who were masters at salting meats, labored to do so with processes of solar evaporation by boiling sea water to produce salt, the Dacians were able to export "stones of salt" of exceptional quality for which they could ask any price.

Dacian salt was exported from Transylvania mainly on rafts that floated downstream and flowed into the various collection points along the Danube. From there it was loaded onto the ships or caravans heading outward to the needy world. Because there was such a shortage of it elsewhere and because it was an expensive commodity, any waste triggered a quarrel. We still today warn that spilled salt is an omen of bad luck.

Besides exporting blocks of salt, Dacians used it to prepare salty butter, cheese, lard, fish (the most valued in Rome was sturgeon), caviar, meat products, sausages, pickled legumes, and vegetables (most notably sour cabbage), all preserved in clay pots, in wooden barrels containing salty solutions, or in boxes interlaced with layers of salt.

In brief, the Dacians were the main salt traders of Europe. Their best client was the Roman Empire whose most prized products—olives and cheese—required salt. The biggest consumers were the legions since their food rations needed to be salted so they could carry it hundreds of miles and remain independent in the foreign lands they occupied. Each soldier carried a large quantity of salty cheese, ham, and sausages, the main army food. The legionaries often were paid in *salarius,* chunks of salt (the only edible rock), which was their *salary* or salt money.

As valuable as salt was, the Dacians possessed something even more precious—gold. Their mines, located in Transylvania, were the most numerous and the largest in Europe. The Apuseni Mountains, with what today are named Zlanta, Rosia Montana, and other locations, were indeed the "gold mines" of Dacians who used their precious buying power to crush any commercial competition. Gold was used to buy powerful allies, to pay off unwanted military conflicts, and to maintain a strong domestic market. Dacian gold was legendary, and because of its gold and salt, the area of Transylvania became the object of many predatory imperial ambitions.

Copper and silver mines also were abundantly present in Dacia. As mentioned, they attracted the early Celtic migrants who specialized in working with such metals. But Rome was interested as well in a metal that held little interest for the Dacians—lead. The Eternal City needed lead in huge quantities for the production of water pipes that conveniently brought water inside the villas and palaces. Lead conduits delivered water for huge public baths and into large plazas for washing, drinking; it was also used in creating the much prized artesian wells.

Iron ore was another Dacian export that was in great demand by the civilized world.

Most Dacians were shepherds by tradition, and this occupation developed into a thriving industry based on wool that women spun and then wove into textiles. A woven blanket made of shaggy wool and named *plocad* (cerga) was greatly valued as a wedding gift—a tradition that remains today. Linen was also abundant, obtained from the vast fields of hemp that thrived in the flatlands of Dacia. Fabrics were dyed in mineral and vegetable colors and either sewn into high quality clothing which was worn locally or exported to western markets in rolls. Beautifully made cloth and bales of wool were both in great demand by the Greeks and Romans. Hemp was also used to make ropes and sails needed by the commercial vessels and war ships.

More than 90 percent of Dacia was covered with forests, and the wild and often impenetrable environment was the source of plentiful hunting that provided beasts for Roman circuses and furs for domestic and external markets.

The majority of the Dacian population was engaged in agriculture, cattle and horse breeding, raising cows, goats, sheep, pigs, and cultivating the river valleys in the mountains or the large plains of the Danube. Dobrudja was renowned for its vineyards. The agrarian industry generated an abundance of goods, with the greatest export demand being animals and cereals, mainly oats and wheat, as well as barrels of excellent wine.

Bee-keeping was a popular occupation in Dacia as well, and both honey and wax were in high demand by the Romans. Honey was a natural sweetener, and huge quantities of wax were needed as wax was used as a sealant and for hair removal. (Hairless individuals were considered superior to others.)

By any criteria, the Dacians lived in a land of plenty and were extremely prosperous. These people who were able to produce and deliver so many valuable items for export were not "barbarians" or "primitive." Even though their country was at an intersection of culture and trade, they were considered backward by the Greeks and Romans primarily because of what they were not able to produce. The Dacians had to import prized olive oil, fine ceramics and porcelains, glass articles, mirrors, art and decorative objects, jewelry, rare spices, and silk, all of which the Greeks and Romans considered "civilized" goods.

The Dacians used the barter system in their domestic market. This included exchanges based on the weight of nuggets of gold and silver. Coin currency was not popular even though they minted their own coins as early as the invasion of Philip II in the fourth century B.C. Such Dacian silver coins were copies of the Macedonian *tetradrachmas,* as well as of Greek coins. Celtic immigrants used their design for a better quality coin, another mark of their artistic taste. By using coins, the Dacians began to pay different taxes to the royal treasury that helped to govern and unite a tribal society. The Daco-Celtic coins were a boon to international trade, even though they were melted down in Athens and Rome because of their high gold, silver or copper content.

With the rise of Roman power, the silver denarius became the main coin of international exchange in Europe. Still, the Daco-Celtic coins that were minted from Transylvanian gold were worth at least twenty-five times more than the Roman denarius. Because of that, Dacia was so flooded with the Roman coins that it became its currency. This enormous disparity was taken by Rome to be a sort of Dacian economic insult, and Rome was renowned for its unwillingness to forgive.

An important economic event took place in Dacia after Caesar's assassination in 44 B.C. when his nearly adopted son and co-assassin, Marcus Brutus, took refuge in the Balkans. He settled in Macedonia where once he had been a commanding general. He there tried to raise an army to fight the new emperor-turned-dictator, Octavian Augustus. As this army needed to be paid and Brutus did not have the necessary resources, he looked for a rich and powerful backer, one which he found north of the Danube River.

It just happened that after the assassination of King Burebista (in same year as that of his sworn enemy Caesar) the new Dacian king Coson welcomed Brutus's ambition to conquer Rome and dethrone Octavian. Since he was willing to buy peace for Dacia, Coson agreed to finance Brutus. The new army would be paid in the latest minted *coson* coin of 8.5 grams/.3 ounces of pure gold. There were Dacian and Roman versions of it, both minted in

Sarmizegethusa in Transylvania. The Dacian coin bore the king's inscription, while the Roman one featured the anti-monarchic symbols of an eagle and three senators in togas. Women wore *salba* (gold coin necklaces).

Since Octavian's armies proved invincible and Brutus committed suicide, it is not known how many of these *cosoni* were made or and how wide their circulation was. For sure, their republican messages were not welcomed in imperial Rome. Apparently most of these coins never left Dacia. A large quantity became part of King Decebalus's treasure[7], which, during the A.D. 105-106 war against the Romans, was buried under one of the Transylvanian rivers, never to be found again. Emperor Trajan captured the rest of coins and took them as booty to Rome where they were melted down.

At the end of the first century A.D., King Decebalus, who wanted to stimulate an already strong economy by strengthening existing commercial ties (his goal was to make Dacia a leading economic force in Eastern Europe), minted his own *coson* made of 22-karat gold and weighing 10 grams/.35 ounces. This Dacian coin was superior to all other "gold" coins since they were made of too much alloy. With a currency that dwarfed the weak Roman denarius, any commercial business with Dacia made it richer and more powerful.[8] Economically speaking, however, this proved to be sort of double-edged sword: Dacia, especially Transylvania, became the main target of the increasingly needy and greedy Rome.

The Dacians' economic and commercial organization was maintained by an overlapping web of their military fortresses. Later, *murus Dacicus*, or walls of andesite and limestone, were built with a precise construction technique that was specific to the Dacians. These strongholds guarded the heart of Dacia, which was the land of precious minerals located in Transylvania. A specific military architecture was adopted to provide the necessary defenses—a sort of double massive wall filled with dirt and pebbles. The walls had flat surfaces with crenellated battlements located atop them to offer protection to the soldiers.

More than fifty such well established fortified towns dotted the map of Dacia; these were known to foreign traders. Many survived under the modern names, such as Dealul Cetati (the Fortress Hill) and Intre Cetati (Between Fortresses), along with others that include *fortress* in their names. In case of danger, nearby caves such as those in Cioclovina, Dambovicioara, Geoagiu, and Scarisoara, all of which had secret entrances, provided shelter for the population.

The high priest, Deceneus, became the main adviser of Burebista, and the king decided to reside in Sarmizegethusa. The royal presence and his accompanying army did not change the serene landscape, but allowed it to remain sacred. Nevertheless, the king's move was a major step in the evolution of an embryonic religious creed for a homogeneous tribal federation that later became the kingdom of Dacia. This happened because of a cluster of monastic sites in the area of the Orastie Mountains that were re-built as military forts during the reign of Burebista—the fortresses of Banitsa, Blidaru, Costesti, Capalna, and Piatra Rosie, among others. This area of Transylvania became the political and social center of Dacia, and the patriotic king succeeded in uniting for the first time, at least for military purposes, most of the Dacian tribes. It can be said with reasonable certainty that the anarchic social conditions and self-destructive behaviors of other tribes known as barbarians were not a hallmark of the Dacian tribes.

After Burebista's death, his kingdom was divided into four parts. A military and social crisis soon developed, one that had to be solved by an even more determined king—Decebalus. He had a clear vision of why it was crucial to unite the Daco-Getians, namely to repel the Roman invaders. His wise leadership resulted into a strong, central government that created a more stable and homogeneous society. This society centered to an even greater degree around the sacred city of Sarmizegethusa and the result was a kingdom with a military power that ranked third after the Romans and Germans.

Let us now clarify a few historical misconceptions about Dacia and also revisit the story of the unhappy Ovid, who for nine years lived in the "barbarous land" among the Daco-Getians. He described them as wild men who carried knives and were ready to fight at any time. He was torturously aware that in the area of Tomis "countless tribes surround us, who think living except by pillage a disgrace."[9] The delicate poet, who never served in the Roman army, constantly expected the city to be sacked by "savage Goths, the skin-clad barbarians that terrorize these parts!"[10] He was equally afraid of the Getians "carrying bow and quiver and poisoned arrows."[11] No doubt, Ovid lived in an armed society, one that was always ready to defend the commercial port of Tomis, his new residence. But instead being grateful to his co-citizens who protected his life, he accused them of being dangerous and uncivilized.

In fact, he never mentions any act of cruelty on the part of his hosts. Certainly they were armed at all times, but they constituted an industrious society. Their wagons had spiked wheels, their oxen had yokes, and their horses wore leather harnesses. Ovid knew all too well that the Dacians' "creaking wagon-axles" came across the frozen Danube fully loaded with goods to be traded at Tomis and carried away by the Roman ships. Savage people did not engage in such civilized ways of making a living.

Relentlessly fixed in his role as a victim, Ovid continued writing and lamenting about the natives, only to contradict himself: "No race in the whole world's as savage as the Getae [Getians], yet even they are moved by my woes."[12] Yet, even though the "savages" were cultured enough to be receptive to his elegant Latin (he had to admit "Here I am not hated"), to Ovid the "trousered Getians" were nevertheless "stupid peasants," "uncultured people."

While his poems were (futilely) aimed to evoke feelings of pity from Emperor Augustus, there was not a single paragraph in his *Tristia* and *Epistulae* in which the refined Ovid complained about the way he was treated by "the natives—still barely civilized."[13] Certainly there was no reason for him to complain. As a Roman nobleman, he was exempted from paying taxes, and he received civic honors from the local people He may have been destined to a harsh fate, but not because actions carried out by the Daco-Getians. He was free to do anything he wanted, and all his letters sent from Tomis reached his wife, his literary agent, and his friends in Rome.

Like other writers of his time, Ovid based his knowledge about Getae on mythical stereotypes inherited from Herodotus. To this, he added self-serving lamentations, a subjectivist philosophy, and numerous parochial biases against the non-Roman world which he had acquired in Rome. Herodotus did call the Getae/Getians "the bravest and most law-abiding of the Thracians,"[14] and thereby make a clear distinction between the two nations. It went without saying that people who were "the most law-abiding" could not be savage or socially dysfunctional. Still, adverse legends about the Daco-Getians were perpetuated when ancient historians continued to substitute heroic and mythical stories for facts.

In Ovid's time, a Roman military post was stationed in the city of Tomis in order to ensure a safe conduct of commercial transactions, and this even though that the city functioned according to very unambiguous and reasonable laws. There is no doubt that the native Getians respected these laws because during the summer holidays the city was a popular resort for rich Romans. Tourists rarely vacation in places where their lives are at risk.

The unhappy Ovid never saw Rome again, and he died in Tomis in A.D. 18. A large statue of him still beautifies the center of that Dacian city. His sad epitaph reads, "If you have ever loved, pray for Ovid." His poems were written when Dacia was on its way to becoming a major European economic and military power. It was the time when the Roman borders already extended into the middle of Balkan Peninsula. Roman settlements had begun to spread toward the Danube River in the Dacian land of Moesia. The richness of those "barbarian" lands was an irresistible attraction for the expansionist Augustus who had already made plans to invade Dacia. His death and the civil war that weakened the Roman Empire canceled those plans, and powerful Dacia continued to remain the cornerstone of Eastern Europe.

NOTES

1. Herodotus, *The History*, trans. David Grene (Chicago: University of Chicago Press, 1987), 5. 6.

2. Herodotus, *History*, 5.6.

3. Jordanes, *The Gothic History of Jordanes*, ed. and trans. Charles Christopher Mierow (Cambridge: Speculum Historiale, 1966), 69.

4. Jordanes, *Gothic History*, 71.

5. It resembles the Kukri knife of Nepal; its probable point of origin was ancient India.

6. After thousands of years of continuous exploitation, today the subterranean salt reserves are estimated at 38 billion tons. In spite of this fact, Dacia's salt industry was rarely if ever mentioned in works documenting this industry or in other history books.

7. A treasure of 450 *cosoni* was discovered at Sarmizegethusa in 1803.

8. In the year 2000, one such *coson* was sold outside Romania for 5,000 Deutsch-marks, approximately US$3,500 at the time.

9. Ovid, *The Poems of Exile: Tristia and the Black Sea Letters*, trans. Peter Green (Berkeley: University of California Press, 2005), bk. 5, 10:15-16

10. Ovid, *Poems*, bk. 4, 8:83-84.

11. Ovid, *Poems*, bk. 5, 7:15-16.

12. Ovid, *Poems*, bk. 2, 1:32-33.

13. Ovid, *Poems*, bk. 5, 7:11-12.

14. Herodotus, *History*, 4.93.

Chapter Seven

The Shadow of the Roman Empire

In 250 B.C. the city-state of Rome led a conglomeration of Latin tribes in a successful occupation of the entire Italian Peninsula, thereby forming the Mediterranean's most powerful nation. The Romans were less intellectual, sentimental, and idealistic than the Greeks about the many foreign lands they occupied. Instead, they were pragmatic and determined to exploit their conquests by imposing taxes and ensuring their own commercial and military domination of them. The will of Rome was implemented by the violence of its legions, and it was fully enforced wherever they were present.

After defeating Hannibal in 201 B.C. and conquering the Iberian Peninsula, the Romans became the masters of Mediterranean Europe. Their next aim was to transform the Black Sea into a Mare Nostra as well. However, the powerful Hellenic and Macedonian states had already mastered the southern part of the Balkan Peninsula and so kept the Romans away from Dacia. It was only a matter of time until the balance of military power began to change dramatically.

In 200 B.C. Philip V of Macedonia, an ally of Hannibal, was aiming to increase his borders and expand the scope of his military power by attempting to rule Thracia, his close neighbor. So, when the Macedonians invaded the Greek coastal cities, the Romans stepped in, and, in the year 195 B.C. General Flaminius defeated Sparta which in 146 B.C. was included in the province of Macedonia. Then, in 86 B.C. the Roman General Sulla captured Athens. Greece later came to be dominated by Rome, but the refined Hellenic culture, philosophy, and civilization spread throughout the Italian peninsula in no time. The result was that the Romans became more culturally sophisticated at the same time as they remained determined to establish a New World Order.

With Roman garrisons ensconced in the Hellenic Peninsula, the era of the glorious kingdoms of Macedonia and Thracia came to an abrupt end. Both

143

nations became allies of convenience to the multi-state empire that encompassed more than three million square miles and twenty million people. To control these states and ensure the coherence of its empire, Rome built a vast web of paved highways and military forts. These now extended toward the Danube and Eastern Europe. With Macedonia and Thracia subdued, the path to domination of the rest of the Balkans was wide open for Rome, and Dacia was forced to face this formidable superpower alone.

The Dacians, however, continued their expansion toward the western and southern areas of the Danube until they inevitably clashed with advancing legions who had already planted Roman standards in Illyricum and part of south Moesia. Further expansion on the part of the Dacians was thus firmly halted. They were angered by the fact that the Romans kept approaching their lands; conversely, pan-Dacianism was a permanent source of irritation to Rome.

Eventually, the Roman legions reached the lower Danube after a rapid succession of victories against many Dacian tribes settled on its banks, and arrived at the Iron Gates located at the sharp bend of the river facing the fluvial gates to Transylvania. General Scribonius Curio did not dare to cross the Danube but he had no problem proclaiming Roman ownership of Western Moesia in 75 B.C. Four years later, the Roman proconsul Terentius Varro Lucullus occupied a strip along the Black Sea shore and part of Getia that had many commercial ports.

The new Dacian king, Burebista, would not tolerate this territorial intrusion. In 61 B.C. his warriors defeated General Antonius Hybrida near Histria and recaptured Callatis and Tomis. He continued his victorious campaign north of the Black Sea littoral and established Dacian control of the territory as far north as Olbia (near today's Odessa). Then he focused his efforts southward toward Messembria (Nesebar) on the Aegean Thracian shore. The commercial cities Callatis, Histria, Tomis, Tyras (on the mouth of Danube), and all of Getia, were re-incorporated into his kingdom. If that were not enough, Burebista prolonged his venture by boldly attacking to the west as far as the Dalmatian coast and what are now Austria and Slovakia. During his reign, Dacia had the largest geographic borders in its history, and its army numbered two hundred thousand.

These Dacian conquests diminished Roman commercial control of the lower Danube and cut off land access to the Sea of Azov toward the Scythian grain fields. The valiant Dacians had thereby successfully confronted the majesty of Rome, a first in Eastern European history. Such an economic blow, however, sowed the seeds of great bitterness in Rome and made it ever more determined to subdue the Dacians. A form of brutal punishment was about to be meted out.

Fortunately for the Dacians, Caesar's legions were not in a position to attack Dacia. They were otherwise engaged, fighting the colossal force of some forty-two Celtic tribes that had revolted against Roman domination. The Celtic armies numbered two hundred forty thousand foot soldiers and eight thousand horsemen led by Vercingetorix (the Supreme Warrior), whose father had been executed on the order of Caesar. His fearless soldiers fought naked, wearing only horn helmets and screaming battle cries. After eight years of bitter battle, the Romans leveled eight hundred Celtic towns and villages, killed one million soldiers and civilians, and enslaved three million Celts. Those who escaped to freedom went to Dacia and Britannia.

Vercingetorix was forced to surrender and was taken to Rome to be flaunted in Caesar's triumphal parade, after which he was strangled. By conquering Gaul (most of today's France) the Romans extended the western borders of their empire almost to Dacia.

When he realized that the Dacians had not learned a lesson from the genocide suffered by the Celts at the hands of the Romans, and because he continued to be incensed at the ongoing Dacian attacks on Roman outposts south of the Danube, Caesar decided to incorporate all the Dacian lands into the Mediterranean empire. Anticipating stiff resistance, he moved six legions into Macedonia, instructing them to wait for orders to head north for to invade Transylvania. He intended to assemble sixteen legions and ten thousand cavalrymen and have them march toward the Danube, but as it happened, the closest he came to Dacia was Vindobona (Vienna).

Caesar had become the most powerful ruler in Europe and seemed entirely unchallenged, yet the course of his destiny would change. Resistance began with General Pompey, who wanted to cast him out before he had the chance to declare himself a dictator. Acting quickly to exploit the opportunity that this created, Burebista interfered in the Roman civil war by offering military aid to Pompey in exchange for an agreement to preserve the freedom of Dacia. However, destiny intervened in Caesar's plans. His expeditions against Burebista never took place—he was assassinated in the year 44 B.C.[1]

A short time later, Burebista suffered the same fate, and a tribal-civil war divided his kingdom. Even as they fought among themselves, the tribes knew that the survival of Dacia depended on their remaining unified, and they never failed to unite when faced with the threat of foreign attack

Marcus Brutus, who conspired in the assassination of Caesar, was now in charge of the provinces of Greece and Macedonia and sought an alliance with the Dacians. It would empower him to march on Rome and enforce the republican ideals. His mercenary army was, however, defeated, and Brutus committed suicide. In Rome, civilian unrest was amplified by the power struggle between Gaius Octavian (the nephew and adopted son of Caesar) and

Marc Antony (one of Caesar's favorite generals). This struggle escalated in a civil war and nearly rent the empire.

In his fight against Antony, Octavian-the-future-emperor sought to ally himself with the Dacians. In 35 B.C., he asked for the hand of the Dacian King Cotiso's daughter in exchange for the king's betrothal to Octavian's daughter Julia (who was only six years old at the time). Thus Julia would become the queen of Dacia, and the Romans would help Cotiso (who ruled only Banat and Oltenia in Dacia) to become the king of all the Dacians and of the Thracians. When Antony was unexpectedly defeated by Octavian in Actium in western Greece in 31 B.C., plans for these two marriages were canceled.

After Antony and Cleopatra committed suicide to escape capture by Octavian's legions, the legacy of the Roman republic declined into a monarchical dictatorship. Five centuries of democratic tradition ended and the long list of *imperators* (victorious commanders) was begun.

With the state treasury exhausted by so many foreign and internal wars, Rome was badly in need of gold. At that time, the main source of gold for the Roman mint was Gallia Comata (Portugal and Spain) and Noricum (south of the Panonian Danube); still, nothing could match the quantity of this metal that was being extracted from the Transylvanian mines. With the shadow of Rome already extending over the Danube and with Burebista's powerful empire having been split by tribal warfare into five smaller kingdoms, the land of Dacia now faced an unprecedented military danger.

Yet, Dacia stood firm once again, this time under the leadership of Deceneus, the supposed priest–turned-king who ruled from the area of the Transylvania's mountains that were rich in gold and silver. Other Dacian kings who ruled at the same time were Scorillo, who reigned for forty years in Transylvania; Dicomes, who was a relative of Burebista and ruled a kingdom from the Carpathians to the Dniester River; and Dapyx and Zyraxes, who ruled in Dobrudja. Each was able to inflict severe military blows on the Roman outposts, and when they were united, they constituted an army second only to the Germans in size and effectiveness.

The increasing Dacian military strength caused Rome to order five generals to march their legions toward the Danubian border. Generals Crassus and Lentulus would advance from the south, Catus from the southwest, Tiberius from the west, and Vinicius from the northwest. But plans for these simultaneous attacks had to be put aside in order to deal with the "Scythian" invasion south of the Danube in 29 B.C.

According to the Roman historian Dio, Dacians and Bastarnae "occupied Moesia and crossed the border into Thracia, a Roman ally."[2] Indeed, the Bastarnians/Bastarni (a German-Scythian tribe which had been assimilated into eastern Dacia), led by King Deldo and the Dacian allies, carried out marauding expeditions in Thracia and threatened to enter Roman-controlled Macedonia. General Crassus, who led legions IV and XX, took prompt action and repelled the invaders. The Getian king Roles and his cavalry came from the area north of the Danube Delta to help the Romans and played an important role in defeating the Bastarnians, who were erroneously identified in Rome as Scythians.

The main battle between the barbarians and the Roman coalition took place on the Cedrus River. It ended in a duel between Deldo and Crassus, probably in front of their troops. Deldo was killed, and thousands of Bastarnians were left without a king and then slaughtered. Crassus's legions then raided Moesia and that portion of Getae that was not under the control of Roles; the latter had already ensured immunity for his land.

Dio dedicated several pages of his Book 51 to these truly knightly events. According to his description of what happened after the victory: "Roles, when he visited Caesar, was treated as his friend and ally because of this service; and the captives were distributed among the soldiers."[3] Clearly, Caesar (Octavian) tried to bring the Getians into the Roman camp in order to separate them from the Dacians.

The determined Crassus then persisted in fighting the Dacians of Moesia, a task that proved to be very difficult. According to Dio, the general applied force and persuasion to pacify them "after hardships and dangers." When winter was approaching, Crassus withdrew to Macedonia, an area which was continuously being harassed by Dacian guerillas.

Confident in his achievements, Crassus declared part of Dobrudja a Roman colony; he then named it Scythia Minor. Octavian, who was about to be named emperor, did not, however, allow him to continue his campaign in the main land of Dacia. The reason for this decision was purely political: the emperor did not want a supporter of Antony to be triumphant and so become a second Caesar. Crassus was therefore the first victorious general not to be proclaimed *imperator*; the jealous Octavian kept the title for himself alone. From that point onward it was reserved only for Roman emperors.

Quick to exploit the power vacuum that developed after the withdrawal of the Romans, the Bastarnian and Sarmatian tribes rushed to fill it in Getia and Moesia, joining older relatives already living around the mouth of the Danube. Thus a Dacian territorial alliance was created and further resistance against Roman power was ensured. Crassus was forced to campaign again, and, annoyed by the fierce barbarian opposition he faced, he proceeded to cut off the hands of many prisoners he took, as a warning to those who would keep up the fight.

Crassus continued his march through Dobrudja where his legions fought against the warriors of Dapyx and Zyraxes, two Dacian leaders who had separated from the kingdom of Burebista. After the Romans crushed their resistance, Crassus had to turn around and fight the Moesians who had instigated a revolt in the wake of his troops' movement. This was a nightmarish campaign, one that convinced other Roman generals to stay away from the complicated affairs of the Daco-Getians and their allies. Still, the uneasy relation between Dacian and Roman powers was destined to result in a collision sooner or later.

In 27 B.C., Gaius Octavian became Augustus (considered sacred/semi-divine), a new Caesar of Rome. He proved to be a competent statesman and his economic and military reforms prolonged the life of the empire. At its outset, Augustus's reign was troubled by many distant wars and much civil unrest; also, an empty state treasury that forced him to reduce the number of legions from sixty to twenty-eight, all of which were stationed outside the Italian Peninsula.

To ensure his safety, Augustus created the Praetorian Guard. It would soon become a military and political institution that would make or break emperors. The enormous civic and religious edifices he constructed brought him a great deal of public admiration, but they created an even larger financial deficit for the state. Rome itself was a poor territory with few natural resources, including a scarcity of drinking water. Since its main revenue came from the pillaging that went on in conjunction with foreign wars, the conquest of Dacia could not have come at a better time. The Roman generals began to plan the much desired invasion, but first they would be tested.

From 10-2 B.C. General Vinicius continued to push the remainder of the Bastarni into what is today Moldova, and for the first time Roman military outposts were built on the southern shore of the last leg of the Danube stretch of Getia, only a mile from the Dacian mainland. However, the unmistakable sign of the imperial presence on the great river did not stop the local Dacians from remaining indisputably in control of their territory while Vinicius entered Western Dacia. There in Pannonia he fought and routed the Anarti, Catini, Teurisci, and other Dacian tribes, parts of which crossed the Theiss/Tisza River into the shelter of Transylvania.

In spite of the military threat this entailed, the Dacians began to reclaim the Moesian areas. They fearlessly conducted devastating raids against the Roman garrisons and settlements south of the frozen Danube. But Rome still had the most powerful army in Europe and responded with full punitive force. In fact, a new legion was formed from Moesians as proof of Roman occupation. Its animal emblem was a Capricorn, yet the legion, led by Roman officers, sported the famous Dacian standard of the flying dragon with a wolf's head and a serpent's body. This legion fought under General Crassus against the Scythians (hence its name, the IV Scythica) on the lower Danube.

Thus far, the Dacians had escaped a well planned military invasion against them primarily because the Roman legions were needed elsewhere in Europe. In A.D. 9, for example, General Publius Varus crossed the Rhine into Germania in an attempt to display Roman strength to the barbarians. Within in a few days, however, his powerful legions (XVII, XVIII, and XIX) were massacred in the Teutoburg Forest; he subsequently committed honorable suicide.

The age enfeebled Augustus never recovered from such a humiliating loss of men and outright defeat. With his death, plans for an invasion of Dacia were postponed indefinitely. But the situation in Moesia and Pannonia got out of control when the Dacians rampaged against the young Roman colonies. Punitive campaigns of the Romans did not discourage any further attacks. Many Sarmatian tribes who were in need of better land crossed into Dacia, e.g. the Iazygi who settled in Pannonia, west of the Theiss (Tisza/Tisa) River. Because they seized Dacian land, they became long lasting enemies to the Dacians.

At this point, Dacia was spared the burden of any further Roman aggression. Taking full advantage of a generally favorable situation, however, the Dacians raided the Roman strongholds south of the Danube and ransacked their colonies on the coast of the Black Sea. In return, Rome stationed Legio III Gallica on the lower Danube as part of an effort to prevent the Sarmatian Roxolani and Iazygi from advancing deeper into Moesia. Because the Romans were at war in other distant lands not many legions were available to deal with the Dacians.

The Dacians of Transylvania may have lived a relatively isolated and happy life, but south of the Danube there prevailed a state of continuous warfare. This segment of Dacia was gradually conquered and occupied by the Romans.

While the Romans had total contempt for the *barbaricum* (barbarian world) of the Eastern Europe, at the same time they feared it. The disciplined Roman legions were not trained to fight against troops using primitive clubs, arrows, and lances—weapons that were handled with brute strength by the barbarians. Most of the barbarian victories were attributable to the sheer number of their equestrian warriors who wildly trampled and raided the civilized world. The Romans had to ensure a long and painful battle experience before they could accept the fact that the same weapon was ten times more lethal when used by a rider than it was in the hand of a foot soldier. The speed, strength, and size of the Daco-Getian horses were intimidating and created instant panic and disorder among the Roman infantrymen. A mounted man-at-arms became several times stronger than a regular lancer, even if he were clad in mail or wearing plated armor. The Celts, Germans, Getians, and Sarmatians proved this fact repeatedly.

Inflicting sizable human and material damage on the groups they confronted, the barbarian invasions eroded the power of Rome even as they were themselves decimated in bloody fights that were almost invariably carried out to the end. The only winners in these man-made disasters were the Dacians, who would then offer shelter to the defeated barbarians as a means of gaining control over them and also benefiting from their war plunder.

Thus, in a short time, Dacia became a sort of base of operations, a point from which the Eastern European barbarians could initiate attacks against other areas. Since they were unwilling to have them on their land too long, the Dacians encouraged these barbarians to invade the Roman provinces south and west of the Danube. They used any known enemy of Rome to inflict damage on the ranks of the Roman cohorts and legions occupying the Dacian lands. Yet, however strong the barbarians and their Dacian protectors may have been, they still faced the Roman army, a military that had raised the empire to the status of a superpower in the ancient world.

As for the making of the Roman military machine, the army was a vital institution of the empire. It was the first regular army ever to be paid by a government for its services, and so also the largest user of funds from the state treasury. It provided certain yet risky employment along with numerous benefits and a retirement plan. Numerous conditions had to be met in order to be admitted to the army. Only Roman citizens could serve as legionaries, which were a springboard for career advancement for future politicians and emperors (they had to serve at least ten years). Most of the generals were tribunes; they were usually in command of one legion of five to six thousand soldiers, divided into *cohors* of one thousand men and *centurias* of one hundred—the real backbone of the Roman Army.

Discipline, loyalty, and obedience were enforced with deadly precision, and the legionaries feared their superiors more than they feared the enemy. Any deserter, rebel, or sentry caught sleeping on duty was stoned to death by his comrades. Any unit that demonstrated cowardice on the battlefield was decimated by the fact that each tenth soldier was killed.[4]

The legionary was a soldier unique in the history of mankind: during the war he was a fighter, and in peacetime he was a builder and a colonist. He was an ambulatory arsenal, and a sort of tool shop on the move. He carried with him all the equipment needed to both destroy and build, including his *gladius* (short double-edged pointed sword, no longer than 60 centimeters/2 feet) on his right hip. The latter distinguished him from the barbarians, who carried their swords on the left hip, under the shoulder, stuck in the middle of their belts, or hanging between their shoulder blades. Thus the legionary was forced to pull his sword with his body turned toward the left, but he was ready to strike the enemy with a single sharp swing. His entire body was therefore behind the strike, which made for an efficient and lethal move. The *gladius* was not a slashing sword, but a thrusting one. On his left hip the legionary carried a *pugio* (dagger) that was no longer than 30 centimeters/1 foot.

The strength of the Roman army, unlike that of the barbarian warriors, was not based on individual fighting skills and daredevil tactics. It was rather the deliberate result of having been trained to be a fighting monolith. The impact of the Roman legions was enhanced by virtue of the fact that they were well educated in *esprit de corps*. Their cruelty in war was legendary and in many ways exceeded that of the barbarians.

The Romans were of the firm conviction that they were a superior nation that had the right to lead the world and subjugate uncivilized lands. Like the Greeks, they considered any war against the barbarians to be a just one because it led to the extermination of sub-human peoples. The Roman rule of conquest was simple: force the enemy into submission and make him a slave for the good of the empire.

The appetite for expansion into faraway lands actually had its roots in the permanent financial crises to which virtually all the Roman emperors were subject. Given that there were sixty-six days of festivities each year, the Romans had to find money to feed their lavish appetites. Since the legions were stationed in all the occupied territories and near to nations that were scheduled to be invaded, the Roman army was essentially the economic foundation for the ever-expanding empire.

The year A.D. 1 found Dacia having collapsed into small kingdoms; yet it remained an enemy of the Roman Empire, one which was too strong to be tolerated and one whose borders crawled ever closer to the Lower Danube. General Marcus Vinicius specialized in renewing attacks on the Upper Danube area. He attempted to consolidate Roman power there, at least in Moesia and Pannonia, areas which became Roman provinces. When he defeated King Maroboduus of the German Marcomanni, Vinicius imposed Roman control over this portion of the Danube region as well.

Three Roman legions were stationed in Moesia in an effort to discourage Dacian raids from across the Danube, but the great river was too long and the Roman forces too few to cover it. The Dacians showed no respect for imperial power and kept crossing the Danube into Moesia Inferior—the northern segment of modern Bulgaria that was intensely populated by Dacians. The response from Rome was stronger than expected. In the year 6, Proconsul

Gaius Curio defended the Dardani, thereby opening up a path toward Transylvania for the Romans.

In the years 11-12, General Sextus Aelius Catus led an expedition across the Danube. After repelling scattered packs of rebellious Dacians, he occupied what is today the south of Oltenia and Muntenia between Calafat and Giurgiu. During this brutal campaign, many Dacian settlements were destroyed, and at least fifty thousand of inhabitants were enslaved and relocated in southern Moesia. The Roman depopulation tactics were aimed at retribution and part of an attempt to discourage any future Dacian military incursions into the area. General Catus reinforced the fortresses of Oescus and Novae across from the mouth of the Olt River on the southern bank of the Danube, thereby creating a border and two bridgeheads. The latter would facilitate future Roman invasions into Dacia at the end of the first century A.D.

Legions IV Scythica and V Macedonica were stationed in Moesia Superior, 100 kilometers/62 miles east and west of the Iron Gates of the Danube. They built the *castri* (military camps) of Ratiaria (Artschav, Bulgaria) and Viminacium (Kostolac, Serbia), thus providing two more bridgeheads. Still, no invasion took place. This was primarily because the Romans were busy with other wars, one of which was with rebellious Thracia. After defeating the Thracians, the legionaries re-entered Scythia Minor in Dobrudja and incorporated it into Lower Moesia.

For a brief time, the rich, fortified city of Histria, which governed an area of 140,000 hectares/346,000 acres, was under Roman protection. Histria was not conquered by force; instead, its population was lured into accepting Roman rule by a system of tax exemptions and other economic privileges.

Legions VIII Augusta and XV Apollinaris were transferred to Pannonia for the purpose of stopping any invasion by the free Dacians or any attempted revolt in the occupied regions. General Severus, who was already familiar with the Dacian "problems" in Moesia, became governor of this area. Meanwhile the final stretch of the Danube, from the Iron Gates to its delta, remained entirely under Dacian control.

Eager to demonstrate the power of their flying dragon, large packs of Dacian warriors took part in the German war against the Romans, aided by some mutinied Roman legions. In the year 14, General Drusus was sent to rebellious Pannonia with his troops in an effort to restore order there. He could not subdue the German tribes, but he did found the strong military base of Mainz on the Rhine; he also forced the Germans to recognize the power of Rome.

The Dacians still were not intimidated by the imperial might, even though in the last years of Augustus's reign a total of ten legions were stationed on the Sava River, on the Rhine, and in Pannonia. Their mission was to hold the Dacians and Germans at a respectful distance from the Roman borders. Ironically, it was the Dacians who repelled the invasion of the German tribes of the Chauci and Chiati when they attacked from the northeast.

Still, the Dacian presence was an intolerable thorn in the side of the Roman Empire. This unpleasant fact was confirmed by Cassius Dio, who was the governor of Pannonia Superior and therefore a neighbor of Dacia. Dio was very familiar with Dacian history, and he confirmed the events that took place during the times of Caesar and Augustus. He mentioned the frustration of General Tiberius who, unable to arrest the Dacian rebels, burned their crops and devastated their settlements; after this, however, he retreated with his legions to safer land. Seven legions were re-stationed south of the Danube in Dalmatia, Moesia, and Pannonia to keep the bridgeheads open for a planned invasion of Dacia.

During this time, the Pax Romana became Pax Augusta, and the Mediterranean Sea became Mare Nostrum (Our Sea), basically a huge Roman lake. The border of the Roman Empire was longer than 2,000 kilometers/1,243 miles and stretched from the Baltic Sea to the Black Sea. It was impossible to defend it with twenty-eight legions that were at one and the same time engaged in conflicts in Africa, Asia, and Britannia. Strategically, Dacia was ideal for establishing a military base for the campaign toward Germany and Eastern Europe. It also was advantageously positioned to repel the barbarians from the desolate steppes of Russia, whose attacks became increasingly intense.

In the meantime, the Dacians continued to trade heavily, almost invariably to their own benefit, with the expanding Roman Empire. Even the Chinese were aware of the powerful empire that they called Da Qin/Dakin, a name that sounded closer to Dakia/Dacia. With all her Danube allies defeated or subdued by the Romans, Dacia suffered a period of weakness—especially after General Lucius Piso crushed the Thracians' revolt in a three-year campaign; for this, he was received in stately triumph in Rome. By this point in time, no military power stood between the imperial legions and the Dacian lands.

At the age of seventy-two and in his royal twilight years, heartbroken over the loss of legions in Germania, Augustus was not able to impose his will on the Dacians. When he died, Dacia was still an independent kingdom, Thracia had a semi-dependent status, and Macedonia was regarded by the Romans as a sort of poor relative. In fact, many officials and governors were punished by Rome for plundering Macedonia. And, Dalmatia, Moesia, and Pannonia were already under siege. A clear historico-demographic distinction must be made between the province of Pannonia (which encompassed the land between the Danube tributaries, the Dravus/Drava and Savus/Sava), and the flats of Pannonia of today's Hungary. During the time of Augustus, the flatland of Pannonia was inhabited and controlled by the Dacians.

The next emperor destined to wear the purple robe and implement the New Roman Order was Tiberius (r. 14-37), the former general who had fought the Germans at the Dacian borders. He could not match the glory of his stepfather, Augustus, and, troubled by a sort of identity crisis as emperor, decided to take a peaceful approach to ruling rather than a bellicose one. It was for this reason that he brought the best legions to Rome. They served for his own protection as opposed to being used to thwart the barbarians or the Dacians.

Involved in many forms of cruelty against suspected internal enemies and afraid to live in his own royal palace, he moved at the age of 69 to Capri, where he owned twelve villas. From there he tried to consolidate his power through a reign of terror. Neglecting his imperial duties, Tiberius solved the volatile problem of Moesia and Pannonia by bribing the Dacians with an annual stipend in goods, industrial experts, etc. The next emperors—Caligula, Claudius, and Nero—took no interest whatsoever in the military problems of the empire. Certainly, they were not concerned with Dacia, which continued to receive a substantial annual bribe from Rome in order to remain peaceful. In fact the brother of King Scorilo was freed from captivity under condition that Dacians would not interfere in the Roman domestic problems.

All of these later three emperors set unprecedented records for greed and brutality as they emptied the imperial treasury to fund extravagant games and to build palaces that defied the imagination. Nero's statue, gilded in gold, was higher than the Statue of Liberty. His decision to move Legions IV Scythica and V Macedonica from Moesia to Parthia was a relief to the Dacians, who had become aware that Rome was preoccupied with still other military issues. These issues were compounded by fires that burned out of control in Rome for six days in the year 64 and by the civil war that followed Nero's death. Needless to say, all of these developments produced a period of quiet for the Dacians.[5]

In his descriptions of the tumultuous political and social life of Rome, Tacitus reflected on how the Dacians took advantage of Rome's misfortunes. He concluded that Rome's military might had ceased to intimidate them. This historian was aware of Dacia's aggressive tendencies and wrote: "...so many armies in Moesia, Dacia, Germany, Pannonia either through the rashness or cowardliness of the Generals cast away: so many good soldiers, with so many cohorts defeated and taken."[6] He believed that the Dacians might enter into the battle on the side of the Germans and thus be able to attack the Roman legions from opposite directions simultaneously. Mostly, however, he feared a Dacian-Sarmatian coalition. Indeed, in the near future, such a coalition would prove its deadly military might against the Roman armies.

Watchful for a sudden invasion by the Dacian army, Rome kept Legions I Italica and VI Alude in Moesia Superior, and Legions V Macedonica and VII

Claudia in Moesia Inferior. Pannonia, which was less likely to be attacked by the Dacians, was controlled only by Legion VII (the future Galbian Legion). Before long, Legions XIII Gemina and XV Apollinaris were stationed at Poetovio (Ptuj in Slovenia) and in parts of Pannonia in an effort to contain the Dacians within their own western border.

These powerful military units never encountered the Dacians because in the year 69 Emperor Otho's civil war in Rome against his rival Vitellius (who was very popular with the Danubian legions) was in full revolt. Five legions were decimated during this fratricidal conflict; in its ironic aftermath, the brave legionaries conquered Rome instead of Dacia, and Vespasian became emperor.

Tacitus also referred to what became known as "the year of four emperors." The Emperor Vitellius died in the civil war that shook Rome in A.D. 69, and that same year the Batavi/Batavians (much admired by Tacitus for their bravery) revolted on the Rhine. Tacitus vividly pointed out how well informed the Dacians were concerning what had happened inside the Roman Empire. They knew that Consul Gaius Licinus Mucianus was already in Palestine commanding legions III Gallica, IV Scythia, VI Ferrata, and XII Fulminata against the Jewish rebellion. Practically, the Balkan Peninsula hardly had any Roman troops stationed in it. Certainly they wasted no time in taking advantage of their neighbors' misfortunes so as to extend their territory and control, especially south of the Danube.

Confident in their mission to free Moesia, which was traditionally considered part of Southern Dacia, the Dacians crossed the Danube where they unexpectedly meet up with General Mucianus's army that just arrived, marching from the Balkans toward Rome to save the city. The Dacians were pushed back, but the Sarmatian Roxolani crossed the frozen Danube into Moesia and slaughtered two of the cohorts of Roman auxiliaries sent to repel the Dacian invasion. The Roxolani's next raid was plagued by rain that soaked their leather armor and left their horses stuck in the mud. Forced to fight as foot soldiers without shields, they were brutally defeated by the properly equipped legions. The incident was taken to be a victory against the Dacians, and Marcus Saturninus, the governor of Moesia, was celebrated in Rome.

The Roxolani who escaped from this confrontation took refuge in Dacia. Because they had proven themselves to be sworn enemies of Rome, they were allowed to settle in the grasslands of what are today the Braila and Ialomitsa regions. They never forgot their humiliating defeat, and from that time onward allied themselves with the Dacians in a common fight against Rome.

General Fonteius Agrippa was recalled from Asia and assigned the governorship of Moesia. His weakened troops were enforced with cohorts from the remaining Vitellian army.

In the meantime, Vespasian set about creating a new civic order. Given that funds were lacking, he reduced the army to twenty-eight legions and then dispatched them to troubled spots in an effort to restore order inside the empire. Aware of the military threat posed by the Dacians and their allies, Vespasian reorganized and increased the Roman military fleet on the Danube. But there were too many wars going on along the Rhine and in Britannia, and only a limited number of legions to work with. This forced him to make concessions to the Dacians, who would restrain the rebellious actions of the Sarmatian Roxolani and other barbarians they sheltered. Thus, north of the Danube, Dacia had repeatedly proven itself to be a land that was fundamentally impenetrable.

The Dacians wisely realized there was more to gain by increasing their annual allowance in money and products and by trading with the Romans than by fighting them. They therefore bartered large quantities of grains and began to make advantageous transactions with famine-ridden Rome, transactions for which the city paid in pure gold and valuable services.

During this period, successive emperors were placed on the throne by the Praetorian Guard, with each candidate amply compensating the military. The legions were used temporarily to extinguish numerous revolts within the vast empire, and not for the purpose of conquering new lands. Other cohorts simply marched on Rome, led by generals with imperial ambitions. This was an historic low point as far as imperial power was concerned, a fact which was fully grasped by the Jews of Palestine. Their revolt against Rome in 66-70 was to have deadly consequences.

All the disasters that plagued Rome were exploited by the Dacians who behaved as the absolute masters in Moesia, along the Danube, and on the western coast of the Black Sea. Their raids were so effective that in the year 70 the Moesian Governor Agrippa was killed fighting the Dacians. The mutilated Legio I Italica was stationed at Novae on the Danube to be refitted so it could repel future attacks from its northern bank.

Apparently, at this time Rome also ceased to pay off the Dacians, who began to tax foreign traders, taking in any revenue they could from Danubian commerce. It was only a question of time as to when Rome would retaliate and regain its position of authority in Moesia. This happened in the year 85 when, during the reign of Duras, a Dacian raid was promptly repelled. Roman imperial prestige in the Balkans seemed to be restored.

The first Roman emperor committed to solving the "Dacian problem" once and for all was Domitian (r. 81–96), the brother of Titus, whom he most likely assassinated. He directed his attention to Dacia not because of military ambition, but rather because he had emptied the empire's treasury. As the self-appointed "Lord and God," he planned to rebuild Rome that had burned. He would begin with his palace, which was to cover a surface of 41,000 square meters/441,300 square feet and be overlaid in marble and mosaic. The doors and the gold-gilded roofs of three temples alone cost today's equivalent of $22 million; $3 million was needed to adorn the Jupiter Capitoline in gold, and much more was needed to finish the Colosseum.

Because Dacia was the main source of gold in Europe (fifteen tons were extracted per year), Domitian decided to move against it. A victory there would also give Rome unlimited access to the salt mines of Transylvania, the granaries and wine of Dobrudja, and a huge stock of horses and cattle greatly needed by the Roman army. Besides, occupying Dacia once and for all would eliminate annoying hostilities from the lower Danube and provide huge revenues in the form of commercial taxes.

Subordinating the Dacians would also send a message to the Sarmatians, Germans, and Gauls who also persisted in defying the power of Rome. Most importantly, as Nero had envisioned, the occupation of Dacia would be the first step toward occupying the southeast portion of Eastern Europe and it would ensure that the barbarians could be stopped before they reached the borders of the empire.

Domitian was a typical case of a son and brother who could not match the fame of either his father, Vespasian, nor his sibling Titus, the latter having consolidated the borders of the empire. His idol was Nero. From Tacitus and Pliny the Younger, we learned that Domitian's biggest mistake was to envy and punish capable generals. And, instead of making the wise choice to use honored commanders in his campaign against the Dacians, the emperor retired them, exiled them, and later murdered them.

To his credit, Domitian increased the salaries of the legions before he ordered them to fight the German Chati tribes; he made peace with them in A.D. 83, but it proved to be unsustainable. Still, he claimed victory, celebrated his triumph in Rome, and took the title of *Germanicus*. Despite a lack of sufficient funds, he then focused on occupying Dacia, counting on Legion I Italica, which was positioned in the middle of the Danubian border with Dacia at Novae (today Svishkov east of Nicopol), and Legion V Macedonica, nearby at Oescus (Ghinghen). As a reserve, Legion VI Victrix (Victorious) was deployed some 50 kilometers/31 miles south of the Danube.

The presence of the legions on the Danube's southern bank infuriated King Duras. His ambitious nephew, Decebalus[7], a commanding figure in the Dacian army, was even more offended. In previous years the latter had led many packs of warriors across the frozen Danube, putting Roman settlements in Moesia to the sword and destroying them by fire. His sequence of victories and his acquisitions of land had made him the regent of Dacia.

Rome was neither in a position to conduct a punitive military expedition, nor to pay the annual tribute in materials and experts instituted by Tiberius. Eager to prove himself, Decebalus invaded Moesia in the winter, and his army slaughtered units of Legions I Italica and V Macedonica, including their commander General Oppius Sabinus. The Dacians subsequently plundered and destroyed numerous Roman settlements.

When the news came to Rome that the governor of Moesia had been killed in battle, the outraged public pointed to Domitian's excessive lifestyle and gambling addiction as a cause. The emperor was forced to act quickly in order to preserve his self-respect and his position, not to mention his life. He entrusted generals Cornelius Nigrinus and Vettonianus Funisulanus to lead punitive expeditions that stabilized the situation in Moesia.

Instead of being intimidated by this, Decebalus (according to Dio) agreed to make peace if every Roman would pay two *obols* (1/3 of a denarius) yearly tribute to Dacia. Rome was outraged and demanded action.

The timing turned out well for Domitian, who was eager to prove his military genius and was confident of his ability to conquer Dacia. With three legions already stationed in Pannonia, four in Moesia, and one in Dalmatia (all of which were position to prevent the Dacians from invading these territories), he had a solid base from which to operate. A Roman military fleet was harbored at the fortified city of Ratiaria, a settlement which had been built by Tiberius fifty years earlier. More warships were also anchored at Oescus, another major military base. With additional legions under his direction, Domitian was ready for a war that he believed would bring him imperial glory along with the desperately needed gold, silver, and salt of Transylvania.

Under Domitian, each legionary was thoroughly motivated to fight: he received twelve gold coins per year, and after twenty years of service, three thousand dinars—a small fortune. The Praetorian Guard was promised double benefits. For this reason, the emperor was popular with his troops, and he proudly wore the military uniform even in his Rome palace.

The Roman army was clearly superior in equipment and military training to the Dacians', which is why Domitian hoped for a quick victory. It would make it possible for him to claim personal glory and silence his critics. Intending to occupy Dacia in a single stroke, he recalled the career of the famous Gnaeus Julius Agricola, who had conquered half of Britannia. The presence of this general who enlarged the empire under Vespasian gave the legionaries still greater confidence. But Agricola fell victim to palace intrigues. He was pushed out of command, a political error which may have saved Dacia much hardship at a later point. Cornelius Fuscus, the commander of the Praetorian Guard, replaced Agricola—an obvious arrangement between the emperor and his chief guard.

In order to consolidate the fighting spirit of the legions and build their confidence in victory, Domitian ordered at least eight elite legions to take part in the invasion of Dacia. Nothing seemed to taint the Romans' war plans. Still, the calculations that had been made in Rome did not match the reality on the ground in Dacia.

The first Dacian campaign began in the early summer of 86. Domitian departed Rome with a great deal of royal hubbub, traveling by water to meet the Balkan legions whom he planned to lead across the Danube into Transylvania. He tried to convince the German tribes of Quadi, Marcomani, and Suebi from Pannonia to join a Roman coalition to attack Dacia, but like the Sarmatians, they refused. Nevertheless, five legions continued their confident march toward the Dacian border under the command of Fuscus. He had been considered a capable general under Nero and Vespasian, but had not seen combat in fifteen years.

From the beginning, this campaign was plagued by logistical problems. The lack of Roman roads leading to Dacia forced the legions to travel on dirt paths, and when it rained these changed into rivers of mud. Under such adverse conditions, no heavy equipment, including the artillery and siege weapons, could be transported by the troops. Fuscus therefore ordered his headquarters to be set up in Sirmium (Mitrovitza) in Pannonia Inferior. The encampment was close to Transylvania, yet far from the dense Dacian settlements of Moesia that were not loyal to Rome and likely to attempt surprise guerilla attacks.

In their characteristic manner, the legions marched along the Danube River, waiting their turn to cross the pontoon bridge near the Iron Gates. Then they pressed into the Banat region with their regimented and close ranks, following the Timis River corridor northward. Domitian was anticipating an easy victory and a triumphal return to Rome, so he partied and prematurely celebrated the campaign in the middle of Moesia.

The legions advanced some 75 kilometers/47 miles toward Transylvania, meeting only sporadic resistance along the way. As the roads became reduced to forest paths in narrow valleys, the units were spread dangerously thin. Still, they marched confidently onward. Only after they had advanced into the Bistra Valley and approached the entrance to Transylvania did they become aware of the reality of their situation.

Packs of Dacian horsemen began to attack the open flanks of the invaders and their isolated units. The legions desperately tried to regroup and attack the fortified city of Tapae (near village of Bucova). The unlucky Legion V Alaudae charged through the gorges of the Bistra River, only to be trapped there and heavily attacked, an incident that resulted in their near annihilation.

General Fuscus was ambushed and killed. The imperial flag with its gold eagle on top (it belonged to the Praetorian Guard and was likely the most prized standard of the empire) was captured by the Dacians. This was a unique moment of dishonor in Roman history.

It was probably after this resounding victory that Decebalus became a king and Duras stepped down. The heads of Fuscus and other captured officers were paraded on spears and displayed to the Dacian warriors and the local population. Rome's humiliation was later satirized by the poet Juvenal (ca. 60-140) who lived under Domitian's reign and detested him and the conditions that prevailed in Rome. He wrote of "... Fuscus, who planned battles in his marble halls, keeping his flesh for the Dacian vultures,"[8] hinting that a palace was not the appropriate place for a general to do his soldierly duty.

Obviously, invading Transylvania in a state of overconfidence and with an improvised strategy was an unpardonable mistake—one for which the general paid the ultimate price. From this point onward, the Roman military invasion of the heavily forested mountain areas of Dacia was doomed. They soon had to return to the safety of the Danubian line. Regardless of the outcome, Domitian, in his eagerness for victory, declared the campaign a total success. He even carried with him a fake letter of submission from Decebalus.

Dio described the emperor's "victory" celebration in Rome:

> ...with many exhibits appropriate to a triumph, though they came from no booty that he captured; on the contrary, the truce had cost him something besides his losses, for he had given large sums of money to Decebalus on the spot as well as artisans of every trade pertaining to both peace and war, and had promised to keep on giving large sums in the future. The exhibits which he displayed really came from the store of imperial furniture, which he at all times treated as captured spoils, inasmuch as he had enslaved even the empire itself.[9]

The celebration included infantry and cavalry units fighting against each other and even a staged naval battle, most likely in the newly finished Colosseum. Yet Domitian knew the facts of the situation, and since his ego was deeply hurt, he resorted to an almost unthinkable measure, one that was intended to stimulate the legions' commanders to actual victory. This was a decree that would change the course of history: he promised to give his generals part of the conquered land. Domitian had thereby laid the foundation for what would become the feudal system.

One year later, the Danubian legions received orders to march to Dacia again, and Decebalus began once more to organize counteroffensives of significant proportions. Since he was desperate to secure victory, Domitian convinced the Iazygi tribes, the Dacians' well-established enemies from the Pannonian flatlands, to join the fight. He also hurried to move Legion IV Flavia Felix from Dalmatia so that they could participate in the invasion. Legions VI Victrix and XIII Gemina arrived from Germany. In all, some nine legions were summoned for this new Dacian campaign.

The Roman's chief commander this time was General Tettius Julianus, the newly appointed governor of Upper Moesia, someone who would not accept defeat at the hands of the barbarians.[10] According to Dio, he trained and disciplined the legions to the point that each soldier had to carry a numbered shield, so his fighting performance could be easily identified and evaluated. This new invasion proceeded along the same routes as the other had, and, after an intense battle in the year 88, the legions pressed towards Tapae, the gateway to Transylvania.

The Dacians put up a formidable fight. Indeed, their resistance was so fanatical that Vesina, Decebalus's most trusted lieutenant (probably the name designated a military rank or a high priest), faked death in order to escape. Many of the Roman cohorts were slaughtered, but the charging army still conquered Tapae. The number of casualties incurred by the Dacians is not certain, but it must have been significant because Decebalus is known to have cut an entire forest to the height of a man and dressed the tree trunks in armor in an effort to frighten off the advancing Romans. This worked for a short while, but the legions persisted; undeterred by the bluff, they pushed forward. Regardless of the losses they had suffered, the rest of the troops were determined to continue their campaign toward Sarmizegethusa.

Most likely, Decebalus pulled back toward the Dacian capital where he set up a firm line of defense. Nevertheless, he sent his brother Diegis to negotiate an acceptable peace with the Romans. It was either because of this, or because the Dacians made it impossible for the legions to advance farther, that General Julianus changed the direction of his attack from northward to eastward along the Danube. This portion of the campaign proved victorious in the Danubian plains (Baragan). The Dacian strongholds were subdued and Roman authority was reinforced.

A Roman victory was declared, but the aftermath of this inconclusive campaign favored the Dacians who found occasion to revive their Sarmatian and German tribal alliances. This alone amounted to a major threat to the Roman presence in Pannonia, which was now squeezed between powerful enemy forces. It required urgent military action—action that could not be undertaken in conjunction with a long campaign in Transylvania. Domitian was therefore more than pleased to receive Diegis, who was given a diadem symbolizing the benevolence of Rome in accepting another client king. It implied that an annual subsidy was due to Dacia from Rome and that Decebalus was expected to prove his allegiance. It also signaled that the Romans were afraid of the Dacians.

A temporary peace was concluded, and Decebalus was allowed to continue ruling. The Romans retained their military posts along the Danube and partially occupied Scythia Minor (Dobrudja). Clearly, Domitian was trying to steal time in order to carry out a punitive expedition against Antoninus Saturninus, Governor of Germania Superior, who with his legions, had revolted from the Mainz garrison. Suddenly, a second front was opened up in western Dacia. Decebalus was quick to take advantage of this new opportunity and urged the Marcomanni and Quadzi (from what was Czechoslovakia) to join the anti-Domitian coalition.

Eventually the mutiny in Mainz was put down by Rome, and Legion VII Gemina, led by the young General Ulpius Trajanus, arrived from Spain and restored order. For his bravery and loyalty, Trajan was named consul. This was the beginning of a brilliant career and would eventually lead to his becoming emperor.

Due to the ongoing adversity the Roman military faced in central Europe, the intensity of the Dacian threat increased. Tacitus concluded that the all the bloody campaigns against Sarmatians and Dacians had brought only an inglorious peace. In spite of the reality of the army's situation, Domitian made a triumphal return to Rome, acting as if he had won the war. The Senate felt obliged to offer him a laurel, but not the laudatory recognition of *Dacicus*.

The urgency of the Roman wars against the Germans resulted in Dacia's becoming an equal partner of Rome in its northern Balkan affairs. Domitian inspected the Danubian zone three times and was even able to cross Dacian territory into Pannonia. In order to keep the Dacians in check, sixteen auxiliary formations were posted along the Dobrudja border at fifteen locations. The northernmost point of Roman expansion was the town of Noviodunum (Gherghina), where the Danube becomes a delta.

In order to further secure Dacian peace, Domitian transferred Legion XXI Rapax (Predator) from Germania to Moesia Inferior. They had the mission of repelling any invasion that might occur and protecting the many Roman commercial ports along the lower Danube and on the Black Sea. It is likely that cohorts of this legion were stationed in various garrisons along the Danube around Durostorum. To Decebalus, the deployment of troops in these areas indicated Rome's unmistakable intent to occupy the Dacian land.

In the winter of 92, an armed Dacian-Roxolani coalition carried out a number of precipitous raids into Moesia, and their cavalry packs pushed the Roman units back so that they were forced to fight from distant locations. The combat unity of the legions had been broken, and the centurias were lured into a no-man's-land and then slaughtered one-by-one. The final battle took place in the Banat area and resulted in the annihilation of Legio XXI Rapax, whose emblem was a predatory bird attacking a victim. The name of this legion, formed by Octavian in 40 B.C., was never to appear in Roman military records. It was later replaced by Legio XIII Gemina.

This crushing defeat convinced Domitian to delay any further invasions of Dacia indefinitely. In A.D. 96 Empress Domitia Longina plotted the assassination of her megalomaniac husband. This was the last event about which Tacitus wrote.

Until they were routed in Dacia, the Romans had seldom lost a battle, and they had never lost a war. Now, for the first time, they had lost both, including two entire legions. This was a humiliation that needed to be avenged at any cost.

Emperor Nerva, the next to wear the royal purple robe was, at age 66, busy avoiding being assassinated. Fighting the Dacians was therefore his last wish. Instead he bought their peace with a yearly tribute in money and materials. Meanwhile the Dacians were enjoying another golden age under the rule of Decebalus. In a tribal world, one in which alliances were made and broken overnight along with the continual migration of populations, the kingdom of Dacia remained undeterred in its claims to be the center of Eastern European political, military and economic power.

NOTES

1. Caesar's legacy continued, and his very name became synonymous with supreme, uncontested authority, as did "Czar" in Russia and "Kaiser" in Germany. The month of July was also named in his memory, as was the term "cesarean section" because he was born through this type of surgery.

2. Cassius Dio, *Roman History* (Loeb Classical Library: 1917), vol. 6, bk. 51, http://penelope.uchicago.edu/Thayer/E/Roman/Texts/Cassius_Dio/51*.html (12 Feb. 2008), 23.2-3.

3. Dio, *Roman History*, vol. 6, bk. 51, 24.7.

4. The word "decimal" became associated with mathematics through the European metric system, in which it meant "one-tenth" or "base ten."

5. Given his megalomaniac state, Nero dreamed of invading Getia, occupying Alania and the kingdom of the Bosporus, and thus transforming the Crimea into a second Italian Peninsula. His military plans ended with his suicide.

6. Tacitus, *The Annales of Cornelius Tacitus, The Description of Germanie* (London: printed by F. L. for Richard Whitaker, 1640), 200.

7. A conical dish was discovered containing the Latin inscription, *DECEBALUS* and *PER SCORILO*. This caused many historians to believe that Decebalus was the son (*puer*) of King Scorilo/Corylus who reigned before Duras. It is reasonable to assume that Scorilo and Duras were closely related, *per* meaning "because of Scorilo". Some historians speculate that Diurpaneus was the original name of Decebalus, "the Brave One" being an epithet he acquired after his victories against the Roman invad-

ers. His nickname is also translatable into vulgate Latin as "Strong as Ten Barbarians/wild men".

8. Juvenal, *Juvenal and Persius*, trans. G. G. Ramsay (Cambridge and London: Harvard University Press, 1999), Satire 4, 111-112. Another version of the translation reads, "Fuscus, who then was studying war in his Tuscan villa, saving his flesh to provide a feast for the Dacian vultures."

9. Cassius Dio, *Roman History*, trans. Earnest Cary (Cambridge: Harvard University Press; London: William Heinemann, 1955), bk. 67, 333-335.

10. Julianus had deserted his Legion VII during the Civil War of A.D. 69 and crossed lower Dacia from Pannonia to escape capital punishment. Officially rehabilitated by Vespasian, he wanted to prove the value of his generalship at any cost.

Chapter Eight

Two Major Wars

In his short reign, Emperor Nerva did one notable thing: he adopted the Iberian-born Marcus Ulpius Trajanus, who was the loyal governor of Germania Superior, and set up a line of succession that would have enormous ramifications for the Roman Empire. When Nerva died in A.D 98 Trajanus/Trajan was officially nominated as the new emperor by a young tribune for whom he was the legal guardian—Hadrian. Trajan would become known as one of the most ambitious and competent rulers of empire, and his successor, Hadrian, would have an equally illustrious legacy, having been catapulted to fame by his performance in the Dacian wars.

Instead of engaging in the customary triumphal march through Rome, Trajan consolidated his royal position while he was still in Germania where once he commanded Legion VII Gemina. He began by executing the arrogant Praetorian commanders who had been summoned to Cologne. After touring many of the garrisons, thereby increasing his popularity with the legions, he fought and defeated the Suebi on the Danube, for which he received the title of *Germanicus*. (A portion of the free Suebi/Suevi tribes lived in the Banat area of Dacia.) One year later, he entered Rome as a proven leader, inaugurating a dynasty of non-Roman emperors.

Trajan was the first emperor to put the law above his throne and make it work for the good of the empire. Entirely dedicated to serving his people and the Roman army, he was loved by all of his subjects and held in high esteem even by his enemies. He was a battle-tested emperor with a solid military reputation in Britannia and Germania, where he had served in all of Domitian's and Nerva's campaigns. As a former governor of Moesia, he was also undoubtedly familiar with the growing problems in Dacia, and with its wealth of resources and stubbornly independent people.

165

Since he planned to invade Dacia, the warrior emperor began to properly train and equip many of his twenty-eight legions (less than a quarter of whom were born in Italy). His first priority was to assemble a supply of heavy artillery and to strengthen cavalry contingents.

The impressive Roman catapult could throw 50-killiogram/110-pound stones or burning projectiles over fortress walls that were 400 meters/1,312 feet away; and the scorpion, a large arch powered by twisted cords, could shoot heavy iron bolts across the Danube. These war machines were mounted on mobile carriages for easier transport to efficient positions; they could release some one hundred volleys a day. Thirty men, under the command of a military engineer, handled each of the thirty artillery pieces assigned to each legion. Smaller versions of these war machines named *carroballistae* (ballista in carts drawn by mules) could fire large arrows at a deadly 300 meters/984 feet. These efficient weapons were each served by eight men. Ten carroballistae were assigned to each cohort of five hundred men.

Iron bolts, sling bullets, and projectiles were imprinted with the legion's number or name and sometimes short messages. This made it easier for future historians to trace the location of the various legions' camps and identify the battles they had participated in. Mounted battering rams on wheels for breaking down gates and walls, as well as mobile siege towers with floors from which legionaries could attack over high fortifications, completed the war arsenal.

Equally important was medical care. Each Roman legion had twenty-four surgeons and orderlies that provided the most advanced field treatment in the world. Each legion had the support of some five thousand auxiliary troops, most of whom were barbarian prisoners of war or volunteers whose ferocity was taken advantage of by the Roman army. Their shields bore no insignia or military ornament, and their body armor was made of leather, not of metallic strips or mail. Considered to be inferior humans, they were over-worked in peace time and over-exposed to danger as sacrificial troops in war time. They all spoke the common language of international trade, the Latin vulgaris of the poor or foreign people. Their motto was *Legio, Patria Nostra Est!* (The legion is our country!)

Other highly qualified staff, such as engineers, sappers, clerks, tent-makers, equipment craftsmen, cartographers, supply attendants, and centurions/drill-masters completed the legion; it was commanded by tribunes with ranks from major to general. A vast web of paved roads throughout the empire ensured the rapid deployment of troops.[1]

The legionaries were traditionally foot soldiers, and the Roman army excelled at fighting on the ground. The cavalry was greatly improved by the addition of barbarian horsemen, mostly Celts, Germans, and Thracians. The Roman troops owed their victories to their discipline, their ability to move, and their compact formations fighting shoulder to shoulder. The legionaries were willing to die for the honor of Rome, which often deteriorated into mass plunder, rape, indiscriminate massacres, and other unspeakable forms of violence. Any brutal means to keep order in occupied territories was acceptable.

Unlike the barbarians who tended to fight spontaneously, the Romans considered war to be an art and a source of revenue. Conquered people were immediately put to work, strictly supervised by the Romans, who governed them as a ruling class would.

In sharp contrast to the Roman military arsenal, the Dacians' was simple. It consisted mainly of the long scimitar (sword) with its tip curved toward the sharpened interior—a formidable two-hand weapon for hooking and slashing. Its curvature added extra swing and striking power that could split a shield while it ensured firm blockage from an enemy blow. A shorter version was the one-hand *sica* (dagger) finely honed on both edges to a razor-sharp point. It was an extremely maneuverable weapon and probably copied from the Scythian sickle.[2] The side-arm arsenal was completed with a smaller dagger called the *cosor* (pocket or belt knife, also curved), a name retained in modern Romanian language. They did not have sheaths (as is shown accurately on Trajan's Column). These slashing weapons were intended for hand-to-hand combat and were much feared and despised by the Romans, who used stabbing weapons to keep the enemy at a distance.

The Dacian bow with its arrows, kept in an ornamented leather quiver, was considered a defensive weapon as well, as were the shields made of oak and covered with richly decorated copper worked by Celtic craftsmen. The Getian horsemen were expert archers. In close combat, they used a lance and battle ax. Packs of *arcasi* (archers) on horses engaged in swift hit-and-run attacks with devastating results for the enemy's foot soldiers.

In spite of its small size, the Dacian shield was heavy but easy to handle; it was therefore also an efficient striking weapon. Both of these facts indicate that Dacians preferred to engage in close combat. Aside from conical fur hats (only worn by noblemen) and long sheepskin coats or capes worn with the shaggy fur toward the outside to deflect the impact of sharp blades, the Dacians had no other form of protection. In contrast, the Thracian soldiers wore body armor of Greek or Roman type, proving the unlike common identity between the two nations.

Realizing that war was imminent, King Decebalus did not hesitate to spend Dacian gold to bribe the most skillful Roman engineers and even the best officers, some of whom had been sent by Domitian as part of the annual tribute. The pay evidently was so good that many auxiliaries and even legionaries deserted their Roman units and enrolled in the Dacian army.

While the increasingly popular Decebalus did not have a regular army, he did have something equally important: the geographic area of Dacia crisscrossed by rivers and mountains was unmapped and so favored him. The layout of his kingdom would force the Roman legions to make long and exhausting detours, passing through gorges that were easily defended by the Dacians. Additionally, the Dacians would be fighting a war on their home turf. They had the advantage of determining when and where battles would take place, and so fought valiantly to protect their families. Their ultimate goal was to remain free, and they were willing to die for that cause.

Their best defense was to attack the invaders. Packs of Dacian horsemen proudly showing their dragon flag raided the Roman colonies in Moesia, mostly in the winter. The audacity of their contemptuous actions was observed by Trajan, who, according to Dio, "grieved at the amount of money [the Dacians] were receiving annually [in tributes], and he also observed that their power and their pride were increasing."[3] In response, Trajan accelerated his war plans for the invasion of Dacia in the spring of 101.

He chose a safe and original way to move the Roman infantry from Western Europe to points at which it could cross into Dacia. He ordered a large contingent of stoneworkers to cut a passage along the right bank of the Danube in the area of Cazane (Canyon).[4] He then had a suspension bridge constructed whose beams were embedded in the canyon wall. These made it possible for ships to be towed and for legionnaires to march toward Central Dacia on the southern bank of the Danube.

Leaving nothing to chance, the emperor ordered two of the empire's ten fleets, Classic Moesia and Classic Pannonica, to bring his heavy artillery, cavalry, and a massive war arsenal in from Germania and Pannonia. The ships' cargoes consisted primarily of the troops and equipment of Legions I Adiutrix (Helper), VII Claudia, and XIII and XIV Gemina (Twins). They were transported from the Sava River to Sirmium (Mitrovitza), and from there to the Danube Iron Gates, the first point at which one could cross into Transylvania.

The Roman legions already conveniently stationed in the Balkans included II Italica, II Adiutrix, IV Flavia/Felix, and V Macedonica. Trajan ordered them to march north, and one by one they arrived at the Danubian collection points. Legion XI Claudia was stationed at Durostrum (Silistra) and built a fort north of it at Capidava to control part of the lower Danube. In all, nine legions, as well as veteran cohorts of earlier Dacian wars—nearly one hundred thousand men—were poised to cross the Danube into the Banat region of Dacia.

Trajan established his headquarters at Sirmium and Viminacium with the Praetorian Guard for his personal protection. He also stationed reserve army units there. The emperor wanted to be accompanied only by generals he could count on in the event of an emergency. One of them was Claudius Livianus, the commander of the Praetorian Guard, and his devoted adviser Lucius Sura, who was in charge of a body of troops.

Decisions on which commanders would lead the troops were made based on their fighting records and their proven capabilities against unpredictable enemies. Lusius Quietus was case in point. His military expertise, combined with his legendary cruelty, expedited his promotion to the rank of general.

In the past, Quietus, a black chieftain of the Moors, had agreed to fight for Rome. His career would culminate in his victory in the Parthian wars, during which he indiscriminately slaughtered both war prisoners and civilians. His excessive zeal was punished by the Romans, and the sadistic general was dismissed from the army. But Trajan believed him to be the perfect commander to lead the storm troops in an invasion of Dacia, so Quietus was rehabilitated and his rank restored. With all preparations completed, the wolf-dragon warriors were about to face the Roman eagle of legions at the peak of its glory, at a point in time when it controlled much of the known world.

The first invading column to cross the Danube on ferry boats at Lederata (Rama) was that of the infamous General Quietus. His auxiliary troop of savage Moors (barbarians who could be readily sacrificed) terrorized the Dacian land. Trajan's Column illustrates this by detailing the longest uninterrupted sequence of cavalry charges backed up the movements of auxiliary infantrymen. These soldiers are all portrayed as stepping over the fallen Dacians, whose comrades continue to fight with determination and courage. One by one, the strongholds of Jidova, Arcidava, Berzobis, and Aizis were stormed and conquered. Then the Roman troops turned eastward toward Tibiscum/ Jupa, the junction for their other advancing columns.

The second military column was led by the governor of Pannonia, Quietus Agricola, who may have been the son or a relative of the great veteran general. It crossed the Danube on a pontoon bridge at Drobeta and advanced along a parallel route with the column of Quietus. Its only bloody encounter took place a few miles north of the Iron Gates Bridge, where the Dacians had anticipated an attack. Their line of defense was destroyed by the legionaries, whose emperor and Praetorian Guard followed at a close distance. Agricola then marched through the Timis valley that led to the Jupa stronghold on the river (near today's Caransebes).

A massive clean-up operation eliminated any remaining resistance in otherwise Roman-friendly Banat. The conquering troops began to build castri to signal their occupation and then headed toward Jupa where they would merge with the rest of their forces. It had already been evacuated by the Dacians.

Trajan's Column shows that, at this point, while he was surveying the battlefield, barbarian auxiliaries were presenting him with the severed heads of Dacians. In the background, Decebalus is shown watching his warriors with their dragon flags flying high, pushing back the Romans. Other Dacians carry their wounded away from danger into a fortified camp. The wall of a Dacian fort was adorned with impaled skulls, probably belonging to Romans prisoners from the previous war. Trajan and his lieutenants are depicted watching their soldiers set fire to Dacian houses, most likely as a punishment for the siege of that fort.

The Dacians, who rode on horseback, conducted lightning attacks and speedy retreats in the lush forests they knew so well. It is for this reason that most of the battle scenes on the Column are separated by trees, symbolizing the importance of the forests that protected the defenders and made it difficult for the invaders to chase them.

A Roman side thrust along the Cerna Valley was intended to split the main Dacian forces, thus preventing them from organizing a single, massive line of resistance. This route was also chosen as an alternate means of entry to the Hateg Depression, the vital center of the Dacian kingdom. Trajan had launched a well-planned invasion with pincer-like attacks that would enclose Sarmizegethusa.

After winning the first of several scattered battles, the core of the invading Roman columns united to attack fortified Tapae, the gateway to Transylvania. But the anticipated and potentially brutal confrontation never happened. Fate played an unexpected trick on the Dacians. They were the victims of set of adverse circumstances unleashed by Mother Nature.

The darkness of the spring night was crossed and stabbed by huge bolts of lightning, and claps of thunder split the sky. One lightning bolt killed a top commander of the Dacians, possibly a relative of Decebalus. Interpreting the storm and deadly accident as an omen and a warning from their god Zamolxis to quit fighting, the heavily entrenched but superstitious Dacians broke off their defense and left the city hurriedly. The Column shows them conducting an orderly retreat while heading to Sarmizegethusa.

The Dacians' unexpected retreat made their Celtic, German, and Sarmatian allies think twice about continuing the fight. The Column depicts a delegation of ten Buri and Sarmatians asking for peace. Dio wrote otherwise, however. He stated that they brought with them a large mushroom with a message written in Latin, advising the invaders to turn back. Trajan is shown with a proud and contemptuous attitude, turning down their plea. The delegation clearly had not been sent by Decebalus, but by local leaders who were unimportant to him. Trajan decided to press on.

After the easy victory in Tapae, the Romans entered the Hateg region and the Gradistea Valley. Its rough terrain and roads had been flooded by late summer rains, making forward movement difficult for the cavalry and virtually stopping the advance of mobile artillery. The foot soldiers advanced slowly, only after units of carpenters and other constructors had fixed or built bridges across the flooded streams. Other crews were busy converting mountain paths into regular roads on which the mighty Roman war machines could advance. Suddenly the heavy armor and artillery proved to work against the legionaries.

Meanwhile, as was typical for the Roman army, units of soldiers who were wounded, sick, or near retirement age were deposited at strategic points to build forts and castri. These either served as defensive strongholds or were used as *hibernaculum* (winter garrisons). Thus far, the Romans had made only a slow and difficult advance toward the heart of Transylvania. The land would soon be covered by snow. But unlike previous wars, they showed no intention of retreating to the Danube and waiting for more favorable weather.

At this critical point, some of Decebalus's tribes may have begun to doubt that victory was possible. The Column depicts a delegation of five bearded and long-haired Dacians, wrapped in long mantles hemmed with tassels, standing in front of Trajan. The men are *comati* (common folk), who would have represented neither Decebalus nor his army. Just as prior and later Dacian delegations had done, they spoke without an interpreter. The reason for their humble appearance before the emperor is explained in another image in which the Romans are destroying Dacian villages. The next frieze shows how the merciless auxiliary troops massacred Dacian civilians or torched their dwellings, while Dacian captives, most of them women, were led to ships to be resettled.

Why did the Romans commit such crimes? Another section of the Column may provide an answer to this question: it shows sheep and cattle being killed by the Dacians since they were unwilling to let the Romans use them for food. The Dacians probably also poisoned the wells and other sources of potable water, thus infuriating the Romans carried out deadly reprisals. The rows of Roman heads displayed on the top of hill forts also seem to require mortal retribution. It is no wonder the emperor ignored the five submissive peasants who were asking for mercy.

With the Banat region having been conquered and Dacian resistance diminishing as their troops retreated toward Sarmizegethusa, the Romans began to encircle the Dacian capital. Yet, there was no sign that Decebalus was willing to negotiate an end to the war. He knew that the Romans avoided fighting in the winter, especially under such hostile conditions as those of the Transylvanian mountains. He calmly waited for the cold to return since it would change the course of the war and put him in charge of the campaign.

His hope did not materialize, however, and the invaders persisted in building military encampments around the besieged capital. They clearly intended to maintain their position during the coming winter, and this time the weather seemed to be on their side. If communications were cut off, Sarmizegethusa and the fortresses around it would eventually face starvation. The legionaries knew this, so they confidently waited for Decebalus and his entrapped garrison to surrender unconditionally.

The rest of the empire was peaceful. It seemed that nothing would interfere with a victorious campaign in Dacia, which was now covered in snow. The emperor sent his confidants, Generals Livianus and Sura, to negotiate an honorable peace. But the defiant Dacian king did not even bother to receive the two envoys. Decebalus was up to something unforeseen that would soon horrify the Romans.

Dacia was a large kingdom. Its Buri warriors of the mighty tribe of Buridavensi from Muntenia/Wallachia took advantage of the fact that the Roman legions were locked in position in Transylvania and carried out their own invasion across the frozen Danube into Moesia. The Roxolani, Getians, and Daco-Moesians joined the lightning raid. One frame of the Column shows a Roman castrum from Moesia being assaulted by the Dacians who were led by a Roman deserter (identified by the fact that he is without a beard). The Dacians are depicted wearing their traditional clothing, holding their distinctive weapons and round shields, and ramming the fortress walls.

Nearly everything was going well for the Romans in the Transylvania campaign until desperate messages for help came from the commanders in Moesia. Trajan divided his army, and, leading the mounted troops that were still in the Iron Gates camps, he rushed to the area of the disaster. Fortunately for the Romans, the winter climate suddenly became mild, and the cargo ships cruising down the Danube hurriedly brought more reserves, including the Praetorian Guard.

Unfortunately for the Dacians, the ice over the Danube became so thin that many of their horsemen returning with plunder or heading out to raids were swallowed by the cold, deep river. The Column illustrates the dreadful details of how the Dacians and their allies tried to save themselves from the deadly water.[5]

Decebalus took full advantage of the movement on the second front that removed the legions from Transylvania, and he successfully attacked the winter encampment of the Romans surrounding Sarmizegethusa. It was a brilliant military move that freed the Dacian capital from the jaws of defeat and briefly restored his prestige and the public's confidence in him.

However, exactly as had happened at Tapae a few months earlier, a stormy rain in the middle of the winter led the surviving Dacian raiders to believe Zamolxis was giving them a message to give up the fight. Unwilling to anger their deity, they and some of their allies speedily retreated from Moesia. When they were searching for a portion of the Danube with thicker ice, they encountered the Roman fleet waiting to hack them to bits in the water. Meanwhile, the Roman cavalry on the ground, probably the Aelia I Civium Romanorum and the cohort II Hispanorum Scutata brought from Spain, annihilated the last remnant of Dacian resistance. Many prisoners were forced to build Nikopolis ad Istrum, known as "the fortress of victory."

The victorious Romans continued their march toward the wealthy and fortified cities of Callatis, Histria, and Tomis, as these were also under the threat of invasion by the Dacians. Their timing was perfect. The army corps was led by Trajan, its mission being to intercept more of the heavily armored Roxolani cavalry coming from above the Danube Delta as well as the Getian archers of Dobrudja who were heading toward precisely those Roman-held cities. The confrontation between them took place on the old battlefield later known as Adamclisi, not too far from an altar erected by Domitian's soldiers. In no time, initial scuffles degenerated into a major savagery.

The friezes on the Column dedicated to this brutal confrontation show numerous incidents of hand-to-hand combat. Of course, the Romans are depicted as surrounded by the dead bodies of Dacians and their barbaric allies. Most notable are the Sarmatian horsemen wearing their fish-scale armor made of horse hooves. For the first and last time, the legionaries are shown treating their wounds. A carroballistae is shown in full action, but Dacians continue to fight undeterred even as their comrades litter the ground. This battle was so bloody that Trajan offered his imperial attire in order to supply his wounded men with more bandages.

At this point, the Dacians almost turned defeat into victory; still, it was not to be. It is likely that cohorts of Legion XI Claudia stationed only miles away at the newly built Durostorum arrived with fresh troops in time to influence the outcome of the battle. Unable to match the superior numbers and equipment of the Romans, the Dacians and their allies tried to escape, only to be hacked to death or captured by the auxiliary cavalrymen. A frieze shows one prisoner being pushed in front of Trajan who seems impressed by the Dacian warrior with his hands tied behind him.

This excessively bloody campaign in Dobrudja ended with a clear victory for the Romans. They lost four thousand men in a few hours, but Dacian losses were believed to be larger. As for the surviving Buri, Sarmatians, and other Dacian allies, their morale was temporarily broken. Decebalus, however, was far from defeated. In the meantime, Trajan led his army back to the main target, Transylvania, for the rest of the winter. For the time being, the war remained at a stalemate.

As soon as the spring of 102 arrived, the new military camps that had been destroyed by the Dacians were rebuilt, enlarged, and better organized by the Romans stationed in what is today the Banat region. Undeterred in his plans for a conquest, Trajan ordered still more reserves to enter Dacia. Legio I Minervia and many thousands of auxiliary troops, under the command of General Hadrian, arrived just in time from Germania and Pannonia. The column shows him advancing with many legion standards by his side along the Mures River, and Trajan meeting a Dacian embassy. The emperor reinforces the morale of his troops with numerous speeches, rewards, and sacrifices to the benevolent gods.

Construction of roads, bridges, and camps then commenced at a feverish rate throughout the occupied territory, the aim being to accommodate the speedy arrival of reinforcements. New Roman fortifications could be seen everywhere with impaled Dacian heads on their walls—a dramatic indication of a shift in the tide of the war in favor of the Romans. Yet, one scene on the Column clearly depicts the Dacians with their beloved dragon standard flying high above them as they watch the enemy's activities from a hilltop.

Eventually all the Roman forces met up in the Hateg region. The zigzag front lines in the mountains now merged and pushed again toward Sarmizegethusa. The troops leading the march were the unmistakable African cavalrymen of General Quietus. They are easily recognized on the Column because of their long, braided hair. Additional auxiliary sacrificial troops joined the fight as well. Heavy infantry continued to advance at a steady pace, exploiting the fact that the cavalry was surrounded or forcing their way through the front breaches created by the Palmarian archers and the Syrian lancers.

It was obvious that the Dacians did not have a siege mentality. One by one, many of their fortified settlements were occupied by the Romans, culminating in the conquest of the main fortress, Costesti. There the Romans found much of the plunder (including the imperial standard) that had been taken by the Dacians from General Fuscus. This evidence of the shameful defeat they had suffered earlier made the blood of the proud legionaries boil with anger, and they became even more determined to achieve victory at any cost.

They captured Decebalus's sister, who is clearly portrayed on the Column as Trajan benevolently greets her before she goes into captivity. No doubt, this provided the emperor with enormous bargaining power. This noble woman carries a baby at her breast. Dressed in a long gown with long sleeves, with her hair held in place by a scarf, she appears to command royal respect from her captors. Many other mothers with children and older civilians joined the forced exodus. Decebalus's sister was taken to Rome, where she inspired much adulation and victory propaganda.[6]

The Dacians continued to fight as they retreated, seeking shelter in the wilderness of the mountains. Unfortunately, they also headed away from their capital, where Decebalus was mobilizing the rest of his warriors. Meanwhile many tribesmen and their chieftains were willing to surrender rather than continue a hopeless fight. Cassius Dio believed "Decebalus had sent envoys even before his defeat, not the long-haired men this time, as before, but the noblest among the cap-wearers."[7] Indeed, the Column shows a Dacian nobleman kneeling in front of Trajan. The worried Dacian king had sent his first emissaries but Trajan had refused to negotiate with them. Since he was entirely confident of winning the war, the emperor wanted to see Decebalus's power destroyed.

After conquering many of the hill forts around Sarmizegethusa, the Romans began to build fortifications atop them, thus allocating more time to work than to fighting. The auxiliary horsemen methodically attacked one Dacian stronghold after another, and one point of resistance after another was annihilated in the hot summer of 102. The Column shows the Dacians suffering heavy casualties with mortally wounded troops lying on the ground and the rest of them fighting while in retreat under the dragon flag they struggle to save. More Roman constructions consolidate their power over the occupied land while two more Dacian noblemen come to kiss the emperor's hand.

At the same time, another Roman expeditionary corps entered Transylvania from Wallachia through the Olt River corridor. It quickly surrounded the Dacian resistance there. The scrolling scenes on the Column show the progression of the war: how the legionaries in compact formations hold their large shields above them—the famous "testudo" defense—as they attack the gates of a fortress.

It is likely that at this point Decebalus knew in his heart that he had lost the war, even as the Dacians defended their position by showering the Romans with lances and stones and by operating a ballista. This battle probably occurred near Sarmizegethusa given that it is the most detailed of the Column's fighting scenes.

The German auxiliaries, with their long hair tied into side-knots by their ears, are shown engaged in hand-to-hand combat. A few of them hold Dacian heads in front of Trajan who is flanked by Sura and Livianus. In another frieze, Dacian heads are atop poles. It is interesting to note that in all of the Column's war scenes the Roman legionnaires are behind the first line of attack, pushing the sacrificial troops forward. The barbarian auxiliaries had only one choice: to win or to die.

The Dacians are shown fighting with the same determination, using their main weapons, the curved sword and dagger. For its own glorification, the Column shows the battlefields littered only with fallen Dacians. Mistletoe motifs were placed at various points on the Column to indicate that Celtic warriors also participated in the war on the Dacians' side.

To illustrate the strength of the Roman offensive, the Column depicts some Dacians as running from their fortified settlements into the mountains, with legionaries in pursuit. Sarmizegethusa had finally become surrounded. The city was besieged, the Romans were pushing in from all directions. Finally, Decebalus, advised by the great Vesina and unwilling to sacrifice any more of his army and people, surrendered and asked for peace.

A long sequence of events followed this surrender, which is lavishly carved in the Column. Trajan is shown sitting on his throne looking down at the kneeling Dacian leaders who plead for mercy. Standing behind them is Decebalus, the royal standard of flying dragons at his side, with his arms outstretched in gallant capitulation. This was the glorious moment the emperor had long awaited.

Decebalus's distinctive face with his large crooked nose is clearly portrayed on the sculpture. He has trimmed hair and a beard and wears a nobleman's hat. Behind him is a large group of civilians, mainly women holding babies, small children, and older men. The king surrendered in order to save their lives. This scene takes place outside the fortified walls of Sarmizegethusa, a clear indication that the Romans did not enter the Dacian capital.

The end of the Dacian war of 101-102 is shown on the Column with Trajan, flanked by Sura, Livianus, and the imperial standards, as he receives a group of Roman noblemen who salute his victory. He holds a rolled-up document, probably the senatorial acclamation that rewarded him with the title of *Dacicus*. Next to them are magnificent trophies: four captured Dacian dragon standards, weapons, shields, and uniforms, markedly distinguished from the angel-like statue of victory that witnesses the end of the war.

Roman military power in Dacia had been secured by a few cohorts of Legio IV Flavia and XIII Gemina garrisoned in what are today the Banat region and the southern portion of Oltenia. Obviously, Trajan believed that he had pacified the Dacians and that there was no need for additional occupation troops. He was wrong.

The conditions imposed by Trajan were severe but not unbearable for Decebalus: an end to all the hostilities, total military demobilization, and surrender of all weapons. The Dacians were forced to destroy their forts and extradite all deserters and Roman collaborators. They also had to return the war plunder taken from Domitian. Finally, they had "...to withdraw from captured territory, and furthermore to consider the same persons enemies and friends as the Romans did."[8]

Decebalus agreed to these terms. He recognized the Roman control of all occupied territories, Moesia included, and he committed to paying for the occupation troops. But he set one condition: he must be allowed to continue to rule the country. After all, his presence in Dacia would calm the many tribes who respectfully took orders from him. This made sense to Trajan, who, after a good look at Decebalus's nose, decided to leave him in power. (According to Roman mythology, all predestined rulers were born with a crooked nose.) Trajan granted the king's request to keep his throne, and Decebalus opportunistically accepted the imperial sovereignty. Besides, his submission was purely formal—only one-sixth of the Dacian Kingdom had been occupied by the Romans.

The Roman traitors (easily identified because the legionaries were distinctively tattooed upon entering the army) were handed over by the Dacians, and they were executed in front of the legions as a lesson in loyalty. Trajan and the greater part of his triumphant troops returned to Rome with war plunder and thousands of enslaved Dacians. According to his physician Crito, "the emperor brought back fifty thousand prisoners who were promptly put up at auction."[9] Among them were many women. He celebrated the victory for several days with the customary public feasts and circus games.

The occupied Banat region was formally annexed to the empire as a Carpathian protectorate with the name of Colonia Dacica. The rest of Dacia remained a free country under the rule of Decebalus who took orders from General Decimus, a Roman governor in name only. Because the war had resulted in no clear victory, Roman success was short-lived. It had only marginal benefits, most of which served only for propaganda purposes.

From the start, Decebalus behaved independently of the will of Rome, ignoring the commitment he had made. Dio wrote:

> This man was shrewd in his understanding of warfare and shrewd also in the waging of war; he judged well when to attack and chose the right moment to retreat; he was an expert in ambuscades and a master in pitched battles; and he knew not only how to follow up a victory well, but also how to manage well a defeat.[10]

The peaceful interval that followed was used by Decebalus to prepare for a new war. He knew too well that freedom was to be gained by conquest, and that was not offered freely. Of course, Trajan, the veteran of so many battles, was not fooled by Decebalus's fake submission. Since he was aware that most of the Dacians were free, rich, and still very powerful, the emperor ordered Apolodor/Apolodorus, his favorite architect from Damascus, to begin building a permanent bridge over the Danube. That highway across the great river was intended to connect Moesia with Dacia and to allow for the speedy intervention of Roman troops in Decebalus's kingdom; of course, it was also built for the purpose of systematically exploiting Dacia's numerous natural resources. It would ensure total Roman control of the collection of taxes from Danubian navigation.

The bridge was built at Drobeta[11] for a good reason: here there was a large sandbar in the middle of the Danube. Water could be drained on one side of the island and then the other, thereby making it easier to build the needed pillars. The construction site was guarded by a military garrison under the command of General Hadrian, who was interested in mathematics and architecture. But his amateurish advice received, at best, only polite smiles from Apolodor who frequently did not hesitate to put the future emperor in his place. (Later the great architect would pay mortally for his lack of tact.)

The bridge, which took three years to complete, was a unique combination of engineering precision and monumental architecture. Dio described it as having "twenty piers of squared stone one hundred and fifty feet in height above the foundation and sixty in width, and these, standing at a distance of one hundred and seventy feet from one another [that] are connected by arches."[12] Massive pillars of stone and brick were connected by braced timber arches that supported a wooden deck and rails. Each arch between the pillars was 50 meters/164 feet long and stood at least 20 meters/66 feet high above the water. Hundreds of acres of oak forest were cut for scaffolding and to provide the floor and the rails of the bridge, which had been precisely planned, foot by foot[13] and built with Dacian hard labor.

It stretched more than one kilometer across the water (almost a mile from one bank to the other). It was also wide enough for two heavy vehicles to travel in opposite directions and still allow space for a column of foot soldiers. It took six hours for a legion marching six abreast to cross the bridge. The monumental entrances on each end incorporated military forts. They guarded the bridge with its large piers and its warehouses for barges that unloaded troops and supplies. Needless to say, this bridge was the most ambitious engineering feat of the time, and its image was proudly stamped on a Roman coin.[14]

While the Romans were busy building their spectacular bridge, Decebalus was preparing for another war. The Roman colonists settled only in a limited area of the Banat region, making the Roman presence in Dacia merely symbolic. Decebalus became even more authoritarian than he had been previously. He was "acting contrary to the treaty in many ways, was collecting arms, receiving those who deserted, repairing the forts...even going so far as to annex a portion of the territory of the Iazyges."[15] In other words, he re-armed his troops, built new fortifications, and broke each of the stipulations Trajan had dictated. Moreover, he campaigned against Rome's strongest allies, the Iazygi, and pushed them out of Western Dacia.

In the winter of 104 squadrons of Free Dacians not only attacked south of the frozen Danube, but also turned on some Roman garrisons stationed in Dacia. When General Longinus, the commander of the occupation troops, wished to protest against this violation of peace, he fell into a clever trap and was captured. According to Dio, Decebalus tried to negotiate the general's release in exchange for the independence of occupied Dacia and payment for all war expenses. Trajan turned down any and all negotiations. He even refused to take back the body of the general who, by then, had committed honorable suicide.

The die having been cast, the Dacians attacked the advanced Roman positions, tore down the walls of their fortresses, and killed the defenders. The cohorts of the occupation troops retreated beyond the Danube, using the great bridge that was firmly defended against Dacian attack. One of the most heavily fortified Roman garrisons was the newly built Durostorum. It sheltered at least one legion and became the target of Dacian raiders, but nevertheless held on. Rome received this disturbing news with predictable indignation.

Trajan traveled to Spain to put down some attempted revolts. While he was there, he granted the restless Gauls economic and commercial favors and thus ensured peace in the remainder of Europe. Many of the troops that had been stationed there were freed, including Legion Hispania Tarraconensin. He formed two new legions, II Traiana Fortis (the Brave) and XXX Ulpia Victrix (the Victorious), and trained them for a new Dacian campaign. To build morale, he had coins minted in Rome with the inscription, *IMP NERVA TRAIANVS AVG GER DACICVS* (Emperor Nerva Trajanus Augustus Germanicus Dacicus).

In Transylvania, Decebalus had reached the peak of his popularity. He decided to hire an assassin to murder Trajan while he was inspecting his troops in Moesia. When the emperor learned of the plot, this was the last straw for him. He declared war on the Dacians to the roaring applause of the Senate. This may have been the only time that not a single senator argued against a proposed decision. Indeed, the Romans were unanimous in describing Decebalus's actions as beyond contempt.

The second Dacian war began on June 4, 105 when Trajan again left Rome with the customary hubbub of parading troops. The Column shows him performing numerous animal sacrifices to ensure the help of the gods in the upcoming campaign. After his fleet arrived in the Adriatic port of Dures, Trajan offered still more sacrifices. From there, he traveled east with a cavalry corps and met part of his army (twelve legions with more than 120,000 soldiers total) at Drobeta where he was greeted by Hadrian. All-out war—coupled with vengeance—had returned to Dacia.

The main Roman forces hurriedly crossed Apolodor's bridge. The column shows the emperor riding on horseback and intervening in a timely fashion to save the bridge from a Dacian attack. From there, the main expeditionary forces under the command of Trajan and Hadrian followed the Timis and Cerna rivers. They arrived unopposed in the Hateg region where they met at Tibiscum, then marched westward along the Bistra River. The Column also depicts the population of Tapae, obviously Roman loyalists, greeting Trajan as he entered the city; subsequently he offered more animal sacrifices.

The campaign continued as the legionaries cleared a dense forest and approached a hilltop fortress into which the Dacians rushed and took up their fighting positions. The Romans attacked. The next friezes on the Column show dramatic hand-to-hand combat and Trajan's timely arrival with his equestrian Praetorian Guard, which ensured victory. Most likely the sieges were carried out against the rebuilt and heavily fortified cities of Blidaru, Costesti, and Piatra Rosie, all of which lay in the proximity of Sarmizegethusa.

The focus of the story narrated by the Column then changes to the next Roman army under General Quietus that was ferried across the Danube by the Roman fleet and advanced on the Jiu Valley. Roman auxiliary troop destroyed Pelendava (Craiova) and had additional orders to eliminate any Dacian military help that might be on its way to the Orastie region of Sarmizegethusa.

Another attack was spearheaded at Sucidava (Corabia) and then followed the Olt Valley that divided Dacia in half. The Romans occupied Buridava (Ocnele Mari), the second largest city after the capital, and thereby discouraged an attack by Buri warriors. A powerful garrison was left to secure the volatile region of the Buridavensi tribes. Battles commenced and skirmishes erupted along the path of the victorious Roman march through the Turnu Rosu Pass, into central Transylvania, and west toward Sarmizegethusa.

It is likely that in order to intimidate the remainder of the Dacians and prevent another Sarmatian military move towards the Danube, an additional Roman contingent crossed the river into Wallachia. Since it followed the Arges River, this expeditionary force would have entered the Bran pass and headed into eastern Transylvania. Hence the Romans would be fully engaged in an invasion of the Carpathian plateau, exactly what Trajan had strategized and Decebalus had not foreseen.

Taking advantage of the new turn in development, the Iazygi invaded Dacia from the northwest and became instant allies of the Romans. These same Sarmatians who, two decades earlier, had been defeated and exiled by Decebalus now hoped Trajan would compensate them for their help by giving them a portion of the Dacian land.

Just as in former wars, the Romans advanced and attacked in compact formations, following up on the actions of their auxiliary troops, who continued to be used for suicide missions. The Dacians employed their usual guerrilla tactics of harassing the Roman units, forcing them to spread out along the narrow roads or valleys. The defenders knew all too well where to wait for the exhausted, marching invaders, namely, in the most vulnerable spots of deep gorges. The ambushes rained arrows, stones, and lances from the slopes and abrupt hills above. The thickets that surrounded the invaders were set afire, and falling trees helped finish off the enemy.

Other fierce battles took place in unfamiliar types of terrain and under unusual circumstances, thus throwing the Roman fighting routines off track. Essentially no organized battle formations or maneuvers were possible, and officers were unable to lead their troops effectively. Since they were jammed tightly together in narrow passes, they could not swing their swords. Hand-to-hand combat gave the Dacians a great advantage: they were shorter and could run faster than the Romans, and they used smaller weapons. The Column is very keen to ridicule the physical size of the Dacians, their weapons, and their petite horses, one of which is shown throwing off its rider.

Indeed, it is true that the Dacians did not stand a chance in a dual against the body armor of their enemies. However, the knees of the Romans were not protected and they were the primary target for the Dacian blows. When they were unable to move or even to stand up, the wounded Romans became an additional burden to their own troops. Such massive damage shocked the unprepared and confident Romans, who were being crushed to the ground. Yet, the Column hardly portrays a single fallen legionary.

The Roman army was plagued at this point in time by the lack of a regular cavalry. Most of the horses were either of an inferior breed or too old, and they were used to pull the luggage trains and the heavy artillery. The only important mounted force was Numerus Maurorum with its *equites* units from Africa. But the desert horses could not adapt to the rugged land and unfamiliar climate of Dacia and so provided little assistance. Their frustrated raiders were better off dismounting and fighting as foot soldiers in testudo formations. Many of the Roman gains therefore remained unexploited since no cavalry was able to pursue the retreating Dacians.

Due to these hit-and-run tactics and the almost randomness of the lines of attack and defense, the Romans experienced a type of hardship they had never anticipated. All too often the legionaries found themselves buried alive under crumbling cliffs or falling into large pits with deadly spikes at the bottoms. In the dense Transylvanian forests, the Dacian *sagetasi* (archers), well camouflaged in the trees, proved to be amazingly accurate snipers and they took the lives of many officers. Still, the heroics of individual Dacians who won skirmishes were not a match for the highly organized Roman war machine that kept inching its way toward the heart of Transylvania.

Decebalus's defeat was expected with each passing day, yet his warriors continued to fight. In fact, the Column clearly shows how the Roman avant-garde is held back by the Dacians, although they are ultimately forced to retreat. It is important to underline that in almost all of its friezes, the Romans attack from left to right (west to east) while the Dacians fight from the opposite direction.

The Romans appear civilized, clean cut, and shaved, immortalized in the clear postures of total victors. They conduct an ideal war, with no images that might diminish their prestige as the masters of the world. The Dacians are shown with beards and mustaches, reaffirming the notion of "barbarian" as it was understood in Rome. But unlike other barbarians who tied their hair in tight knots, the Dacians combed their long hair over their heads. Roman hair was cut short, mostly for practical reasons: it could not be grabbed by the enemy in close combat.

Nevertheless, a winner cannot be a hero if his adversary is not strong and brave, too. And, a victory means very little if the enemy does not have equal combative merits. For that reason, the Column illustrates Decebalus marshalling his forces on the battlefields. His warriors, physically fit and with intelligent countenances, are clearly determined to die fighting. Their bravery is obvious and impressive.

Special attention was paid to the Dacian women, who are shown to be taller and even more war-like than the men. The women urge their men to fight, they torture the prisoners with lit torches and knife stabbings, and even execute them. Indeed, they seem to confirm the legend that no Daco-Sarmatian woman could get married if she did not kill an enemy. The Column also illustrates the fact that Dacian women were highly respected, even when they were taken prisoner by the Romans. It is likely that high-spirited Dacian women stood behind many heroic actions.

The Column reserves some twenty scenes for the siege of Sarmizegethusa, the vital stronghold of the Dacians. Roman units are shown pouring in from all directions, most of them belonging to legions II Adiutrix (Supportive), VI Ferrata (Ironside), and IV Flavia Felix (Fortunate). Many Dacian warriors and their families are seen trapped inside the fortified city where Decebalus is still in control.

In one spiral scene, the Column portrays the assault on the Dacian capital. First, it clearly shows the Dacians defending their fortress with gallantry and blind courage, even throwing themselves at their attackers. One frieze shows a kind of "infernal machinery" that was used to cut through fortress walls. Its many wheels are encrusted with a variety of tools appropriate for cutting and crushing the stone wall. When a breach was cut in the defensive wall, the Romans rushed in, but the Dacians immediately repelled them.

Still remembering the conquest of Masada in the year 73, the Roman engineers used cut timber to build high platforms that could reach the top of the battlements. Soon Sarmizegethusa was sealed off by *circumvellatio* (high walls of earth with wooden ramps around them). The Column depicts Trajan refusing to listen to a kneeling Dacian negotiator, while inside the city the people set their houses on fire. Because dead bodies are shown strewn everywhere, it has been speculated that many chose to drink poison rather than surrender.

Determined to starve the city, Trajan ordered the water supplies cut off. This deadly measure affected the defenders more than any attack. One frieze shows the warriors and the civilians rationing the last drops of water from a cauldron. When their prayers for rain were not heard by Zamolxis, the Dacian defenders believed they had offended their god; they panicked and became demoralized. In a moment of desperation, the able warriors and noblemen, including Decebalus himself, are shown trying to fight their way out of the encircled city. They seek shelter in their religious edifices that are now fortified terraces above the unoccupied Sarmizegethusa Regia. Immediately, the sacrificial auxiliary troops under General Quietus, backed up by four powerful legions, engage in an all-out assault. They storm the capital and achieve the sought-after breach in the battle line.

Finally, at the end of the hot summer of 106, the biggest prize of the Roman campaign, Sarmizegethusa, had been captured. Trajan and his court entered the city and accepted the official Dacian surrender. His soldiers are shown on the Column looting the city.

Nevertheless, those Dacians who had escaped continued to put up a hellish fight, most likely in an attempt to cover the retreating civilians. The Column also shows Decebalus holding a war meeting with his trusted commanders. Even at this point and against all odds, he managed a most zealous resistance and succeeded in dividing his remaining army and stationing them in two strategic areas—the Orastie Mountains, site of the Dacian religious center, and the Sebes Mountains that guarded the entrance to the gold mines, the ultimate target of Trajan's war.

Although his army had been drastically reduced and scattered and many of his fortified cities and their populations captured, the king still did not cease his efforts at reorganizing his army and buoying the spirits of his warriors. Sadly, his efforts were to no avail. Their desperate defense could not produce the much needed victory, and the Column shows many Dacians committing suicide with their daggers rather than surrendering.

The last Dacian military encampment was at Porolissum (Zalau). It was conquered and destroyed by the legionaries who were anxious to keep the war from going on for too long. Since he had exhausted his options as far as maneuvers were concerned and was anticipating an uncertain end, Decebalus decided to bury his treasures under a river bed. Its water had been re-directed during the process of excavation, and the river was then allowed to run its regular course.

As the auxiliary troops cleared out the remaining pockets of Dacian organized resistance, it was clear that Decebalus's defeat was pending. A scene on the Column shows how the horsemen protected their fugitive king. Many fallen comrades hold their shields, refusing to give up and thus illustrating their ferocious resistance. It was this spirit that caused Emperor Trajan to give credibility to the legend that the Dacians were happy to die fighting.

Overwhelmed by the enemy's superior numbers and power, Decebalus and his faithful warriors and courtiers managed one narrow escape after another as they fled and were hunted down throughout the northern mountains of Transylvania. Soon, the inevitable happened. The Column shows the encircled Dacian leaders committing suicide. Even the king, his clothes ripped, kneeling near a tree, brings a curved dagger to his throat. His round shield, probably ornamented with gold, has fallen next to him.

A Roman cavalry officer, Tiberius Claudius Maximus, with his right arm outstretched, dashes forward on his horse to stop Decebalus. But the king has already jumped in the opposite direction to avoid being captured. Another Roman infantryman is shown running to take Decebalus's dagger away, but is too late: the king has already slashed his neck. Not wanting to share the humiliating fate of Vercingetorix, Decebalus has chosen the heroic end of the other Celtic royal, Queen Boudicca, who had also been defeated by the Romans.[16]

Whether he died in this way or by taking poison (as is often speculated), the carvings detail Decebalus's appearance—not appreciably different from other Dacians or from today's Romanian shepherd. He wears tight pants held at the bottom with the strings of the leather peasant moccasins, a tattered shirt down to his knees, a cape over his shoulders, and a conical hat made of lamb fur. Despite his age (approximately sixty years), the bearded king has a strong physical constitution and his face reflects a firm character and a great deal of suffering. He looks every inch a royal hero, one who inspired fear in those who attacked him.

Decebalus's head and right hand were placed on a platter and taken by Maximus to Trajan, who was stationed at a fort in the center of occupied Transylvania. They were displayed in the middle of the hippodrome race track in Rome. This gesture officially confirmed the defeat of the dreaded enemy of the empire and also proved that the Dacian king had not been captured alive. His head was later rolled down the Gemonian steps of the Forum, a treatment given to criminals to delight the mob. No doubt Decebalus was considered a treaty-breaker and a double-crosser, a violator of Roman trust.

There is no indication of the fate of Vesina, most likely a great Dacian priest and the king's main adviser. It is also unclear why Decebalus and his warriors did not take refuge in Moldova, part of Free Dacia, which already may have made a separate peace with Trajan. In any case, the king's honorable suicide opened a new chapter in the history of Dacia. It marked the origin of a Daco-Roman nation, baptized in blood, that would never vanish. The Romans may have won the war, but they soon discovered that they had lost the peace in Eastern Europe.

The end of the Dacian wars brought about a chain of events worthy of brief review. With the death of Decebalus, Dacian resistance lost all of its power to mobilize and quickly dissolved. Many of the tribal chieftains went to Trajan and asked for mercy, as the Column proudly illustrates. Their body language shows that they had suffered a major defeat. Other sequences on the Column depict the legionaries plundering Sarmizegethusa and the royal palace treasure, at the same time as they are annihilating the last elements of fanatical opposition. The main message of the final friezes concentrates on the captured Dacians being driven into slavery. Their defeat supplied an abundance of prisoners who were put immediately to good use rebuilding their own country or adding glory to the architecture of Rome.

The clean-up operations of the armed resistance and the efforts of the Romans to extend their occupation lasted another seven months after the fall of Sarmizegethusa. Their push for new territories was promptly stopped by the firm resistance of the Greater Dacians in the Crisana, Maramures and Oas regions, as well as in Muntenia, Moldova, and half of eastern Oltenia. The Column accurately shows how in the last days of the conflict the Dacian warriors retreated to save the rest of their country, which would never be occupied by the Romans. Still, the Dacian kingdom and its confederacy had been irrevocably broken.

During the winter of 106-107 Trajan and his legionaries remained in the castra-hiberna and other settlements they had already built. One reason for their staying was the actions of the Iazygi. These former Roman allies occupied many areas of Transylvania that they believed rightfully should be theirs. The problem was that they chose precisely the areas where most of the Dacian gold, salt, and other mines were located. When they refused to leave, Trajan ordered General Hadrian to "pacify" the rebellious Iazygi—to throw them behind the Dacian border to the west of Tisza River, into Pannonia.

Trajan, however, was busy looking for Dacia's treasury, evaluated at more than one thousand tons of gold.[17] The emperor was also busy collecting much needed horses for his feeble cavalry and recruiting new troops from the among those young Dacian warriors who were willing to become mercenaries of Rome. When one of Decebalus's royal lieutenants, Bicilis, was captured, Trajan knew he was close to finding the hidden treasure. Indeed, either under torture or of his own free will, Bicilis divulged the location of the king's gold—under the waters of the Sargetia. Thus the river became the target of the final Roman looting campaign.[18]

Trajan stayed in Dacia until the spring of 107. Only after he finalized his objectives did he leave, naming General Decius Terentius Scaurianus the first governor of Dacia. At least three legions and many auxiliary cohorts stayed as well. Their mission was to impose the will of Rome and supervise the extraction of precious metals. Dacian workers, especial miners and smith craftsmen, were in great demand and fugitive natives were encouraged to return and be productive for the benefit of Rome. They greatly outnumbered the foreign labors and other colonists brought by the Roman administration.

The plunder from Dacia brought to Rome riches of biblical proportions. Crito, Trajan's physician, presumably valued the spoils at 150,000 kilograms/165 tons of gold, 330,000 kilograms/364 tons of silver, and 700 million denari. Roman registers indicate that the gold that was brought in from Dacia alone exceeded three times the annual treasury of the empire. The entirety of the goods taken from the war would amount in today's dollars to $50 billion. Tens of thousands of slaves completed the largest war plunder in the entire history of the Roman Empire. The war with Dacia was, without a doubt, the pinnacle of its conquests.

The victory against the Dacians was officially announced on August 11, 106 when transports from Dacia began to pour into Rome. The entire booty would be part of Trajan's triumphal parade. No such display had previously been seen nor would it be seen again in Rome. Trajan was declared the greatest conqueror since Caesar and named "Father of the Nation" for the sixth time.

Dacia's gold made possible a victory celebration that according to Dio lasted for 123 days (there were already 135 legal holidays in Rome). It was filled with feasts, festivities, and games in the amphitheaters. The free games of *Panem et Circenses* (Bread and Circuses) cost the lives of ten thousand gladiators (many of them Dacian prisoners) and eleven thousand wild and tame animals. Many Christians were also eaten by the hungry lions in the arenas. General Hadrian was commissioned to oversee all the victory celebrations, including the construction of four triumphal arches and the minting of seven different commemorative coins. One of them shows Trajan on horseback spearing a presumably fallen Dacian.

Furthermore, three hundred thousand Romans were given the sum of 650 denari/$260 apiece to increase their appetite for the victory celebration.[19] These denari bore the inscription *Abundentia Daciae*, homage to the "Abundance of Dacia." Also, in celebration of the victory, Trajan minted a bronze coin with his head on one side and the Goddess of Victory on the other. The winged goddess was shown holding a shield on which was written, "The Victory in Dacia." Another coin showed the Column with one eagle on top of it and others around its base. An *aureus* featured the emperor's head with laurels, and on the reverse side of the coin a nude warrior holding a lance and a scroll above a child with "Conservatori Patris Patriae," confirming Trajan as the Father of the Country. In memory of his triumph, Trajan officially accepted the title of *Dacicus Maximus*.

The war booty from Dacia made it possible to found centers for the distribution of free food for poor Roman citizens. Thus began *alimenta*, the charitable organization that later became the only public source of food for Roman orphans. But the most impressive and lasting contribution from the plunder was the construction of the Forum Traiani complex, designed by Apolodor, the omnipotent architect of the empire.

In order to build the Forum in the middle of Rome, Trajan ordered a large section of Quirinal Hill to be excavated to a depth that would match the height of the future Column. Thousands of Dacian prisoners dug into the earth by hand and completed the sensational excavation. The newly leveled area offered a great advantage for the entire Forum, as gravity would bring a continuous supply of water to the new public complex. The Forum included temples, libraries, and other stately buildings destined for eternity. Among them was the first shopping mall in Europe, a huge building with five terraced levels in the form of a semi-circle. This mammoth complex of brickwork also served as a retaining wall to keep the remains of the Quirinal Hill in place. Adjoining it was the Basilica Ulpia, the largest room under a single ceiling ever to have been built in the ancient world. It served as a model for all later cathedrals and palaces.

Trajan's Column was erected behind the basilica. It was flanked by the Latin and Greek libraries and the temple of Trajan. The monument, 38 meters/125 feet tall and Doric in design, whose shaft measures 3.5 meters/11.5 feet in average diameter, was built of eighteen massive blocks of Parian marble, each weighing thirty-two tons. Its twenty-three spirals were initially painted in sharp colors, and 155 friezes covered an area of 220 meters/722 feet.

The Column was set on massive blocks weighting fifty-six to seventy-five tons each, beautifully ornamented with weapons and armor that had been used in the war. Dacian dragon flags adorn its sides and frame the Dacian and Sarmatian uniforms; shields, daggers, axes, swords, arrows, and lances are shown around the base. Roman eagles dominate each corner of the monolithic base. The entrance to the chamber is guarded by two angels of victory flying over more Dacian and Sarmatian uniforms, shields, and weapons.

This chamber eventually came to serve as the resting place for the urns containing the ashes of Trajan and his wife Plotina. An interior spiral staircase, lit by forty-three small niches cut in the marble of the Column, leads to the top of the monument. The giant round shaft was capped with a towering bronze eagle (replaced after Trajan's death with a statue of him measuring 6 meters/19 feet high, of bronze and gilded with gold). Below the statue is a square platform that once offered panoramic views of Rome, much as the Empire State Building today offers a bird's eye view New York City.

Initially, the reliefs on the shaft of the column were painted. The friezes followed Trajan's war memoirs, *Commentarii de Bello Dacico*, a work that was stored in the two libraries located in the Forum on opposite sides of the Column. In fact, by reading the book and walking upstairs inside each library, it was possible to follow the narrative contained in the frames on the spiral ribbon of the Column. Toward the top of the monument, the marble drums are smaller in diameter but the figures increase in size (from 0.60 meter/24 inches to 0.80 meter/31 inches) to ensure better viewing.

The base of the Column was surrounded by a splendid portico with marble floors; also its many ornate colonnades suspended a balcony around the column. Many statues of Dacian noblemen were originally placed on the portico, as if they were witnessing the events portrayed on the triumphal Column. Judging by their body and head positions (downward looking), they were probably originally placed at the balcony level of the portico. Their enduring presence would be an indication of the ever increasing prestige of Trajan, their conqueror.[20]

All in all, the Forum of Trajan measured 300 meters/984 feet long and 185 meters/607 feet wide; it was the most grandiose of all the forums in Rome. And, it was the most prestigious cultural, economic, political, and religious plaza of the entire Empire—and built with the gold and slave labor of Dacia, as confirmed by the inscription *Ex manubiis* (constructed from the spoils of war).

The breathtaking Column was inaugurated on May 12, 113, exactly twelve years after the invasion of Dacia. Sometime later, when the colors began to run and fade, the same scenes were carved into it again. The result was that more than twenty-five hundred human figures were downsized to one-third of their natural dimensions. Dedicated to Trajan's victory, the Column glorifies the emperor: he adorns it more than fifty times.

Years after the war had ended, the huge plunder from Dacia allowed many public works to be extended undertaken outside the city limits of Rome, such as drying swamps and constructing new roads and bridges. Ostia, the far western port of Rome, was rebuilt and enlarged. Aqueducts were built or improved to satisfy the thirst of Rome's one million people who required more than a million cubic meters of water daily. This same war plunder was also used to pay the legions who, in the year 117, conquered Parthia (Armenia), Iran, and Iraq. The wealth of Dacia enabled the Roman Empire to extend its conquests of Asia into the Persian Gulf. Trajan was the first and the last Roman general or emperor to reach the Indian Ocean. His empire measured 5,700,000 square kilometers/2,200,000 square miles and had a population of more than fifty million.

The victory in Dacia expanded the empire to its largest geographical size ever and marked the zenith of its power. The world map was redefined or completed in accord with the Trajan's victories. Thus Dacia Traiana appeared on the new map of Europe as Dacia Felix (Fruitful). It was a buffer colony against barbarian invasions from the area northeast of the Roman frontier. It was also the sole, and most vulnerable Roman outpost in Eastern Europe.

NOTES

1. The best highway in Albania is part of Via Egnatia—800 kilometers/500 miles of road built by the Romans twenty-two hundred years ago. The first British and American railroad gage was 4 feet 8 inches long and ½-inch wide, to accommodate the axle of the Roman chariot wheels.

2. In shape and size, it resembled the *kukri* used in sacrificial ceremonies in Nepal during Dashain festivals. These continue today.

3. Cassius Dio, *Roman History*, trans. Earnest Cary (Cambridge: Harvard University Press; London: William Heinemann, 1955), bk. 68, 369.

4. This remarkable six-foot wide road, cut in stone, was used until the 1960s when it was covered by the waters of a dam. Today, the inscription *Tabula Traiana* is still visible. It was moved up on the vertical Danube wall.

5. Years later, when the stone carvers from warm Syria immortalized the event, they left out the ice in their depiction and showed the Roman auxiliaries fighting half-naked—an unlikely scenario in the freezing Dacian winter.

6. An existing Romanian legend offers another version of the story of this sister who was known as Dochia. The princess with her baby and a few ladies-in-waiting escaped the besieged Sarmizegethusa and climbed the mountains. Because the winter was warm, the path was steep, and the Romans were in close chase, they took few warm clothes. The legend places the time in the first week of March, when the Romans almost caught the exhausted and desperate Dacians. Alas, an instant snowstorm changed the fugitives into ice statues, saving them from a humiliating captivity. This miracle is still celebrated in Romania as the Week of Babele (Old Women), suggesting the power of destiny and the capricious weather.

7. Dio, *Roman History*, bk. 68, 375.

8. Dio, *Roman History*, bk. 68, 377.

9. Jerome Carpino, *Daily Life in Ancient Rome*, trans. by E. O. Lorimer (New Haven: Yale University Press, 1958), 61-62.

10. Dio, *Roman History*, bk. 67, 329.

11. In the Dacian/Romanian language, *drob* means "a chunk of something"; in this case it refers to the Simian island that used to split the Danube in two halves.

12. Dio, *Roman History*, bk. 68, 385

13. The Roman *foot* became the basic measuring unit in England and the United States (30.48 centimeters/12 modern inches).

14. The remains of one pillar connected with the fortress can be still seen on the left bank of the Danube. The bridge was built with red mortar specific to the Roman style of construction. Its mortar mixture remains a mystery. It has been speculated that the indestructible mortar was mixed with human blood; more likely it was mixed with volcanic ash that made it waterproof.

15. Dio, *Roman History*, bk. 68, 379.

16. In 1965 the grave of T. C. Maximus was discovered in the village Grameni near Drama, Macedonia. A sculpted funeral stone illustrates how Maximus's horse jumped on the fallen Decebalus, who has dropped his weapon but still holds his oval shield. A detailed inscription explains the event in a version convenient to Maximus, who presumably took Decebalus prisoner. Both this scene and that shown on the Column may be inaccurate. It is more likely that Decebalus and his entourage followed the Dacian tradition and took poison in order to avoid the inevitable humiliation of captivity.

17. This quantity may not be an exaggeration because, fifteen centuries later in an underground vault near the Mures River, forty thousand gold coins and large chunks of gold were found. Later, 1,600 kilograms/3,500 pounds of gold and 250,000 denaris were found near Gherla. After 1800 more than two thousand gold coins were unearthed, half of which were cosons from the time of Decebalus.

18. Many historians believe that the Strei and Sargetia are the same river. Considering that Decebalus's last organized effort at resistance was carried out along the Mures River, any of its tributaries could be the river in question. The royal treasure has never been found.

19. One denarius was a day's pay for a skilled laborer.

20. A few of these statues were rescued after the plundering of the portico after A.D. 400 by invading barbarians. They ended up on the top of the later Arch of Constantine. Nothing is known of the whereabouts of the equestrian statue of Trajan, gilded in bronze, that once marked the center of the Forum.

Chapter Nine

Dacia Felix

The new Roman province in the middle of Central Dacia functioned like a large wedge, while the entirety of Dacia formed a bulky salient directed toward the barbarian lands of Eastern Europe. Dacia Traiana included today's territories of Banat, the middle corridor of Transylvania, and the western half of Oltenia; it had a population of less than half million people. Still, most of Greater Dacia remained free. It included Bessarabia, Bukovina, Crisana, Galicia, the southern part of Maramures, the Oas Mountains, the eastern half of Oltenia, Muntenia/Wallachia, and Moldova, and had a population of more than one million.

The smallest free area was Maramures, with a surface area of 10,000 square kilometers/3,861 square miles stretching deeply into what is today's Ukraine; it had more than one hundred villages and one hundred thousand natives. For pragmatic reasons, Trajan bestowed on unoccupied Dacia the status of a Roman client. This served primarily for trade exchanges, making them equal partners and confirming that Free Dacia's independence had been formally accepted by Rome.

Trajan stayed in Transylvania for one more year after his final victory at Sarmizegethusa. His aim was to find Decebalus's treasury and coordinate the transports of the new war booty to Rome. His concern for the safety of the Romans who were now living on barbarian land moved him to reinforce many of the garrisons from Drobeta (Turnu Severin) and Nicopolis to Napoca (Cluj). A web of more than one hundred fortified castri and new settlements covered occupied Dacia. Its new capital, Colonia Ulpia Traiana Dacica Augusta Sarmizegethusa,[1] was placed at a distance of 40 kilometers/24 miles southwest from the original Sarmizegethusa Regia, now laid to waste.

The Roman strongholds were connected with a network of military roads that began at Apolodor's bridge and stretched into Banat and Transylvania.

Most notable were Via Traiana and Via Pontica. They mainly connected Drobeta and Lederata with the new capital as well as with Tibiscum (Jupa), Lugio (Lugoj), Apulum (Alba Iulia), Potaissa (Turda), and Napoca (Cluj).

Initially, Ulpia Sarmizegethusa served as a command post for the Legion XIII Gemina. But Trajan decided to transform the military fort into a model city in order to demonstrate the superiority of the conquerors. Again he entrusted Apolodor with this important task, and soon an amphitheater for five thousand spectators, temples, plazas, and a public bath with elaborate mosaics adorned the Roman-style city that encompassed some 30 hectares/74 acres.

A governor's palace with colonnaded courtyards was the center of political power, and a stone-paved forum was the physical center of the new city. A plant for making glass and a Schola Gladiatorum (School for Gladiators) were constructed. Eventually the square's fortified walls were extended to house twenty thousand inhabitants, most of them public servants, military personnel, and colonists. A nearby military base provided living quarters and a drill area for the stationed legionaries.

The modern city was surrounded by the military castri and smaller forts. The inauguration of the new metropolis in the Carpathian Mountains in 110 was immortalized on the sesterius coin. It contained Trajan's profile and the inscription *Felicitas August* (Fruitful Emperor). His newly acquired province was named *Dacia Felix* (Fruitful Dacia or Happy Dacia).

Far away from Rome, in Dobrudja, which was essentially in the middle of nowhere, a triumphal *tumulus* was completed in the year 109 at Tropeum Traiana (later known as Adamclisi). The impressive monument and sacrificial altar (12 x 12 meters/39 x 39 feet) was dedicated to Mars Ultor (the Avenger) and commemorated the famous battle that had taken place eight years earlier between the victorious Romans and defeated barbarians. It was the only monument erected by Trajan on a battle site.

The Tropeum Traiana monument was almost an exact copy of Augustus's mausoleum; the latter had been built fifty years earlier on the Field of Mars in Rome. The one in Dobrudja has a diameter of 40 meters/131 feet, and it is as high as the Column (further evidence that Trajan rebuilt the mausoleum). It is based on seven circular steps and is made of beautifully cut and ornate limestone, all of it fixed in cement; its mausoleum is capped with a cone-shaped tiled roof. Whether it was intentional or not, the circular roof resembles the scales of a fish, very much like the Sarmatians' armor. In the middle of it there stands a hexagonal column showcasing a huge symbol of the weapons used by the Roman legionaries, additional proof that the mausoleum was not conceived by the Dacians.

Carved plaques containing fighting scenes similar to those of Trajan's Column in Rome, but smaller in scale, surround the oval monument. Many of them show the fighting spirit of the Dacians and Sarmatians, as well as of their allies, the Buri and Bastarnians. The Dacians use the typical sword with a reaping hook; the others use the larger sword held with both hands, an impressive and devastating weapon at the time. One of the friezes clearly shows a legionary defeating two barbarian warriors—a Dacian and a German.

Unlike Trajan's Column, the Adamclisi monument does not contain any complex battle scenes. Judging by the battle garments worn by the warriors, the battle was fought in the winter. All of the Adamclisi stone carvings lack the artistic sophistication of the Column, but the scenes it depicts are closer to historical fact. The stone carver for this monument was not a sophisticated sculptor, but a military artisan. Most likely the entire battle was described in *Trajan's History of Dacian Wars*, a work which is known to have been written but has never been found.

Aware of the ongoing danger presented by the Free Dacians residing nearby, Trajan continued to enlarge and re-fortify the strongholds of Bononia (Vidin) and Oescus (Pleven); he also built Ratiaria (Arcar). All of these were safely located on the south bank of the Danube and were soon to become Roman colonies. Across the Danube, he built a second line of defense against eventual attacks by the Free Dacians. One of its strongholds was Marcianopolis (formerly the Dacian settlement of Rexidava), named after Marcia, the emperor's sister.

The occupied sections of Dacia were governed by General Decimus Terentius Scaurianus, who proved to be a capable administrator. He issued laws that were acceptable to the natives as part of en effort to peacefully merge the two worlds. He knew that most revolts were ignited either by exorbitant taxes or by religious repression. To forestall problems, therefore, he imposed low taxes—one percent for commercial transactions and a five percent inheritance tax. This constituted a drastic reduction of traditional Roman taxes, and it appeased the population because Dacia Traiana was immensely wealthy. Rome netted all of the tax revenue it needed.

Decimus closed his eyes to the fact that the Dacians moved their temples inside caves, e.g. Sinca Veche, in order to be able to practice their old religion. He was keen to recruit Dacians for the auxiliary Roman legions and to provide workers for the massive fortifications. Under his wise administration and the traditional Roman efficiency, the new imperial province of Dacia began to flourish in all aspects.

The Daco-Roman wars had a huge financial impact on the economy of the Italic Peninsula. Transylvanian gold had paid for the construction of Aqua Traiana aqueducts, Via Traiana, a new Forum with a majestic commemorative Column, Trajan's Market, and numerous temples and public dwellings. The abundance of Dacia Felix resources satisfied the Romans, including

Pliny the Younger who had served under Domitian. After he had become a high priest and senator, Pliny wrote to Canninus Rufus, a fellow writer:

> It is an excellent idea of yours to write about the Dacian war. There is no subject which offers such scope and such wealth of original material, no subject so poetic and almost legendary although the facts are true. You will describe new rivers flowing over the land, new bridges built across rivers, and camps clinging to sheer precipices; you will tell of a king driven from his capital and finally to death, but courageous to the end; you will record double triumph, one the first over a nation hitherto unconquered, the other a final victory. There is only one difficulty, but a serious one. To find a style of expression worthy of the subject is an immense undertaking, difficult even for a genius like yours.... Another problem arises out of the barbaric names, especially that of the king himself, where the uncouth sounds will not fit into Greek verse.[2]

This correspondence suggests a romanticized version of the wars against the Dacians, but it also indicates the Roman contempt for the Dacian leader Decebalus. He is elsewhere mentioned as "some native king." Meanwhile, opportunists and adventurers began to flood into Dacia Felix and quickly became rich. News of this spread throughout empire.

After conquering numerous lands and defeating armies that previous emperors had been unable to subdue, Trajan suffered a massive stroke in August 117 on his way to Rome. He had just reached the age of sixty-four when he died in peace and well-deserved glory. He had been elected consul six times; tribune, sixteen times; and he had been proclaimed emperor six times. One of his greatest achievements had been defeating the Dacians whose wealth allowed him to pay all the imperial debts that had accumulated and cancel all the mortgages of the citizens of Rome.

At the time of the emperor's death, the Roman Empire had a population of fifty million (with an army of five hundred thousand, of which only one hundred fifty thousand were legionaries). At the time, Japan had a population of twenty million; India, fifty million; and China, sixty million. But Asia and its giant empires did not interest the Romans. Nor are they reflected on their maps, most of which were drawn by the famous astronomer Ptolemaeus/ Claudius Ptolemy from Alexandria. For the next thirteen hundred years, his map of Europe showed Dacia/Datia merely as a large country north of the Danube.

Trajan's purple mantle was taken by his adopted son Publius Aelius Hadrianus, known as Hadrian. He inherited an empire whose borders had expanded into three continents; it contained many provinces whose names he did not even know. But he knew Dacia well. He had participated in wars against it, and he was still in Transylvania when he received the news that he was to become the new emperor. Confident that his troops would complete the occupation of Dacia, Hadrian transferred Legion IV Flavia from Ulpia Sarmizegethusa to Berzobis and then back to Singidunum (Beograd) in western Moesia. This was a mistake—one that kept him in Dacia instead of allowing him to enter Rome in imperial triumph.

Because the frustrated Iazygi felt greatly betrayed by the Romans, who did not live up to the tribe's expectations, they decided to revolt again and take back their portion of the promised Dacian land. These Sarmatian horsemen had helped the Romans conquer Transylvania. Now they stormed the area of today's Bucharest and destroyed four Roman strongholds. In their powerful winter raids in Moesia, they were supported by their cousins, the Sarmatian Roxolani, who were refugees in Free Dacia. The Getians from Dobrudja also joined the fight against Roman occupation. To deal with their raids, cohort II Hispana was employed along the Olt River on both sides of Buridava.

When he was unable to leave Transylvania, Hadrian called upon his friend, General Quintus Turbo, who had just crushed a Jewish uprising in Palestine. The general promptly responded and shortly thereafter put an end to the Iazygi revolt and the military raids of the other Sarmatians. Turbo's victory was so crushing that he forced the Roxolani king Raspaganus and his son Peregrinus to become vassals in Rome, where they lived in fear as royal hostages.

As for the Iazygi, their military power was divided as they were allowed to settle east of the Prut and west of the Tisza Rivers in Free Dacia. The event marked the beginning of an historic shift: Free Dacia became a haven for enemies of Rome. Soon it reached the point that Hadrian returned some Wallachian areas (along the Olt River) to the Free Dacians in exchange for their promise never to initiate attacks against the Romans. A consummate barbarian hater, the new emperor was so unhappy with the festering problems north of the Danube that at one point he considered evacuating Dacia. Its gold mines were sufficient incentive to remain there, however.

Instead of withdrawing, he divided the occupied territory into two colonies—Dacia Apulensis (Superior), including the Transylvanian Plateau with a capital in Apulum, and Dacia Malvensis (Inferior). The latter incorporated Banat and almost half of Oltenia and had its capital in Drobeta. When Apulum was just about to be rebuilt, Drobeta was extended by thickening the walls that formed a one-kilometer square. Because of its important strategic position guarding the only Danubian bridge, Hadrian declared Drobeta a municipality. Later it became a colony.

Impressed by the bravery of the Dacians, Hadrian recruited many auxiliary soldiers to serve in Legion III Gallica. It had been stationed in Moesia and subsequently returned to Syria. The military's recruitment lists and payroll receipts were filled with Dacian names like Bitus, Butus, Sassa, and Tarsa. Having learned a valuable lesson from the Dacian wars, Hadrian was the first emperor to employ heavily armored cavalry in the Roman army, a mode of operating similar to that of the Sarmatians.

After he had declared a total victory north of the Danube, the emperor left Dacia. Escorted by the Praetorian Guard, Hadrian made his royal entrance into Rome on July 9, 118. Meanwhile Turbo continued to liquidate revolts in Moesia, accomplishing his mission by the end of 119. The following year, the victorious general of Dalmatian origin was named the new governor of the now subdued Dacia Felix.

The unparalleled power exercised by Rome during this time period could be compared to the economic and military strength of the United States in our time. Each time peaceful negotiations failed abroad, the Roman legions promptly intervened. Pre-emptive strikes in distant, troubled lands were motivated by the need to gain control of potential enemies before they became too strong or came close to attacking the Empire. Having decided to install their own New Order in foreign lands, the Romans used the terror of their weaponry to enforce it.

Hadrian was, however, different from the previous Roman emperors. His vast military experience was combined with a cultivated intellect and Herculean physical strength—he was said to have killed a lion with his bare hands. He was also an accomplished musician and dancer, and wrote poems and treatises on Latin and Greek grammar. Thanks to the Dacian immense booty, he was the first leader to use state money to pay university teachers and institute many other public services. He was the first emperor to tolerate the Christians, and the first Caesar to sport a beard (many speculated that his beard hid a scar received in battle). Hadrian was proud to present himself as a Greek philosopher; he was even nicknamed "Greekling." All of these facts made it possible for him to relate to the Dacians more easily than any emperor before him had.

He knew that an overextended Roman empire meant a weak one, one that was already on the verge of war with most of its neighbors. Wisely, therefore, Hadrian-the-Pacifist decided to consolidate what his predecessor Trajan-the-Conqueror had achieved through so many wars. Firm in his determination not to engage in costly wars and hugely supplied with gold from Transylvania, he canceled many taxes and debts of the Roman people. Such measures made him enormously popular. Life was never better for the Romans who now lived in a true Golden Age.

The restless emperor proved to be the most traveled person of the empire, visiting thirty-eight out of the forty-two Roman colonies. Hadrian became the most recognizable face of that time. Since he was obsessed with fortifying the borders and wished to keep his legionaries busy in peaceful Britannia/Britain, the emperor ordered the construction of a stone wall 115 kilometers/74.5 miles long across the width of the island. In the Balkans, he built his own city, Hadrianopolis, later known as Adrianopole (Edirne), on the ruins of Uscudama.

The legions stationed in Dacia kept the flood of Eastern Europe's barbarians at bay. At the same time, they created a new breed of Romanized indigenous people. The Dacian warriors who enlisted in the Roman army became Latinized, but they were sent abroad. Cohorts Primae Dacorum (of Dacians), such as II Ulpia Dacorum and Aurelia Dacorum, were stationed in Pannonia. Others served in Britannia: Alea Dacorum could be found at Deva (Chesters) and Camboglanna (Stanegate), while cohort I Aelia Dacorum miliaria was based at Birdoswald.[3] The cohort I Ulpia Dacorum marched to Syria, and Vexillation Dacorum Parthica took part in Septimius Severus's Parthus campaign. Because of their religious experience in the Roman army, many Dacian soldiers became devout Christians.

Hadrian stationed the best of his troops in Dacia Felix. Legion V Macedonica was brought to the gold and silver mining zone; Legion XIII Gemina was stationed in Apulum; Legion IV Flavia Felix at Berzobis (Resita); and Legion VII Claudia was garrisoned by the Danubian border.

He paid particular attention to the mining industry, assigning a special contingent of commercial guards to the gold and silver sources in Transylvania. The Pirusti tribesmen from Dalmatia settled around the gold mines of Ampelum (Zlatna), Albunrus Maiori (Rosia Montanta), and in what are today Baia Aries, Brad, and Bucium, all of which were under strict Roman control. Dacian miners continued to work inside the iron mines which are today located at Rosia and Vadul Dobrei, or in the salt quarries of Ocna Dejului and Uioara. Others found new employment in extracting lead, a metal which was in great demand for making water pipes needed in the crowded Roman cities and lavish villas.

Attracted by generous Roman salaries, colonists from Egypt and Asia Minor came to work in the mines of what are now Calan, Deva, Hunedoara, Teliuc, and Turda, among others. Some foreigners were also attracted by the numerous commercial opportunities in Dacia, and Transylvania's Metallic Mountains became a sort of El Dorado of that time.

Newcomers to Dacia introduced exotic aliments such as sugar, olive oil, rice, and Oriental spices to the locals. Because so many Dacian warriors had been felled in the recent wars, the colonists found local women welcoming and ready to start families. Legionaries followed the example of the colonists. Latin became the convenient language for everyone, and a new Daco-Roman nation was in the making.

To the pleasant surprise of the Romans, Dacia offered a rich variety of healing springs, and under Hadrian's orders thermal baths were built at Aque (Calan), Arutela (Calimeanesti), Germisara (Geoagiu), Therma Herculis (Herculane), and many other places; these were frequented by the wealthy of Rome. The emperor himself, who suffered from arthritis and tuberculosis, enjoyed these natural spas and expressed his appreciate for the local healers with their renowned herbal remedies during his repeated inspections in Dacia.

Because he loved horses (he had a statue made of his beloved stallion Borysthenes), he was interested in having the Dacians supply the Roman cavalry.

But Hadrian-the-Architect concentrated on what he liked most—building a new colony. His vast construction program transformed large settlements into modern cities, like Ampelum, Apulum, Castra Traiana (Sambotin-Valcea), Castrum Regia (Timisoara), Dierna (Orsova), Forum Novum Siculorum (Targu Mures), Media (Medias), Napoca (Cluj), Potaissa (Turda), and Romula (Resca). Romula, built on the site of old Malava, was one of the cities with a Roman name located in the abundant vineyards of the Olt River region. It was supplied by a three-mile long aqueduct that brought fresh water to the villas and public baths. Its main industries were wine and the carving of semi-precious stones.

In a short period of time, traditional mud and stones were replaced with mortar and baked bricks; Roman arches and vaults covered by tile roofs became a familiar site. Massive, perfectly cut andesite blocks were brought from distant locations via Roman roads on heavy-duty lorries. The quarries, known today as Boita, Luncani, Ruschita, and Vascau, supplied marble for temples and other institutions.

These Hadrianic projects were interrupted in 123 by the Iazygi and other Sarmatians who now invaded the northern part of Transylvania. Once again, General Turbo was victorious. He stationed troops at Potaissa and Porolissum, where one cohort of a thousand soldiers was posted under the command of Octavio Grapo.[4] Most likely this was the point at which the Roman border was pushed northward to Rivulus Dominarum (Baia Mare).

Anticipating additional barbarian invasions, Hadrian ordered a triple fortified line on the vulnerable Dacian border, formed of castri, forts, and watchtowers. The Roman army's custom of stamping their bricks with the name or the number of the legion left historians with clear evidence of their building efforts. They employed Dacian workers who learned how to use new tools, like the long saw, iron clips or grips, pulleys, and cranes. They also adopted the Roman *foot* as a measuring unit under the name of *cot* (elbow), approximately the distance between the wrist and the elbow (30 centimeters/12 inches). The Roman army (and later the Romanians) retained the *prajija/stanjen* measure unit of 1.80 meters/6 feet, most likely the length of the cavalry lance.

Each castrum served as a main garrison. It had hospitals, food, and fodder storage sufficient to accommodate at least five hundred men and their horses. Between distant castris there were smaller forts. A typical fort of 2 hectares/5 acres could shelter up to three hundred men and horses. Each fort was a small town with a shrine, a statue of an emperor, heated barracks, bath houses, indoor latrines, and everything else that was distinctive about the Roman way of life. It was surrounded by a stone wall 5 meters/16 feet high and a ditch 10 meters/33 feet wide and 5 meters deep, as well as by crenellated watchtowers. Each watchtower held ten soldiers who were in charge of surveillance and transmitting smoke, light, or sound signals. At least eighty military camps were built and, as was the case throughout the empire, civilian settlements mushroomed around every Roman stronghold.

In Transylvania alone, this line of defense measured over 100 kilometers/62 miles with one hundred twenty-eight watchtowers connected by horse or foot patrols. The castri of what are today Buciumi, Casei, Copaceni, and Gilau, marked the outermost line of the Roman advanced posts. At Cetatea Fetele Albe and elsewhere, one can still see the ruins of massive walls that are more than 3 meters/10 feet wide, the standard width prescribed by Hadrian.

In 124, for military reasons, Hadrian divided Upper Dacia into two provinces: Apulensis with its capital in Apulum, and Porolissensis, with its capital in Napoca. In 126, he returned to Dacia to fortify the Limes Alutanus, the western borderline of the Olt River and already described as the "Road of Trajan." These defensive constructions stretched some 200 kilometers/124 miles, and the ruins of eighteen forts of the Limes Alutanus still can be found today. One road was cut in the Olt gorge, high above the water, a further example of Roman building determination. One portion of the road was named *La Carlige* (On the Hooks) most likely because the stonecutters worked while being suspended from ropes attached to the cliffs above. Another line of transport, equally difficult to traverse, connected what are today Copaceni and Jiblea. With the strongholds of Arutela (Bivolari), Buridava (Ocnita), and Rusidava (Dragasani), the Olt Valley became a formidable line.

These military works show clearly that Hadrian intended to keep the Free Dacians and their allies away from the eastern side of his walls. Like any other Hadrianic long walls, they also served as roads. They firmly defined Roman territory and controlled traffic through the guarded gateways.

At this point in time, Dacia Felix encompassed approximately 100,000 square kilometers/38,610 miles and had a population of nearly seven hundred thousand. The Roman troops stationed there numbered about the same as in Britannia—forty to fifty thousand men, or 10 percent of the empire's armed forces.

Hadrian proved to be a peaceful ruler. His only defect was his huge ego which made him a prisoner of his own revengeful ambitions; it was as legendary as the memory that consistently supplied it with resentment of others. And, it brought about one of history's greatest ironies from which the Dacians would benefit. The envious emperor decided to subdue Trajan's generals, for whom Hadrian had previously organized so many triumphal parades in Rome. He put Lusius Quietus, the hero of the Dacian wars, to death, as well as Cornelius Palma, the conqueror of Syria, and finally his best friend General Turbo. Nor did he forget that Apolodor had ridiculed him in front of Trajan. The vengeful Hadrian ordered Apolodor to disassemble the wood component of the monumental bridge over the Danube, and then had him executed as well.

Since the bridge had been almost destroyed and there was no possibility of consistent Roman traffic across the Danube, it was now impossible for Rome to transport reinforcement troops to Dacia in a matter of hours. This gave the Dacians an opportunity to once again take up arms against the Romans, their military occupation being confined exclusively to Transylvania.

To prevent barbarian invasions, Hadrian had ceded part of southeast Dacia to the Sarmatian Roxolani—in particular, the land east of the fortified Olt River. This was supposed to be a buffer zone against the eastern barbarians, but the Dacians and their allies from Moesia and Pannonia who could not accept Roman rule took refuge there, and so created a volatile area. Considering that more than half of the mines (gold and other metals) and nine-tenths of the salt mines were inside Free Dacia, the Dacians had again become extremely powerful. They represented a potential danger to Rome, one that could not be ignored. Still, Hadrian could not do much about it.

He did give special attention to strengthening and developing the Roman presence in the Danubian ports of Carsium (Harsova), Drobeta, and Troesmis (Galati), and to the Black Sea cities of Tomis, Callatis (Mangalia), and Histria. In Dobrudja, the Romans built more than thirty castri. The lower Danube and the shore of the Black Sea were webbed with military strongholds. Hadrian rebuilt and enlarged Histria with massive walls, erecting temples and public baths whose ruins can be seen today. Knowing that a tired soldier is a submissive man who is probably without thoughts of mutiny, the emperor kept his legionaries busy in Dacia Felix.

These fortified ports were vital to the shipping industry, the safest way to transport gold, silver, copper, salt, furs, honey, wax, and other goods to Rome. The influx of these goods allowed Hadrian to create architectural wonders, such as Temple of Jupiter and the Dome of the Pantheon. The latter was the largest building in the ancient world made of concrete. It had a vaulted ceiling that that stood at the same height from the floor measuring almost 43 meters/140 in diameter.[5] Hadrian also built a private villa for himself at Tivoli, a lavish estate with every luxury available at the time. It continues to amaze and thrill visitors today. Also, he rebuilt the former Greek spa resort in Crimea, the city of Trebizond. Some ten thousand Roman soldiers were located there to defend this luxurious and thriving Eastern European port and supervise trade with Asia.

However, in 132, when Hadrian wanted to build pagan temples in Jerusalem and banned circumcision, the Jews rebelled. He crushed the revolt mercilessly, and it was said that five hundred thousand Jews were killed during the next three years. Afterward, the "City of Peace" was renamed Colonia Aelia Capitolina. It is noteworthy that such a development did not occur in Dacia with its monotheistic religion. Indeed, the Dacians soon traded the ancient Zamolxis for Jesus.

Hadrian brought numerous Dacians to his imperial court and gave important assignments to those he favored. One of his men, described as a Danubian slave named Mastor, refused the order to kill the dying emperor who was riddled with incurable tuberculosis. He had caught the terrible disease during the long marches when he walked elbow to elbow with his legionaries through rains and snow storms. The emperor had the respect and loyalty of his men until at age sixty-two, when he died inspecting the garrison of Vindobona (Vienna).

Hadrian- the-Pacifist thus realized more with the trowel than Trajan-the-Warrior had with the sword. Hadrian consolidated all the conquests he inherited and implemented the power of Rome, making it the master of many lands. The fortified "Hadrianic frontiers" divided and weakened the mobility of the barbarians, forcing them to move not through but around the empire's border. Under Hadrian, the Roman Empire reached the zenith of its power and glory, and occupied Transylvania began to be transformed into a Daco-Roman nation.

With its borders stretching out more than 5,000 kilometers/3,107 miles in three continents, the Roman super-empire was both overextended and militarily underpowered. But it was still safe from the Goths and the Gepidaes who lived close to the Baltic Sea; the Slavs who were north of today's Poland; and the Huns who were trying to move away from Lake Baykal. All these barbarians were destined to collide along the Danube and in the area of Dacia.

By this point, the grandchildren of the Gauls who had been slaughtered by Caesar were already in the Roman army, many of them occupying important positions. The same phenomenon developed in civilian administration, political life, and other areas that had previously been controlled exclusively by the Romans. After so many conquests and forced annexations, the Roman Empire came to be both formed of and eroded by populations of many races, cultures, and traditions. However, the immediate internal danger was not posed by them, but by the new Christian religion.

Suddenly, the generals found themselves leading pacifist troops who believed in turning the other cheek, a conviction which was less than compatible with orders to destroy the enemy. Moreover, the Eternal City, Rome, had become the entertainment and welfare center of the empire.

The military and political vacuum left by the death of Hadrian was filled by his adopted son Antoninus, who competently and compassionately ruled from 138 to 161. He was given the epithet "Pius" and "Father of the Empire." He kept a watchful eye on the distant frontiers of Britannia and doubled the length of Hadrian's Wall with his own Wall of Antoninus. In Dacia, he consolidated the northern and eastern borders that faced the barbarian world and ruled this province with a steady hand and much wisdom.

Yet, tribulation could not be avoided, and toward the end of his reign the Free Dacians, joined by the Sarmatians, assisted the occupied Dacians in revolting on numerous occasions. The battle-cry of the Free Dacians was felt by the Romans too often and in too many places, proving once again that it was much easier to conquer territory than to hold onto occupied land, especially in Transylvania.

The Costoboci who were scattered throughout Dacia joined the uprising, and Pius was forced to mount a hard-won military campaign to punish the rebels in the years 143, 157, and 158. Legion V Macedonica was highly instrumental in consolidating Roman power in Dacia. Pius re-divided the civilian and military administration of this important colony into Dacia Porolissensis (northern Transylvania) with its capital at Porolissum (near Zalau), Southern Dacia Apulensis (mainly Banat) with its capital at Apulum (Alba Iulia), and Lower Dacia Malvensis (currently Oltenia) with its capital at Romula. All were ruled by military prefects under the same governor.

Pius's adopted son, Marcus Aurelius, followed him. He was one of the most brilliant minds of his time and an extremely capable emperor; he ruled from 161 to 180. However, at the beginning of his rule the Parthians invaded Armenia, forcing the strongest of the legions to introduce Roman control into Asia Minor. They conquered Mesopotamia, but paid a very high price for their victories there—soldiers who returned home brought with them the Bubonic plague, an epidemic that took the lives of untold number of legionaries and millions of civilians. Sensing the weakness of the empire, the Free Dacians again mounted repeated attacks on the Roman posts in Dacia Felix. This in turn encouraged the barbarians from the east and the Germans from the west to attack the semi-defenseless and crisis-ridden empire.

As problems multiplied along the Danube, Free Dacians invaded Moesia, and Aurelius was forced to send in his Praetorian Guard to restore order. Obviously, the emperor was short of troops. The German Quadi and Marcomani, who had forcibly settled in the Pannonian flats, grasped this fact and threatened to invade Dacia Felix. The Longobardi and other German tribes besieged Aquileia and threatened to flood the Italic Peninsula. Taken together, all of these developments paved the way for another Dacian rebellion.

Aurelius was not surprised when an army of Sarmatians, which included the Roman's eternal rivals, the Iazygi, raided Western Dacia in 167 and two years later invaded south of the Danube. They were weary of waiting so long to reclaim the land in Western Dacia from which they had been removed by Decebalus, Trajan, and Hadrian. One year later, to eliminate delay and confusion in the chain of command, Aurelius dissolved the three Dacias and united them into a single military province with its capital in Ulpia Sarmizegethusa. General Helvius Pertinax was named procurator of Dacia.

Unfortunately for the Romans, the Free Dacians persisted in creating military crises. Packs of Costoboci (mistaken by most historians for Germans) crossed into Moesia, raided Thracia, and attacked Greece. They stopped 20 kilometers/12 miles short of Athens where they destroyed a temple; they were then bribed into retreating.

In 170 Dacia Felix was directly affected by the Marcomanic wars. It was invaded by Chauci who first defeated the free Costoboci and then destroyed many Roman castri, among them the fortress of Tibiscum, before they headed towards Sarmizegethusa.

Dio described the routine bribery other barbarians used with the Romans as the Astingi (a Baltic German tribe) "came into Dacia with their entire households, hoping to secure both money and land in return for their alliance."[6] When their bribery attempt failed, they left their families in the protection of Governor Cornelius Clemens and attacked elsewhere. Many others followed.

Aurelius had to return to Dacia in order to restore stability there. Oddly enough, the Free Dacians of Crisana, sandwiched between the attacking Germans and resisting Romans, sided with the latter because the unwanted invaders endangered their nation. This was an historic shift, the first sign of successful Dacian-Roman cooperation against a mutual enemy and a step toward a peaceful co-existence.

The emperor ordered the transfer of Legion V Macedonica to Potaissa, and a road was built between Napoca and Porolissum to facilitate the rapid movement of troops to the troubled northern part of Transylvania. However, the Roman troops deployed there to push back the Iazygi encountered unexpectedly strong resistance. During the winter of 172-173, the coalition of Iazygi and Free Dacians, now united against a common enemy, attacked Roman strongholds on the Danube and Tisza Rivers. General Claudius Fronto, the Roman commander, lost his life during one of these battles. Emperor Aurelius responded by leading a punitive expedition, and he obtained a much-needed victory that led to his being named *Dacicus Maximus*.

Determined to spare his troops from endless fights, Aurelius permitted the Iazygi to leave the plains of Pannonia at any time to visit their Roxolani cousins who had settled in Eastern Dacia; he also allowed the Bessarabian Roxolani to visit Pannonia. Soon the two tribes visited each other so often that territorial disputes developed, and they essentially self-destructed. Thus the Sarmatian tribes, who only a century before had occupied a land larger than the entirety of Europe, became nearly extinct through fratricide wars.

Another danger was posed by the Quadi, Marcomanni, and Longobardi, one that resulted in a four-year war. Aurelius had no choice but to incorporate the Dacian cohorts into the Pannonian legions in his attempt to fight the revolting Germans. The Dacian and Sarmatian horsemen impressed him so much that Aurelius decided to include eight thousand of them in the Roman army. Knowing all too well how easy it was for auxiliary forces to fraternize with a close enemy, he sent five thousand five hundred of the new recruits, together with their horses and families to Britannia. After a long journey across Europe under their wolf-dragon flag, they arrived on the British island. In 175 they were stationed along Hadrian's Wall.[7]

Their Roman commander was Lucius Artorius Castus, born in Dalmatia. He had previously served in Legion V Macedonica and so had been stationed in Dacia. Most probably, he spoke Dacian, a fact that would have made him fit for to command the Cohort Decebalus. The outstanding fighting skills and valor of the Dacians in defending the Romanized Britannia reputedly catapulted Artorius into history as the legendary King Arthur.[8]

After twenty years of successful military duty, the Dacian auxiliaries retired from service of Rome, but their sons replaced them and carried forward the same brilliant military reputation. Headstones found by British scholars in England in the nineteenth century confirmed their presence in the forts of Bremetennacum (Ribchester) and Chesters. It is interesting to note that the Chesters region was called "Deva," reminiscent of a Dacian city whose similar name meant "city of wolves."

In 179 many Sarmatian tribes joined the Roxolani and invaded the western shore of the Black Sea. These hordes would have flooded into Dacia if it had not been for Pertinax, the future emperor, who put them to flight northward. In memory of this decisive victory, the triumphant Aurelius named himself *Sarmaticus*.

He intended to implement the model of government he had used in Dacia in all the barbarian territories of the north, and so to unite them into a confederation called Trans-Danubiana. It was probably during his reign that the giant Limes Transalutanus project was conceived as part of an effort to protect the Olt and Danube borders. It included the extension of Trajan's Wall as part of the ample defense system. Since they were aware of the benefits of Roman occupation, the Dacians were not entirely hostile to Aurelius. When their territories became a clear target for numerous barbarian invasions, the emperor promptly intervened with troops to protect his Dacians.

The problem was the Dacian salient. It represented an obstacle for barbarians coming from what is today Ukraine and heading toward the Balkan or Italic peninsulas. Because the marshes of Danube Delta created a natural defense, most of them were forced to attack around it and so entered Free Dacia. However, the Carpathians were another discouraging obstacle, so they often chose to cross the Danube into Moesia. Others took a long detour through the plains of Danubian Pannonia toward central Europe—precisely the region Aurelius was preoccupied with defending during his entire reign.

While commanding the Danubian campaigns and after bringing the Marcomanni to their knees three times, the emperor wrote his *Meditations*, a work of practical philosophy interspersed with metaphysics introspections. In spite of all of these wars and a plague that claimed millions of people, this stoic and capable ruler succeeded in prolonging the Pax Romana. He was able to do so as a result of the sudden prosperity and stability created in Rome by the riches of Dacia Felix. This made it possible for the Roman coin to have 75 percent silver in its alloy, boosting trust in the Roman treasury.[9] According to Dio, the emperor brought in enough plunder from his campaigns to give each citizen 800 sesterces ($80 in today's currency); he also forgave all debts. Aurelius's death at age sixty-nine interrupted the Trans-Danubian project.

The tendency among the Roman emperors to grow bushy beards reflected the strong influence of the barbarians. Given that the legions were dominated by barbarian recruits, the emperors did not want to look radically different from them. The beard represented power and virility, qualities much desired by the vain emperors, including the next in line for the throne, namely, Commodus.

The reign of Commodus (180-192) marked the beginning of the end of Roman domination in Dacia and of Roman hegemony throughout its vast empire. He was renowned mainly for being the only left-handed emperor thus far in Roman history. Commodus believed himself to be a reincarnation of Hercules. Fancying himself the strongest man in the empire, he appeared in the Roman arenas more than seven hundred times; legend has it that he killed one hundred lions with one hundred arrows in one day. However, he preferred to buy peace from the Germans rather than war against them, and dedicated his life to open debauchery, thus becoming a symbol of Roman decadence.

In an effort to refill the empty treasury, Commodus further exploited Dacia. He entrusted administration of the mines to the military, thereby aiming to increase the workload of the miners. At that time, the population of Dacia Felix was divided between the colonists who lived in the cities, the Dacians who lived in the villages, and the foreign workers who lived in cluster houses around the mines.

Commodus rightfully credited the Dacians for their important role in the operation of the gold mines and also for preventing the Eastern European barbarians from entering the Balkans. In recognition of these achievements, he granted them a semi-independent status. He reinforced the Roman garrison of Napoca and declared Dacia Porolissennsis a Roman colony. It was he who began building the strategic Limes Transalutanus as a part of a second defense system, 30 kilometers/19 miles east of the Olt River.

After he had nearly bankrupted the empire, Commodus died at the young age of thirty-one, poisoned by one of his three hundred mistresses—Marcia, a Christian. Commodus is also remembered for having erected a column in memory of the victories of Aurelius, along the Danube in Dacia. It is a copy of Trajan's monument, placed a short distance from it in the middle of Rome as a reminder of his father's military legacy.

The capable General Pertinax, who was in charge of the legions fighting in Pannonia under Aurelius, took the throne next. As a former procurator of Dacia, he understood its people. Their history would have been much different if Pertinax had not been assassinated by his own Praetorian Guard only eighty-seven days after his coronation.

Pertinax was followed by Septimius Severus (r. 193-211), who put in place the dynasty of emperors chosen by the legions. He owed much of his honor to Legio XIII Gemina, stationed in Dacia, and other Danubian legions. At this point, an internal power struggle deteriorated into a civil war in Dacia, and Pax Romana approached its end. Roman domination of Dacia had become lax and increasingly vulnerable to the predations of Eurasian invaders. The ambitious emperor was determined to change all that.

Many former Dacian conscripts had retired and returned home infected with the spirit of freedom and a desire to overthrow Roman domination. But Rome knew how to crush ethnic revolts, and Severus sent in troops who forced the Roman border westward into the middle of Wallachia (Muntenia).

Septimius Severus continued to build Limes Transalutanus, extending it 220 kilometers/137 miles northward to Cumidava (Rasnov) and creating at least thirteen military forts to repel Carpi invasions. Among them was Jidava (Campulung Muscel), which guarded the road to the Rucar-Bran corridor of Transylvania. This Roman advance post (132 meters/433 feet x 99 meters/325 feet) with high, strong walls and a moat (6.5 meters/21 feet wide) was the main castrum. It became a large settlement that served the Roman military, and a eventually what would become a Romanian city was built next to it.[10]

Severus almost doubled the number of Roman cities in Dacia. He restored Ulpia Sarmizegethusa, which by now had twelve Roman temples and was to become a Dacian metropolis and a vital military, economical, and cultural center of the province. He granted the title of *municipalities* to Apulum, Dierna, Porolissum, Tibiscum, and Potaissa, and exempted five other cities from taxes. This gave an economic boost to the area and attracted new colonists. Under his reign, Dacia Felix reached the peak of its prosperity. But more than anything else, the mammoth fortification and mining works performed by countless Dacian laborers under the supervision of Romans provided the blend of the two people, their language, and their culture.

Severus increased the number of his legions to thirty-three, and provided much needed stability to the Roman Empire. To halt barbarian intrusions into Dacia, he stationed five legions in Moesia Superior and another five in Pannonia Superior. The migratory and military crises within and around Dacia seemed to be fading into the past. In Dacia Felix only two legions were left—the old, reliable V Macedonica and XIII Gemina. The fact that there were very few occupation troops remaining was an indication of the relaxed rule of Severus and his son Caracalla; the latter ensured a good and stable life in Dacia Felix under Governor Marcus Agrippa.

Emperor Caracalla (r. 198–217) was famous for his imperial slogan, "Make your soldiers rich and have no worry!" He doubled their salaries and increased the Praetorian Guard from ten thousand to fifty thousand. Numerous Dacians, Sarmatians, and Scythians, all mercenaries, belonged to the new legions while the army's generals had dictatorial powers and readily abused their privileges.

Because Roman society lacked a large vigorous middle class, state revenue depended on colonial exploitation. Since the emperor wanted to expand the internal tax base and gain increased popularity, he issued *Civis Romanus Sum*

(I Am a Roman Citizen Law). Thus in 212 Caracalla gave Roman citizenship to all free inhabitants within the imperial borders, a move aimed at stripping privileged Romans of their control of the electoral system and expanding the voting power of non-Italic minorities.

This decree would have major unforeseen repercussions in the administrative, political, and military fields. Ultimately, the process of provincialization so affected the Roman government that it undermined the Empire. Its decline was further hastened under the pressure created by the continual influx of barbarians in search of the privileges associated with citizenship. In a matter of years, the Roman way of life was changed forever—and not for the better.

Nevertheless, Caracalla was determined to guard Dacia Felix and its gold against barbarians and so continued to fortify the Limes Transalutanus of Severus in the north. It was a wise decision: the Carpi invaded Dacia Felix once more and were promptly annihilated by Caracalla's legions. The emperor himself led the military expedition from Porolissum, and he was so confident of victory that he took along his mother, Domna Julia. They took a vacation in the secure area of Apulum, and it is likely that, at this point, this city of forty thousand inhabitants was renamed Apulum-Julia, today's Alba-Iulia.

By forcing the barbarians eastward, the legionaries also extended the border of Dacia Felix toward Brasov. In 213, Caracalla continued his sweeping campaign in the Danubian plains. There he may have founded the city of Caracalla (Caracal) near Romula. With the booty from Dacia, Caracalla issued his own *aureus*, a solid gold coin, and the strengthened *antoninianus*, a coin with 50 percent silver alloy that was worth two denari. This new currency allowed him to pay his legions and engage in a large construction program in Dacia.

The most urgent project continued to be the extension of the fortified line Limes Transalutanus, which had been initiated by Severus. This massive defensive wall extended from Bran Pass to the high north of the Dacia Felix border and south to the Danube, and measured 250 kilometers/155 miles in length. The newly built military forts had three or four levels, and round observation towers.[11] Thousands of local recruits increased the army of auxiliaries that manned this second largest Roman line of defense in Dacia. Legion I Italica was transferred to Novae (near Nicopolis), prepared for battle on both banks of the Danube.

By this point, new invaders—the Ostrogothic tribes—had galloped toward Dacia. Jordanes remarked that King Ostrogotha and his Ostrogoths "crossed the Danube and dwelt a little while in Moesia and Thrace."[12] The Roman legions of those two provinces pushed them back into the Ukraine where they continued to build their own empire. In the meantime, Caracalla was assassinated by his own Praetorian Guard. The Dacian problem therefore continued.

Dio mentioned that in 218, "the Dacians, after ravaging portions of Dacia and showing an eagerness for further war, now desisted, when they got back the hostages that Caracallus, under the name of an alliance, had taken from them."[13] Prior to that, he noted that Commodus defeated many German tribes which he did not allow to settle near the western border of Dacia. Moreover, twelve thousand Dacian prisoners who had assisted the enemies of Rome were to be resettled in Dacia Felix.

One year after Emperor Caracalla died (217), the Free Dacians raided Dacia Romana and demanded that their warriors (those taken prisoners during an earlier rebellion against Roman occupation) be released in exchange for peace. As Dio described it, this illustrates the eagerness of the Free Dacians to carry out a war of liberation on behalf of their occupied brothers. But, it also clearly proved that even the mighty Romans were not able to fracture the unity of the Dacian people.

As the middle of the third century approached, a mighty swarm of Germanic tribes, migratory Goths, appeared on the horizon of the Danube. They had their origins in Scandinavia, and, because they were unstoppable, they had launched invasions in multiple directions, toward both western and eastern European territories. Fighters by birth, the blond Goths were tall and strong. They wore colorful animal furs like that of the lions which once lived in Europe. They were also excellent horsemen and used stirrups that allowed them to sit more firmly in their saddles so they could battle the enemy with weapons in both hands. This proved to be a huge military advantage. Skilled with spears and swords, they rode horses that were also giant-sized relative to those of other peoples. The appearance of a pack of Goths instantly provoked terror in any land.

A typical Gothic invasion consisted of some fifty thousand wagons advancing through the middle of huge horse- and cattle-herds. The whole procession extended close to 300 kilometers/186 miles, thus amplifying the terror. Their *laager* (camps) consisted of huge circles of wagons with women and children inside, guarded by mounted patrols. Their Aryan roots and worship of the wolf may have given them an affinity with the Dacians. In the years to come, the Goths would change the history of Dacia, the Balkans, and the entire Roman Empire.

The Goths from Lower Vistula (today's Prussia) launched the first invasions of the Roman Empire while another branch invaded what is now Ukraine, smashing the resistance of the Sarmatians and Scythians. Since they were forced eastward by other Germanic tribes and by the Roman legions, the Goths founded their own nomadic kingdom between the Dnieper and Don Rivers.

In the meantime, the murder of some thirty emperors over the next one hundred years weakened confidence in Roman institutions and the imperial economy. The *antoninimus* coin decreased its silver alloy from fifty to five percent. The military was also in a state of chaos. Its legions were dispatched to distant locations to put down foreign rebellions, and they became entangled in ethnic conflicts they did not understand and could not solve.[14]

What the legions could do was to name emperors, such as General Avidius Cassius, who had crushed the revolt in Egypt; Iulius Maximinus, who successfully fought the Germans beyond the Rhine. In 235 when the Carpi and other Free Dacians raided Histria and other commercial ports, Maximinus proved his generalship and pushed them north of the Danube. For the next three years, he kept the Dacians and Sarmatians out of Roman borders, took the title of *Dacicus Maximus*, and was hailed Caesar by his legionaries. But he could not exploit his gains because this enormous soldier emperor (eight feet six inches in height), who was uneducated and without knowledge of Latin, was declared unfit to rule by the Senate, and an army was sent to arrest him.

Maximinus defeated this army at Aquileia in northern Italy in 238, and it was only his assassination that stopped him from sacking Rome. He was nicknamed Thrax, meaning "the Thracian," although he was born in Moesia. He reigned for three years, after which he lost his throne and his life in a war against the Christians.

Thus began the phase of military anarchy that brought the "garrison emperors" to the throne. These soldier-emperors were incapable of understanding their role in history and sought to compensate for their inadequacies by persecuting Christians. As a rule, these illiterate generals, many of whom had never seen Rome, were intoxicated by their own victories and lured the troops to battle with promises that could not be kept. Evidently, they were victims of their own self-destructive methods of achieving power. At this point in history, Rome's only real option was to pay off the Dacian Carpi, Goths, and other barbarians in exchange for peace in Moesia.

When Philip the Arab refused to pay the annual tribute in 245, the next year the Carpi entered Dacia Felix and destroyed the city of Romula. The Goths followed, and Philip conducted a successful campaign in which the invaders were pushed beyond the Roman borders that had now receded to the Limes Transalutanus between the Arges and Olt rivers. On account of this victory and also in celebration of the first millennium of Rome's existence, the emperor took the titles of *Carpicus Maximus* and *Germanicus Maximus*.

The grand event was celebrated with Olympic Games and other popular festivities.

The Roman Empire continued to be weakened by various forms of internal anarchy deriving from economic inflation and the plague. The dinari alloy now had only half the amount of silver it had contained under Nero. The legions had been decimated by mutinous demands for back payments and, above all, by the deadly cholera epidemic. The Praetorian Guard, which had the power to both crown and kill Rome's emperors, offered the throne of the empire to the highest bidder. The palace coups created social and military havoc that left the empire vulnerable.

Being quick to capitalize on this crisis, the Carpi and Goths carried out destructive raids in Moesia and Thrace, and in 244 they attacked Marcianopolis where they were defeated by General Quintus Decius. Four years later, they invaded the Lower Danube. Only a single military column entered Dacia Felix and Pannonia and another galloped into Moesia. They seized the fortresses of Novae, the main Roman garrison on the Danube, and devastated Thracia.

Philip chose the well-known General Decius to repel them and to shore up the Balkan borders of the empire. Decius fulfilled his military obligations admirably and defeated the army of seventy thousand Carpi and Goths at Nicopolis. By assuming the title of *Dacicus Maximus*, and having received the endorsement of the Danubian legions who were loyal to this Pannonian born general, he proclaimed himself emperor.

The loyal legions helped him defeat Philip and his son, both of whom were killed in a decisive battle for imperial power at Verona in 249. Decius believed himself to be the second Trajan and *restitutor Daciarum* (the restorer of Dacia), and so placed his own statue in the middle of Sarmizegethusa. He also issued a coin featuring a warrior holding the Dacian wolf-dragon standard. In the same year, however, King Kniva of the Goths entered Dacia and Moesia and conducted a siege on Novae and Nicopolis.

Taking advantage of the internal Roman struggle for power, the Goths, who had escaped from previous battles, joined with the army of Kniva and continued southward, besieging Philippopolis (Plovdiv). The conquest of this city resulted in the slaughter of one hundred thousand soldiers and Roman citizens, including Julius Priscus, the governor of Thracia. The united Goths again ravaged Thracia while the new emperor organized his legions to chase them away. This time Decius lost the bloody confrontation and barely escaped with his life.

He regrouped, and the fighting continued at Abrittus (Razgrad). There, trapped in a Moesian swamp, the emperor saw his son killed before his eyes. A little later, at Novae, he himself was killed. Thus, in the year 251, Decius became the first emperor to lose his life on the battlefield. This victory on the part of the Goths destroyed the myth of Roman invincibility.

Eventually, the brave General Valerian (the future emperor) tried to wage a campaign against the Goths, but was halted when a plague weakened his army. The Goths now dominated the territories of the Lower Danube and the western shore of the Black Sea, including Dobrudja. Their influence in Free Dacia and their massive presence around the Dacia Felix salient was overwhelming. Again, Rome's only real option was to pay them tribute so they would not to attack the empire's borders. Meanwhile, other Gothic tribes captured the mouth of the Bug River and with it, Olbia, a fortified city of the utmost commercial importance, one which had previously been under the control of the Dacians. These same Goths attacked Roman garrisons on the shore of the Black Sea, subjugated their populations, and confiscated their ships and boats. The captives were put in chains and forced to row for the Goths, who continued their invasion southward toward Tomis. Thus began, in the year 253, the first naval invasion of the Goths into the Balkans.

Some fifteen thousand Goths entered with five hundred vessels of every size and description from the Black Sea to the Aegean Sea. They conquered every island they saw, and, in 267 they devastated Corinth, Thebes, Sparta, and Athens. During this Odyssean campaign, the Goths lost numerous warriors whom they replaced with barbarians, Roman deserters, adventurers, bandits, and all kinds of criminals who increased the myth of this invader's ferocity. Their atrocities confirmed the veracity of the eternal philosophy of the barbarians: it was easier to destroy than to build, and it was easier to plunder than to work.

Meanwhile, the ancient religion of the Roman Empire was proving increasingly incapable of ensuring the morality of Roman citizens and their democratic way of life. The Christian religion, however, made healthy progress despite the persecutions carried out by emperors Decius and Valerian. One of the major accomplishments of the Christians was to have Sunday set aside as a day of rest. Overall, the impact of Christian barbarians on Roman affairs continued to grow and the world of Trajan and Hadrian was changing rapidly.

By chance, the next emperors were of Dacian origin as the Dacian military power had become an important support for the Roman emperors. Publius Gallienus (r. 253-268) wrote to a general who was spying for him and asked to conduct negotiations with the Germans without the knowledge of the Dacian troops. These troops had already been provoked and undertaking such negotiations overtly could have further ignited their anger. This fact itself illustrates how important the Dacian alliance was for the endless and nightmarish warfare that had to be undertaken by any emperor who fought the

Alamanni, Franks, Goths, Marcomani, Quadi, and other Germans all over the Danube and Rhine areas.

Gallienus was born in Dacia and his mother was named Romula, which coincides with the name of a Roman garrison on the Olt River. He dedicated all of his strength to repelling the invading hordes from Dacia Felix. His many victorious fights against the Carpi and other Free Dacians brought him the title of *Dacicus Maximus*. Unwilling to feed the meat grinder of guerilla warfare, he was the first emperor to withdraw Roman troops from Dacia Felix. He moved many cohorts of legions V Macedonica and XIII Gemina to Pannonian garrisons.

Demonstrating the same determination to restore order on the Rhine, he subdued the Germanic tribes of the Alemanni, Franks, Quadzi, and Marcomanni. In 268 Gallienus destroyed the Heruli power at Naissus (Niss) and then, as was often the case, the brave *Dacicus Maximus* was assassinated by his own Praetorian Guard. So was his rival, Regalianus/Regillia, who stubbornly insisted that he was the direct successor and a grand-nephew of Decebalus. This capable general was proclaimed emperor by the legions in Illyricum in 260. But his pro-Dacian attitude and the enmity of Aurelian hastened his assassination by a group of Roman officers.

No doubt, this was a turbulent time for the Roman Empire, its legions, generals, and emperors. After more than a century of occupation, the Roman situation in Dacia Felix was like that of the British in America before the War of Independence. On the military level, the sons and the grandsons of the first legionaries stationed in Dacia had taken their places in the garrisons. On the social level, the second and third generations of the Daco-Romans belonged to a newly created nation.

The Daco-Roman army was powerful enough to stop the Marcomanni's invasion of Dobrudja, Moldova, and Muntenia/Wallachia. But Free Dacia was flooded by more Goths and Sarmatians, pushed west by the Huns of Eurasia. The Sarmatians who remained in Ukraine absorbed the Vandali and later gave birth to the Slavons.

In the Balkans, only the timely intervention in 268-270 of the legions sent by Claudius II saved Salonica/Thessalonika and stopped the Ostrogoths from heading to Italy. As a consequence, the tribesmen of the Heruli who manned the invading fleet surrendered to the Romans. Their king, Naulobotus, became a Roman consul, the first barbarian to be vetted with such honor and power. The rest of the Heruli engaged in acts of piracy and sought shelter in Free Dacia when they were in danger.

Defeated and driven back by the Romans from their intended route into Western Europe, the Visigoths also crossed the Danube into Free Dacia. They were well received by the opportunistic Carpi, and together they entered the

Roman occupied Olt Valley and used its passage to reach Transylvania. Suddenly, the legionaries stationed there found themselves partially isolated from the rest of the empire. Other Goths attacked Aquincum (Budapest,) forcing the Romans to evacuate the city.

Encouraged by the success of its naval invasion, three hundred twenty thousand Ostrogoths navigated in six thousand vessels toward the Mount Athos and entered Salonica. But again, Claudius II's legions were waiting for them and killed fifty thousand barbarians in one day alone. The Goths' fleet was captured, and they ran for their lives across Macedonia and Thracia, leaving only devastation in their wake.

Eventually, General Aurelian forced the Goths to cross the Danube into welcoming Free Dacia. There the Germans found the defeated Carpi who had also been chased out of other Roman provinces. Soon more than three hundred thousand Gepidi, Heruli, Vandals, and Visigoths entered Free Dacia, which had been transformed into a vast Germanic military camp. Unaware of that they were subject to any danger, the victorious legionaries returned to Rome. Their vast war booty was carried into Rome by the captive Goths. Claudius received the title of *Gothicus* and subsequently died of the plague at Sirmium on the Danube by the border with Dacia Felix.

Another Dacian-born emperor, Lucius Domitius Aurelianus (r. 270-275), took the throne and inherited the endless military quagmire that Eastern Europe had become. Known as General Aurelian he was already a living legend on the battlefields: in a single day he had killed forty-eight Sarmatians, and over his lifetime, he had killed nine hundred fifty enemies. Now that he wore the purple robe, the former cavalry general focused on the use of horses in war and supplied the Roman phalanx with the heavy armored cavalry.

Greatly impressed with the fighting qualities of the Goths, Aurelian enrolled the best of them in the auxiliary legions. He also agreed to have some Visigoths settle in Dacia Felix, and soon other wandering Goths began to pour in. The understanding between the barbarians and Aurelian was simple: the Goths could colonize Dacia, but their warriors had to fight for Rome, not against it. Peace brought the emperor the title of *Gothicus Maximus*. It was a wise deal, as Aurelian faced a huge invasion of the Gepidae, Sarmatians, and Vandals, who carried out incursions in the provinces of Moesia, Pannonia, and Thracia.

During gruesome battles of 270-271, the Roman legions led by Aurelian defeated the Gepidaes and forced them back into Free Dacia. Given that there was little vital space left there, the German chieftains convinced the emperor to allow them to settle peacefully in Dacia Felix as well. The Vandals who refused negotiations were crushed, and their captured leaders were crucified in Pannonia.

Obviously Aurelian tolerated only the Germans who obeyed his orders. He would allow more Goths and Gepidaes to colonize Dacia as long as they made the same pledge—to fight for Rome, not against it. For the time being, the Danubian provinces and Dacia were saved, and Aurelian took the title of *Dacicus Maximus*. In an attempt to boost the confidence of his Roman colonists, the emperor minted coins stamped with *Dacia Felix*. Meanwhile Free Dacia was virtually occupied by the German tribes of Eastern Europe, who had been pushed into the area by the Huns. Once again, the plans from Rome to have two Dacias as buffer against the barbarians failed, since each was too weak to fulfill that military task. Instead of combining their power, they fought against each other.

Realizing that his own capital was poorly defended, Aurelian decided to put his priorities in order. First, he began to build the great defensive walls of Rome. At the same time, he reformed the monetary system, fought government corruption, regulated the food supply, and created a new order of priests who worshipped the Sun god (similar to Mithra, the god-of-light who was very popular with the legionaries). All of these reform measures earned Aurelian the title of *Restitutor Orbis* (Restorer of the World). Then in 271, after defeating the Alamanni who had repeatedly tried to invade Italy, he also took the title *Germanicus Maximus*. Still, the German problem had not been solved.

By this time Dacia Felix was being attacked from the east and west by numerous barbarian tribes. This, along with the massive presence of the German invaders in Free Dacia, convinced Aurelian that he could not fight on two opposite fronts and still defend the stranded Roman province. His first step was to pull back his units and abandon the Limes Transalutanus, a measure that only encouraged the Goths to occupy Central Dacia.

Anticipating still more difficult times, Aurelian expanded the defensive walls of his capital. As an economic measure, he increased taxes and restored the value of the Roman coins. Encouraged by success in these matters, the capable emperor led a punishing military expedition against the barbarians now in Thracia. Then, with the last of the Danubian forces, in 272 Aurelian launched a campaign to rescue Dacia Felix. He tried unsuccessfully to push the Goths and the first wave of Gepidae out of the country. It was too late to seize a golden opportunity for re-establishing the Roman might, which by then was too weak to hold the barbarians in check, and thus the empire was deprived of a solid buffer against the Asiatic invasions.

Facing a massive military power in the making, the emperor tried to find a way out this zone of ceaseless turmoil. He decided to leave all of Dacia to the Carpi, Goths, Gepidaes, and other Germans who now were forced to fight against the new barbarian hordes moving in from Eastern Europe toward the Balkans. Riddled by the plague, the Roman army had already been redeployed and set up a second line of defense in Moesia and Pannonia.

In a desperate attempt to save the rest of the empire, by the year 274 Aurelian began to evacuate his troops and civilian administration from Dacia Felix. Legion V Macedonica was positioned at Oescus, and Legion XIII Gemina was in the old camp of Ratiaria, both on the south bank of the Danube. The rest of the military units were redeployed to defend the Balkan and Italic peninsulas.

For the Roman Empire, abandoning Dacia meant an incalculable loss of gold, silver, copper, iron, salt, and grains. It also meant the loss of 500 kilometers/311 miles of the northern border. It was a big blow to imperial arrogance, but this was the price to be paid in return for peace in Eastern Europe. A large number of colonists and even loyal barbarians followed the exodus of the Roman troops. Yet, they were only a minority compared to rest of the Romanized Dacians who remained in Transylvania. The emperor was very aware that a large Dacian population still lived south of the Danube, and so founded Dacia Aureliana with its capital at Serdica (Sofia) in Moesia Inferior (now Bulgaria).

Aurelian was assassinated in the year 275 in Thracia by a group of suspicious officers, probably of barbarian extraction, who believed that he sought their death. This was also the year in which Dacia Felix regained its independence.

The new province Dacia Aureliana was defended by the powerful Roman military bases of Oescus and Ratiaria. No doubt, these cities constituted a permanent bridgehead for an eventual invasion of Dacia. But this would never happen. By crossing the Danube into Dacia initially, the Romans had opened a Pandora's box. They had created unsolvable economic and military conflicts that would be amplified throughout Eastern European history.

Thus, after one hundred sixty-five years of occupying Dacia, the Romans returned Dacia Felix to its natives. Given that the Romano-Daco society and culture were thriving, it seemed that Dacia was poised to rise again as a world power. Future Romanians were conceived, but not yet born.

NOTES

1. This is not to be confused with Ulpia Traiana on the Lower Rhine in Germania.

2. Pliny, *Letters, Books VIII – X and Panegyricus*, vol. 2 of *Letters and Panegyricus*, trans. Betty Radice (Cambridge: Harvard University Press; London: William Heinemann, 1975), bk. 8, 9.

3. Their ancient dragon flag was found on tombstones in Chesters, England, and adorned later English paintings such as one currently on display at the museum on the site of the Chesters Roman Fort.

4. Grapo's commission, written on a baked slate, was found two thousand years later in that part of Romania.

5. This ingenious construction continues to serve as an example for the great cathedrals and other magnificent buildings in the world.

6. Cassius Dio, *Roman History*, trans. Earnest Cary (Cambridge: Harvard University Press; London: William Heinemann, 1955), bk. 72, 15.

7. Attached to Legion VI Victrix and known as Cohort Decebalus, these mounted auxiliary troops fought under their beloved Dacian dragon standard and retained their ancient traditions. They successfully defeated and pushed back the Caledoni, Picts, and other invading tribes from Free Britannia across Hadrian's Wall.

8. Today a commemorative plaque is attached to Hadrian's Wall at the east gateway of the fort at Birdoswald. Illustrations of a palm leaf, symbolic of victory, and the Dacian Sword flank the script:

Building inscription of the FIRST COHORT OF DACIANS, HADRIAN'S OWN, recording the names of Modius Julius Governor of Lower Britain in A.D. 219, And Marcus Claudius Menander, Tribune of the Cohort.

Presumably, there was an accompanying inscription recording the names and titles of the Emperor Elagabalus.

9. After Aurelius withdrew the Roman military from Dacia in 275, the same coin contained only five percent silver.

10. Due to its strategic location, Longo-Campo survived in time to become the first capital of feudal Wallachia/Muntenia under the name Campulung (Long Field). The author of this book is a native of this picturesque Carpathian city.

11. This new military architecture would shape the future design of feudal castles.

12. Jordanes, *The Gothic History of Jordanes*, ed. and trans. Charles Christopher Mierow (Cambridge: Speculum Historiale, 1966), 83.

13. Dio, *Roman History*, trans. Cary, bk. 79, 405.

14. A historical analogy would be a comparison of the Roman Empire to the Communist empire which also tried the impossible—to retain its domination after 1980.

Chapter Ten

Post-Roman Dacia

In A.D. 275 (year of Rome 1028) the Dacian land north of the Danube River was about to regain its freedom from Roman occupation. At the same time, many waves of Gothic tribes from the Don River and Vandals from the Vistula River began to enter Dacia and forced the last occupation troops of Legion XIII Gemina to leave Transylvania and re-garrison south of Oltenia. This military unit remained there until the fall of the Roman Empire, ending five hundred years of continuous military service in this same Danubian region.

Roman colonists who evacuated from the province settled south of the Danube in a new province named Dacia Aureliana that occupied most of what is today Bulgaria. Its capital was in Serdica (Sofia); and Durostorum, Odesus, and Marcianoplis were its main cities. The native Dacians, later called *Rhomanoi*, to distinguish them from the Greeks and other ethnicities, formed the largest population of that area. They were courted by the Romans who provided them with tax reductions and other incentives to keep them from fraternizing with the free Dacians. They began to prosper and formed the roots of the Vallachians/Aromanians who dispersed throughout the Balkan Peninsula and remain to the present day.

Nearly all of the veteran legionaries of Dacia Felix, now the fourth generation and owners of large tracts of land that had originally been donated to them, decided not to evacuate and instead remained with their families north of the Danube. They provided the basis for a new Romanized culture and language that would dominate the entire Dacian population from then on.

Given that Rome was now ruling Moesia, many stranded barbarians quickly migrated away from this region and sought refuge in Dacia. The brief territorial disputes that erupted between these people and the Dacians were settled in favor of the natives. The wandering tribes that were being squeezed

221

out of Eastern Europe—most of them of Gothic origin—also ended up in Dacia, the first settled nation they came upon. They gladly offered their military power in exchange for land, and soon the Dacians found themselves defended by many Germanic tribes.

Other large areas of Dacia came to be occupied by the Gepidaes, Lombards, and the Visigoths. Transylvania was so heavily populated by Goths that the Romans began calling it *Guthiuda*. Jordannes confirmed this when he wrote in 551: "This Gothia, which our ancestors called Dacia and now, as I have said, is called Gepidia, was then bounded on the east by the Roxolani, on the west by the Iazyges, on the north by the Sarmatians and Bastarnae and on the south by the river Danube."[1]

Dacia turned out to be an area for temporary regrouping for the migrant barbarians. Before long, the Gothic tribes took over the lower Danube, thereby establishing a corridor toward central Europe. After they had joined with other Germanic tribes, they raided the outskirts of Milan where they were defeated by Aurelian's legions. For this military achievement, the emperor was received in Rome with great triumph. His victory parade was preceded by long columns of prisoners who carried rich plunder that guaranteed many days of free entertainment. It was *la dolce vita* again. Thankful Rome conferred on Aurelian the title of *Restitutor Orbis* (Restorer of the World). The Roman Empire seemed to have regained the height of its power.

Because the Goths gave the Roman army two thousand cavalrymen and their chieftains allowed their sons to be held as hostages in Rome, Aurelian allowed the Germanic tribes to settle in the Roman-controlled territories south of the Danube River. It was a decision that solved none of the brewing problems and only invited more barbarians to cross through Dacia and look for subsidized food and shelter. The result was a heavy migratory flow that continued over the next two centuries and had an extraordinary demographic impact.

The Roman Empire still looked formidable on the map. It still celebrated one hundred fifty-nine holidays each year and continued to be convinced of its own pre-eminence in the world. In reality, however, the empire was in a continuous state of decline. Assassination plots threatened every emperor. In ten years, six emperors came to the throne, each of which had a brief and powerless reign. Barbarians were pouring into the Roman territory of Moesia in spite the fact that five legions had been ordered there to seal off the south bank of the Danube: I Italica stationed at Novae (Sistova), IV Flavia at Singidunum (Beograd), V Macedonica at Oescus (near Pleven), VII Claudia at Durostrum (Silistra), and XIII Gemina at Ratiaria (Arcar).

Seeing opportunity in disorder, the Dacians and Sarmatians acted promptly. They joined the Quadi to invade northern Thracia, only to find that the Roman legions in that area were still strong. In the winter of 283 Marcus Aurelius Carus pushed them back across the Danube, but he had to leave for the Persian campaign. The Dacians were pleased to see the Roman danger removed.

The next emperor, Diocletian (r. 284-305), tried to save the empire by initiating a series of major reforms. Although he had been born near the Danube to enslaved parents and was lacking in formal education, the illiterate Diocletian proved to be a superb general of the troops stationed in Moesia. Acclaimed by the legionaries and the civilians on his first day as emperor, he killed a famous criminal with his bare hands. Since he was a strong supporter of the cavalry, Diocletian was aware of the need for the legions to maintain their fighting supremacy. He was surrounded by military elite, consisting of natives of Dacia, Dalmatia, Moesia and Pannonia. This group constituted a new ruling class in the Balkans and eventually created the foundation of the Byzantine Empire.

At this time the map of the Balkans showed Dacia to be an almost square territory, bordered by the Danube, Tisza, and Dniester rivers and the Black Sea. Its square area was larger than that of Thracia, Macedonia, and Greece together. Moesia was densely populated by Latin speaking Dacian Rhomanoi. Diocletian imposed Roman rule in the Danube region in what was known as Dacia Nova (the New Dacia) in Dobrudja. Its boundaries began at the northeast arm of the Danube Delta, continued to the south above Odessus (Varna), and stretched west to east from Durostorum to the Black Sea littoral. Its capital was Tomis, which Diocletian enlarged and surrounded with defensive walls.

The new province protected Roman interests along the shore of the Black Sea and the mouth of the Danube while providing an ideal bridgehead from which legions could invade and reoccupy Greater Dacia. This optimistic plan stood in stark contrast to the large number of legionary units that were in a state of decline. Diocletian would correct this problem.

Despite many barbarian invasions throughout Dacia and then across the Danube, the emperor did not order the demolition of the old bridges at Drobeta and Barbosi, both of which were conduits for massive amounts of grain, salt, and other commodities needed by the empire. This time the formerly occupied Dacians were treated as equal commercial partners and given full payment for all the exports.

Diocletian was well aware of Dacia's role as a buffer against barbarian invasions, and so formed Legions II Herculia and V Iovia and stationed them in the vulnerable province of Dacia Nova, which was eventually renamed

Scythia. In addition, he posted nine legions (out of a total of twenty-three) along the Danubian border of Dacia and Pannonia and gave them orders to defend the northernmost border of the Roman Empire.

To further deal with the barbarian problem, he created *limitanei*, or border troops, trained specifically to defend the volatile fringes of the mammoth empire. Suddenly the army increased to sixty-eight legions with 420,000 men, plus another 150,000 auxiliaries. This proved to be a financial burden that the Roman Empire could not afford.

Diocletian engaged his *limitanei* troops in building fortifications along the lower Danube between what are today Nikopol and Galati, thereby stabilizing the Dacian frontier. The ambitious project triggered a massive Carpian raid from Callatis (Mangalia) to Dionysopolis (Balchic) and Marcianopolis (Devnya). However, Diocletian made good use of the many troops he had garrisoned in Thracia and Macedonia and repelled the invaders beyond the Danubian border he had just built.

Co-emperor Galerius fought the Carpi/Carpians for two years in so many battles that he took the title of *Carpicus Maximus* six times and still was not able to halt their invasion. In 297 he resettled the Carpi prisoners away from their Dacian roots in Pannonia in the Pecs region. The emperor believed he had solved the barbarian problem, when, in fact, it was escalating with each passing day. The Carpians continued to be being pushed by the Eurasian invaders of Dacia, forcing many of them to move south of the Danube where they were known as Carpodacians. Most of them would later be called Vallachians, and later still, they would be collectively known as the Aromanians of the Balkans.

Under these adverse circumstances, the supply of Dacian gold to Rome was interrupted, and the economy slowed throughout the empire. The treasury was low, and citizens of Rome were looking at an uncertain future. The once great imperial capital had become flooded with poor undesirables, and the wealthier citizens were forced to reside in the safety of the quiet provinces. In order to correct this security problem, Diocletian reorganized the tax and education systems, froze the prices of goods, and, using the empire's last gold reserves, put solid gold coins into circulation. But their scarcity and desirability caused the insecure Romans to hoard them instead of spending them.

Overwhelmed by so many problems, Diocletian decided to share the ruling of the empire with his general Gaius Galerius, who had been born in Dacia Aureliana at Romulianum.[2] His Balkan heritage and military merits convinced Diocletian to trust him to oversee the eastern part of the empire. He also empowered General Maximian to be co-emperor of the Italic Peninsula and Western Europe.

Galerius was immensely proud of his Dacian origins and even envisioned renaming the eastern portion of Roman Empire the "Dacian Empire." He worshiped the sun-god Mithra, and when he moved into the heavily Christianized Thessalonica, the determined pagan emperor carried out severe persecutions against adherents of this new religion. He even crucified Christian legionaries. One of the victims was the proconsul Dimitrie, who had refused to carry out punitive orders against Christians. Dimitrie had been in prison where he met Nestor, a Christian legionary officer.

When the western co-emperor, Maximian (r. 286-305), who likewise had fought against a Carpi invasion, visited Thessalonica, Galerius entertained him with gladiatorial bouts. The climax of the cruel show was a demonstration offered by an undefeated giant gladiator named Lyeus. He fought Nestor, who glorified the power of Christian prayer to the spectators. It was Nestor who killed Lyeus, however, and the two stunned and humiliated co-emperors subsequently ordered Nestor to be beheaded. Dimitrie was slain as well.[3] This event initiated the martyrdom of Christian legionaries. Churches were built over the sites of their executions, and so encouraged interest in the Orthodox rite.

As for Galerius, he was struck by a mysterious illness and developed sores that were filled with stinking worms. This was taken to be a punishment for his blasphemies. On his death bed, the frightened and repentant emperor signed a new law canceling all previous anti-Christian proclamations. This was considered to have been an act of divine intervention, and it paved the way for General Constantine, who was promoted to the rank of co-Caesar.

Meanwhile, religious executions, the plague, and the low birth rate of the Romans caused the ranks of each legion to drop from six to two thousand Roman soldiers. The empty contingents were filled with barbarians. Little by little, the legions became less Roman and more foreign, engaging in bloody battles and pillaging on Italian soil, and seriously undermining the defensive capacity of the empire. Moreover, these ethnic legions, nicknamed *Dialectus*, took adversarial positions when the time came to proclaim their own emperors. Needless to say, the population's trust in the "Roman army" reached an all time low.

Eroded by so many internal fights, the empire collapsed and was consequently divided into two parts in the year 285. The Western Empire kept Rome as its capital, and the Eastern Empire chose Byzantium as its capital. Free Dacia belonged to neither. However, Diocletian replaced Dacia Aureliana with two provinces—Dacia Mediterranea with its capital at Serdica (Sofia) and Dacia Ripensis, south of Oltenia, with its capital at Ratiaria (Arcar) and later at Naissus (Niss in today's Serbia). Later these two "Dacias" along with Dardania (which extended to the Kosovo area), Moesia Inferior, and

Prevalitania (Montenegro) constituted the Diocese of Dacia, which became one of the thirteen of the empire.

All of these bureaucratic and territorial reforms could do nothing to stop the invaders who were galloping in from Eastern Europe, mostly Gepides and Goths (whom Jordanes called Getae/Getians). They used Free Dacia as a gateway for invasion of the Balkan Peninsula. By 305 Diocletian was completely exhausted by all of these developments, and, since he could no longer control them, he abdicated—the first Roman Emperor in history to do so. He became a passionate gardener and died six years later after refusing to eat. He was heart-broken over the slaughter of his co-emperors who had killed each other in their thirst for absolute power.

Because so many conflicts had erupted in other distant parts of the empire, most of the Roman troops were withdrawn from the Dacian lands. They were now garrisoned only by Legion XIII Gemina from Ratiaria and Legion II Herculia, across the Danube from Sucidava in Oescus. Meanwhile, north of the Danube Delta, the powerful Sarmatian tribes of Alani began their move south. The Romans took this to be an indication of potential stability above Dobrudja. They hoped to use the Sarmatians to secure the Lower Danube against the Mongol hordes which were now steadily advancing across distant Eastern Europe.

As the Roman Empire continued to deteriorate, a new Roman ruler of mythical proportions, Constantine (r. 306-337), introduced a spirit of revival. He was born in Dacia Ripensis at Naissus, the illegitimate son of Emperor Constantius I Cholorus and his servant Helena, the daughter of a local innkeeper. Young Constantine grew up under modest conditions among the local Dacians and was raised in the Christian spirit by his pious mother. But later he received royal education and grooming, and became an army general destined for a lasting glory.

Constantine I was the first emperor to paint the cross on the legionaries' shields, and from that time on they were known as Christian warriors. The civilian population followed the imperial example. Christianity toppled the pagan gods from their pedestals, causing temples to be transformed into churches. Within a short few years, the Roman heaven had been replaced by the Christian paradise, and now the Romans were the ones being called barbarians.

When they realized that a change in state religion was likely to cause further crises within the empire, the Dacians and Sarmatians formed their typical alliance and invaded the Roman province of Illyricum. Emperor Licinius (born in Dacia Nova from a Dacian peasant family) was unable to push back the invaders. Constantine's half-brother, General Flavius Dalmatius, saw this as an opportunity to distinguish himself and led his troops into Free Dacia, posting garrisons from Drobeta to the mouth of the Olt River.

Claiming to have conquered Dacia and even all of Scythia (obviously a misnomer for Getae/Dobrudja), Constantine and his legions headed toward Adrianople. There his army defeated the Byzantium garrison, and Emperor Licinius abdicated. One year later, in 325, Constantine executed Licinius and his son. Next he abolished the Praetorian Guard. Constantine's aim was to re-unite the empire, restore its glory, and revive the Golden Ages of Augustus and Trajan.

Now that he was in supreme command, Constantine decided to keep the lower Danube zone under Roman control. Free Dacia with its proverbial riches was his next military objective, and he ordered Apolodor's bridge rebuilt to its initial strength. Then, replicating the invasion of two hundred years earlier, Roman legions entered the friendly Banat region still populated with Roman colonists. As anticipated, Constantine's troops successfully carried out short but bloody fights with the Goths' cavalry, and triumphantly proceeded through the well-known passages that led to the wealth of Transylvania.

Facing certain death, the Gothic leaders agreed to an imposed peace, and as a good faith gesture they handed over forty thousand Goths and horses to the Roman army. Constantine did not venture into the rest of Free Dacia, but posted more garrisons in the lower part of today's Oltenia, Muntenia, and throughout Dobrudja. The Dacians were treated as equal commercial partners, and from this point onward, the gold, silver, salt, and other Dacian commodities were again flowing into the empire. This time, however, they went via Byzantium.

Since he was worried about the influx of barbarians from Eastern Europe, Constantine fortified the border between Braila and Drobeta, particularly between the Olt River and the Iron Gates. A massive wall was created out of excavated earth— 2 meters/6.5 feet high, 30 meters/60 feet wide, and 500 kilometers/311 miles long. There was a highway on top of this Constantine Wall—one that incorporated forts, watchtowers, and customs points. Non-stop patrols between watchtowers and forts ensured a strict accounting of what happened on and around the wall facing the Danube.

Constantine also built a new bridge over the Danube at Sucidava (probably on the same foundation as the one built by Aurelian). The formidable bridge measured 2.5 kilometers/1.5 miles and provided easy access to the Olt corridor into Transylvania. Another bridgehead was re-established at Dinogetia (Barbosi) above the Danube Delta. Many Danubian ports like Axiopolis (Cernavoda), Dierna (Orsova), and Istrus (destroyed by the Goths) were enlarged and fortified. The greater part of his efforts were aimed at expanding the port of Tomis, the major hub of shipping activity on the Black Sea.[4]

Since the safety of the Danubian land was now assured, commercial trade in grains and animals was revitalized. These commodities were provided to Byzantium via southern Dacia. To facilitate administration of the territories, the Dioceses of Dacia and Macedonia were included in the Prefecture of Illyricum.

Constantine's high regard for the Dacians is indicated by their immortal presence on the Triumphal Arch he placed near the Colosseum. Atop thirty-foot high columns, eight life-sized statues of Dacians dressed as *tarabostes* (military aristocrats) still observe the Roman activities going on below them. The Dacian statues were likely taken from other monuments that were falling into ruin; similarly, a large frieze showing Trajan leading a cavalry charge against Dacians is known to have been rescued from the decaying Forum and placed on the same arch. This was the only Roman monument to feature barbarians in such proud postures.[5]

It took six years for Constantine to rebuild the old Byzantine city (founded by the Greek navigator Bias in 667 B.C.), and in 330 he renamed it Constantinople (later Istanbul). This new Christian metropolis had a population of seven hundred thousand inhabitants and rivaled the fame of Rome, which was still controlled by the old pagan aristocracy. Soon, the young elite of the empire moved to Constantinople, which became known as Nova Roma.

A large quantity of the supplies that ensured the prosperity of this New Rome came from the Dacian gold, silver, copper, and iron and salt mines as well as from their grain production. Constantinople, in turn, had a huge influence on the Dacians as far as the spread of Christianity was concerned. The only obstacle preventing Constantine-the-Great from occupying Dacia was the Visigoths, who by then occupied Moldova and Wallachia.[6] When three hundred thousand displaced Sarmatians arrived in Dacia, for once Dacia and the Roman Empire shared the problem of the influx of barbarians. Many of them asked Constantine for permission to colonize Pannonia, Macedonia, and Thracia. The emperor granted their request but dispersed them throughout the Balkan Peninsula since this would dilute their military power. Shortly thereafter, Constantine I died (in 337), and his promise went unfulfilled.

His son Constantius II formed an alliance with the Sarmatian leader Arcaragante and repelled a Gothic invasion of Dacia. The Dacians then pushed the Romans south of the Danube, terminating the legacy of Constantine the Great in Dacia. Since it was left with no imperial protection, Dacia was again an open corridor for the Goths and Sarmatians who had been pushed out of Eastern Europe by other advancing barbarian tribes.

With no where to go, the crowded Sarmatians asked Constantius for help, and he let them settle in the Pannonian area where Tisza met the Danube. He took advantage of their numbers and planned to create a whole province of

Sarmatians that would be capable of defending the Danube up to the area of today's Budapest against the Germans.

The emperor called a meeting with the Sarmatian chieftains, but his negotiations ended with his narrow escape on a fast horse. This taught Constantius a lesson—nothing could change the barbarians, and only brute strength brought respect. Eventually he crushed a joint invasion of the Quadi and Sarmatians, chasing them back north of the Danubian border. Three years later, this second Christian emperor would die of malaria, leaving Dacia once again wide open to the flood of barbarians from Eastern Europe.

In the Western Empire, co-emperor Julian scored many victorious campaigns against various German tribes. With sixteen of their kings captured, Julian was able to offer imperial Rome the last shining glimpse of military glory. Ironically, the Germans' defeat led them to enroll in the ever-thinner ranks of the legions.

Julian understood that the Dacian warriors were a reliable force. Hence, in 360 he made sure they would be on his side before he marched to Constantinople to assume the throne of the unified empire. The sudden death of Constantius had prevented a civil war in which the Dacians could have played an important role by lending their support to Julian. The entire historic episode that replicated the Caesar-Pompey saga showed once again the importance of Dacians in European political and armed conflicts.

Even though Julian was raised like a Christian saint (and nicknamed the Apostate), he firmly believed that the glorious gods inherited from Homer's time must be revived to save an empire that was, to an ever greater degree, losing touch with its nationalistic and religious roots. His campaign in Asia forced him to withdraw precious legions that defended the civilized world against the barbarian invasions from the Rhine and Danube borders. At age thirty-two, and after only eight months as an emperor, Julian reached the Tigress and Euphrates Rivers where he was assassinated by a Christian legionary. Thus ended the last effort of a Roman ruler to turn back the religious clock.

Seven other emperors came to the throne between 363 and the end of the fourth century. They all made the same cardinal mistake of including too many barbarians in the regular legions and the palace guard. In their view, accepting the foreigners into the Roman military would discourage their co-nationalists from attacking the empire. The contrary proved to be the case, as the crushing numbers of barbarians always changed history.

While the Roman soldiers were becoming increasingly weaker, the enlisted barbarians advanced through the ranks of military and government. This process itself led the army and the empire into a pattern of free fall. Constantinople and Rome seemed to forget about Dacia and did not notice the names of

Hunia and *Tataria* appearing on the travel maps of areas beyond Scythia. Nor did they pay attention to the continuous flow of Mongol hordes making their way toward Eastern Europe. If the Danube and Rhine rivers or the Alps and Carpathian Mountains were for the Romans impregnable natural frontiers, they proved to be no barriers to stop the barbarian invasions into Europe.

In the middle of the fourth century, the barbarian penetrations caused Dacia to be fragmented into smaller kingdoms. Its ample Roman constructions were dismantled and converted into practical living facilities. In anticipation of violent times ahead, imperial landmarks were stripped of their construction materials. The entrances to the amphitheater in Ulpia Sarmizegethusa were walled up with stones, and it was rebuilt as a military fortress.

The Dacians undoubtedly shared Rome's conviction that the incoming barbarians were a threat to civilization. Recognizing that it was futile to fight them, the Dacians found a way to benefit from their presence.

The warriors of these mega tribes were extremely strong when they entered Dacia and left their families. But they became weak and were fewer in number when they returned since they were often defeated in their raids. This made it easy for the Dacians to impose their laws on their barbarian "guests." Moreover, when the barbarians did return with booty, part of it was demanded by the Dacians. Most importantly, Dacia was neither plundered, nor forced to give up any land. Its solid status in the center of Eastern Europe remained undiminished.

The most dangerous barbarians to cross the Eurasian steppes and invade Europe in the fourth century were the Huns. Sometime after the year 360, they arrived at the Don River and crushed the Ostrogothic kingdom. Then, branching out in many directions, they headed toward Europe.

Short, wiry, and wearing a pony tail on top of their shaved heads, these savages were the quintessence of cruelty in those times. Their reputation for earth-scorching came from their habit of destroying everything that grew or stood on the ground. Their image as primitive horsemen in furs who ate the raw meat "marinated" under their saddles and who drank mare's milk induced both fear and disgust. Their culture was entirely *cabaline* (horse-based), their diet based on meat and milk as they had never tasted bread.

Ammianus Marcellinus (ca. 325-ca. 391) described them in one of his thirty one history books as "unreasoning beasts, utterly ignorant of the difference between right and wrong." They had no concept of religion and worshipped only the horse. By using stirrups to lead their horses, they freed both hands to shoot arrows more often and more precisely. Savage fighters, they used their terror reputation in psychological warfare that never failed to lead to victory.

The Huns destroyed the Gothic kingdom in Eastern Europe. As a result, the Goths were divided into Visigoths, who remained west of the Dniester River, and the Ostrogoths, who lived east of the same river. On their way to the Danube, the Huns smashed into the Alani, "who were [their] equals in battle, but unlike them in civilization, manners and appearance." Exhausted by their incessant attacks, the Alani were "subdued." Thus the strongest military obstacle in Eastern Dacia was overrun by the Huns. Jordanes says they "live in the form of men [but] they have the cruelty of wild beasts."[7]

When defeated, many tribes joined the Hunic invaders to raid the Eastern Roman Empire. Unfortunately for Dacia, most of these incoming savage hordes settled in the nearby Pannonian plains which offered rich pastures for their horses. Their presence forced the Gothic tribes toward the Balkan and Italic peninsulas.

When the co-emperor brothers Valentinian and Valens initiated the Pannonian dynasty in 364, they were essentially attempting to prolong the imperial agony which was being accelerated by countless barbarian attacks. In 370, the Ostrogoths, who were defeated by the Huns, asked Valens's permission to settle along the Danube in the Balkan region. In an effort to protect his natural borders from barbarian infestation already present in Dacia Nova, the emperor denied their request.

With the Huns on their heels, the Ostrogoths invaded Western Dacia and were forced into the area of the Roxolani living in Pannonia. Unable to challenge these Sarmatians who would eventually be backed by their faithful allies, the Dacians, many Ostrogothic tribes joined the Asiatic hordes. Others became mercenaries in the Roman army.

In 376 the Huns delivered another decisive blow to the Goths fighting under their chieftain Athanaric near the Dniester River. This caused mass panic in Dacia, as they were known for destroying cities first. Many Dacians fled from Sarmizegethusa and other important centers heading towards the secluded mountain refuges. Since they were hoping to return, wealthy people buried their gold and silver coins.

Forced westward and southward by the intruding Huns, more waves of Visigoths headed toward the Lower Danube and invaded Southern Dacia which was already saturated with still more displaced Goths. A sort of domino effect in migration dumped everyone into one land—Dacia. It had become a sort of final dam ready to burst and overflow into Pannonia or Roman Moesia.

Emperor Valens became determined to annihilate this Gothic reservoir of military power and sent his legions across the Danube (probably via Constantine's bridges, since the others were either in the hands of the Goths or had been destroyed by them). General Victor led the cavalry charges while

General Arintheus and his infantry liquidated the marginal packs of Gothic warriors who tried to defend themselves.

Pressing with all their strength to rid the Danube line of Goths, the legions destroyed their settlements and captured a huge number of prisoners, warriors and civilians alike. The cold rains of autumn forced the legionaries to march back to the winter camps in Moesia and Thracia. The captured Goths were taken to work in cities or on the farms. This stirred protests from free Goths, who demanded that their nobility be returned. Their demands were refused.

In 370, after three years of continuous heavy fighting, Valens and King Athanaric met in the middle of the Danube, probably at Drobeta on the rebuilt Apolodor's bridge. Since he was forced to accept concessions in exchange for peace, the emperor agreed to allow the Visigoths to settle in the Roman provinces south of the Danube, mainly in Dacia Ripensis.

Some six years of apparent peace followed, during which the Roman administration abused the Goths. Many were used as slave labor to enlarge the fortified cities of Callatis, Histria, and Tomis, as well as thirty-three other Roman fortifications in Dobrudja.

During the harvest season of 375, the Quadi invaded Pannonia from the west; they were supported by the Sarmatian cavalry from Western Dacia. Because the local imperial garrisons failed to coordinate their defensive efforts, the invaders inflicted an appalling level of damage on the Roman communities there. The granddaughter of Constantine the Great, Princess Constantia, happened to be on a pleasure trip and barely avoided the destructive path of the German invaders.

General Equitius, with two legions recruited from Moesia and Pannonia, encountered the invaders and almost decimated the Sarmatian cavalry in Dacia Mediterranea. Dacia Ripensis was also invaded, but the intruders were pushed back by the young General Theodosius (the future emperor). Trying to replicate the example of the Goths in 375, the Quadi asked Valentinian to allow them to settle inside the empire.

The negotiations turned ugly when the Quadi were so disrespectful and demanding that Valentinian suffered a stroke and died. His son Gratian (also born in Sirmium) followed him on the throne of the Western Roman Empire. The Quadi saw this as evidence of Roman weakness and opportunistically changed their plans. Joined by the surviving Sarmatians, the Germans invaded the western Roman provinces.

Far in the Eastern European plains, a new Hunic invasion forced more Visigoths into Dacia. They asked Valens for the privilege of joining the other Gothic colonists in the Balkans. Based on his previous positive experience with them, the emperor accepted their request on two conditions: that all the weapons would be surrendered on the right bank of the Danube and all Gothic children would be raised in the civilized Roman manner. With the Huns following on their heels, the Visigoths accepted these humiliating conditions. This turned out to be a decision that had monumental implications for both sides.

Almost one million Goths, including two hundred thousand warriors, evacuated Central Dacia. They crossed the Danube where it meets the Ordessos (Arges) River, or probably on Constantine's bridge, and entered Lower Moesia and Thracia. Thus the year 376 marked the end of one hundred years of Dacian and Visigoth co-existence.

Valens had not anticipated the massive numbers of Goths that would come into his territory. They represented an obvious threat to the rest of the Balkans. It was too late to do anything about it, except disarm and feed the hungry invaders. Soon, however, the Visigoths found out that free food sent to them by the emperor was being sold to them at high prices by the corrupt Roman administration from Aegyssus (now Tulcea in Romania). Moreover, they had to pay taxes, which impoverished them. Forced to sell everything they had, including their daughters, the Visigoths found themselves humiliated and starving to death.

Meanwhile, the Ostrogoths who had defected from the camps of the Huns requested the same imperial favor, namely, to be allowed to settle in Thracia. Because he was already caught up in the Asian campaign and worried by the huge number of Goths present in the Danubian provinces, Valens rejected their plea. The Ostrogoths, searching for land, then attacked and pushed many Sarmatian tribes out of Western Dacia.

Taking advantage of the inefficient Roman border patrols, many Ostrogoths crossed the Danube in Moesia, thus doubling the number of indigent co-nationalists in this area. But these newcomers were different—they were armed and on horseback. At the same time, Valens ran out of food supplies with which to keep them calm. The Gothic chieftains went to Marcianopolis to plead their desperate cause, but Governor Lupicinus greeted them with contempt. Thankful to have escaped alive, they returned to their anxious camps where collective cries of sorrow and shouts of revolt ignited the flames of revenge. War was immediately unleashed from the lands of Dacia Mediterranea and Dacia Ripensis.

The troops led by the Roman governor were defeated and slaughtered without mercy. The haughty Lupicinus deserted the battlefield, lucky to escape with his life. Tens of thousands of Goths led by Alavius/Alaviv and Fritigern devastated the Roman settlements and proclaimed themselves masters of Dacia Nova in the Dobrudja area between the Danube and the Black Sea. Their families were forced to live in fortified camps surrounded by circles of enchained wagons.

Armed with captured weapons and revived by the food they had plundered, the army of the Goths was thirsting for revenge. It headed toward Adrianople, the imperial administrative center. Since they had a common interest in the outcome the Dacian and Getian cavalrymen joined the invasion. The freed Gothic children told of the horrors they had experienced in Roman captivity. Their stories intensified and inflamed the bloody rage of the Goths. In blind frustration they flattened the Roman towns and killed their colonists.

Valens hurriedly led his troops to Dacia Nova. The first battle took place south of Tomis. In the absence of a clear victory, each army retreated to its respective camps. As anticipated, this encounter led to further battles. Trying to cut off the Visigoths from the rest of their allies, General Sebastian and his cavalry proved successful and blocked passage between Free Dacia and Moesia by spreading his troops along the Danube line. The isolated two hundred thousand Goths redirected their attack south along the shore of the Black Sea, advancing a few hundred kilometers down to Hellespont (Dardanelle). The Sarmatians attacked from the west of Pannonia, thereby marching into the Balkans from the opposite side.

Since he was determined to teach the rebellious Goths a lesson once and for all, and since he was also unwilling to share his victory with his nephew, co-emperor Gratian, who was on his way to provide assistance, Valens did not wait for enforcements to arrive. Instead, he went out to meet the barbarians. He placed his military camp near the walls of Adrianople. On August 9, 378 the supremely optimistic emperor led his outnumbered troops 20 kilometers/12 miles away from the city. Falling into the trap of overconfidence, he charged the Goths who were led by Fritigern.

This was a suicidal confrontation, one that resulted in the emperor's being killed and the massacre of forty thousand legionaries—the largest military defeat in Roman history. It was also supreme proof that cavalry attacks were the way to fight in the future. This one-day battle ended six centuries of imperial military hegemony. It also marked the beginning of the end of Roman rule in the Balkans.

When there were no legions left to defend Moesia, the Alani and Goths thundered toward Constantinople. After they had devastated the suburbs of the capital, Emperor Gratian rushed fresh legions into the battle, and the raiders had to withdraw to hospitable Dacian lands south of the Danube. For the next one hundred years, the Goths and the Alani were a military force in Europe that took part in every barbarian conquest.

The Dacians did not follow their example. Instead, they decided to stay where they were and defend their millennial territories, which were now a sort of crossroads for invasions from all directions. United by the same language and traditions, they firmly defended the valuable territories of

Transylvania protected by the Carpathian Mountains. This seemed to be a first step in uniting the Dacian tribes into a powerful kingdom again. It did not, however, produce much, primarily because internal quarrels erupted over land disputes.

Ultimately these quarrels resulted in feudal division of the land and caused many tiny states to be formed, states which were led by ambitious warriors. Ironically, these local chieftains advised the invaders to attack their neighbors so as to undermine their strength. Another way for a leader to extend his domain was to marry either the daughter of a rival or the widow of a dead leader. Clearly, no royal figure of Burebista's and Decebalus's status emerged out of these convulsive events. Yet, unlike all of the other Eastern European tribes, the Dacians kept a firm grip on their lands.

Forced to subdue the massive Gothic invasions, Emperor Theodosius I agreed to have the friendly Visigoths settle on the edge of the empire. He hoped they would discourage invasions by other barbarians. Theodosius, a former governor of Upper Moesia who fought between 373-75 against the Sarmatians and Goths of Dacia, knew all too well that it was less expensive to subsidize the barbarians than to fight them. Moreover, in 382 Theodosius named the Goths *federates* (military allies) and allowed them to start new colonies in Thracia. Thus, he separated the free Goths from those who were "Romanized"; nearly fifty thousand of their warriors were incorporated into the Roman army, inducing its military reversal.

One of these Goths was immortalized by history as a supreme example of military leadership that happened to hasten the fall of the Roman Empire. This was the extraordinary Alaric, the future king of the Visigoths and the conqueror of Rome.

Alaric was born in 376 in the Danube Delta in Dacia Nova. At the time this area was under the rule of General Julius. Alaric's family name was Balta, of the Balti tribes, and his father was in the transportation business, ferrying Roman troops and traders by boat across the Danube.[8] An orphan and hostage, Alaric was baptized Christian; at the age of twelve, he entered the imperial cadet school. His exceptional military talents were recognized and, at age eighteen, he received orders to form two legions in Dacia Nova and Thracia and present them in six weeks at the governor's palace in Moesia. Naturally, Alaric focused his recruitment activity in the familiar region of Dobrudja, which was full of Goths; his headquarters were in Tomis.

Still faithful to his emperor, Alaric returned to his native land only to see with his own eyes how much the Goths were being exploited by the mercantile and arrogant Romans. Nevertheless, he obeyed his orders and continued his mission along the Hebrus (Maritza) Valley, recruiting more than twelve thousand men. Suddenly, he found himself leading a real army of Visigoths. Taking advantage of Theodosius's death and of the pacific mood of Theodosius II, he raided Thracia, Macedonia, and Greece. Thus, unofficially, he became the ruler of the Balkan Peninsula.

When he reached the gates of Constantinople, Alaric chose to negotiate a reward and accept a prestigious position rather than risk defeat. Theodosius II recognized the huge potential Alaric presented if his army were to be used against his rival Honorius, the teenage co-emperor of the Western Empire. In 397, at age twenty-one Alaric was promoted to the rank of Master General of the Empire. He had already proved to be a first class leader.

At the same time, the Visigoth warriors carried his image on their shields and proclaimed him to be their king. Both titles represented an irrevocable contradiction in terms and a great dilemma for Alaric. (His name meant "Everyone's Ruler" in Gothic.) He was bribed with the province of Illyria and free access to Dacia Ripensis, where the Goths would be able to safely rest between two wars.

In the meantime, as far as the barbarians were concerned, all roads led to Rome. The Roman population of one million was an irresistible target for the hungry hordes looking to plunder or destroy. Rome had become an almost open city, and in 402 Honorius moved his court to Ravenna. The city was surrounded by wetlands that were difficult for invaders on horseback to traverse. The lives of Roman citizens had come to be marked by such uncertainty and harshness that Emperor Theodosius I ordered the Olympic Games interrupted. They had been held continuously for the past twelve centuries.

Within the empire the traditional population of Roman extraction declined and the birthrate of barbarian immigrants exploded. The Romans themselves became a minority and were forced to speak the corrupted Latin of the new settlers. This enormous ethnic mix had developed because of a need for mutual benefits: the Romans wanted cheap labor and the barbarians wanted to improve their standard of living. But the plague and other diseases introduced into Rome by the immigrants killed millions and further reduced the number of legionaries.

Such were the grim conditions faced by the Roman Empire when in 406 the Huns settled in the northern portion of today's Yugoslavia. Their hordes attempted to invade central Europe, but they were stopped and brutally driven off by the Germans. Confused and divided, the Huns displaced the Goths, who migrated to the upper end of Italy—this time not to destroy it, but in search of shelter. Unable to prevent a Hunic invasion, Rome chose to pay the Mongolians a yearly tribute rather than fight them.

It was because of these circumstances that Alaric had no problem replacing the officials of Byzantium with Visigoth leaders. Almost literally overnight the Eastern Roman Empire had become a Visigoth empire—for a short while.

Alaric had plans to attack Rome next, but the city still garnered respect and its legendary military might still aroused fear in the hearts of potential invaders. Indeed, its impenetrable walls were longer than 30 kilometers/19 miles, but it sheltered a population of mostly non-Romans living on the state's welfare. Oddly, these barbarian residents of Rome, along with Chinese, Jews, Negroes, Indians, and other races, now listened each day to a new sound—that of church bells.

Rome was declared the New Jerusalem by the Christians. It became inundated with non-loyal citizens. The *cloaca maximat* (sewer) became a subterranean city of bandits, lepers, and other undesirables who terrorized the population at night. Panic and death were omnipresent, and survival was a matter of luck. Corruption and social decay had reached its peak. Emperors were no longer towering figures, leaders who displayed fortitude and inspired respect. The Roman army, poorly trained, ill equipped, and scarcely paid, was a sort of state within the state. The infallibility of Rome had become a memory. It was only a question of time before the final collapse.

Meanwhile, the Goths from the Roman army and throughout the entire empire rebelled, a development that triggered resentment throughout the rest of the population toward the "Romanized barbarians." In retaliation, Goths and other Germans in Pavia were murdered, and the practice of anti-barbarian genocide spread throughout Italy. This supplied Alaric with a huge number of barbarian soldiers who had escaped persecution. In a short time, the Goths from within the empire united with the free Goths from outside it; these groups joined the Germans and other barbarians whose families had been killed by rampaging Romans. In effect, all of the empire's slaves and deserters had also enrolled in Alaric's army.

At this historic moment, the Goths feared only the Huns. They rushed to conquer lands not dominated by the Mongols. In an attempt to reapply the blackmail tactics he had used in Constantinople, Alaric initiated negotiations that could save Rome. After blockading the city, he received 2,270 kilograms/5,000 pounds of gold and 13,620 kilograms/30,000 pounds of silver. It is not known if he also was given a demanded 4,000 silk robes and 1,500 kilograms/1.6 tons in peppercorn, the latter being thought to be as good as gold. Regardless, he besieged the capital for the next two years. On August 24, 410, before sunrise, something went disastrously wrong for the defenders: the slave Goths inside Rome opened the Salarian Gate (the Salt Gate), and Alaric's hordes stormed in to plunder Rome in the way only the barbarians could do. The forty thousand liberated slaves killed more Roman citizens than the entire invading army did. Yet, none of the churches were touched.

Moreover, none of the thousands who sought refuge in the churches or in their courtyards met the sword, or suffered rape, or plunder by the conquerors. And, any and all treasures that bore the name of a saint were returned to the churches.

The miraculous outcome of this attack was due to Alaric's commitment to Christianity: he was one of the few barbarian leaders who had been baptized in Dacia Nova. The respectful treatment received by Christians and Christian institutions in Rome at this time was probably the most obvious sign that the barbarian world was ready to embrace the Christian religion and to begin a civilized life with new laws and a system of human values. Meanwhile, the captured patricians were sold in the markets for handsome rewards. Statues or ornaments that shone like gold were melted down to ensure easier transport. After six long days of devastation, the Visigoths left Rome with five hundred wagons filled with loot and all the gold, jewelry, or other precious objects they could find.

Thus, after 619 years Rome, the Eternal City, was conquered and became the "Lost City." The imperial court stayed in Ravenna, and Britannia was evacuated, marking a further weakness of Roman militarism. After eleven centuries of global domination, Roman power had reached an inglorious end.

Alaric died on his way to conquer the south of Italy, an event that abruptly stopped the Visigoth's plan to search for a country they could call their own. Eventually they were accepted in southern Gallia, after which they freed Placida, the half-sister of Honorius. In return, they received sixty thousand barrels of grain from Rome. As for the inglorious Honorius, who ruled for twenty-eight years, the only fact recorded about him is that he enrolled any Goths who were willing in the Roman army. However, this, too, proved to be a mistake of imperial proportions.

By the beginning of the fifth century, the greatest danger for the Dacians came from the Huns. Constantinople preferred to pay an annual tribute to then to ensure that they would remain north of the Danube in Pannonia. Taking advantage of the fact that Theodosius II became emperor at age seven, in 408 Uldin and his Huns invaded Moesia. They were, however, severely defeated by the legions already waiting for them. The Huns were driven north of the Danube, a considerable distance westward from Dacia. They, in turn, pushed the hordes of Bavarians and Vandals into Illyricum and Noricum (Dalmatia).

Aware of the gloomy fact that countless tribes of barbarians were amassed on their borders, the Dacians chose to move into their impregnable forests and mountains. This meant that they had fewer problems to deal with. Because the history of the fifth century was relatively quiet, mention is only made of them as being under the occupation of the powerful Gepidaes.

The hordes of Huns were united for the first time by Attila (r. 434-453), who conquered Caucasia and most of what is today Ukraine, thereby forcing a segment of the Ostrogoth population into submission. This ambitious Hunic king, who was taken hostage by the Roman military and educated at the court of Ravena, always envisioned himself as a universal emperor. Moreover, he had already begun his race to dominate Europe.

Arriving in Europe from what is today's Russia, the Huns first invaded the Danube territories. They pushed wave after wave of defeated barbarians into Dacia and so unwillingly created a bastion that they did not want to challenge. Moreover, they needed abundant pastures for their horses, not wooded mountains and so did not intend to advance through Central Dacia. Instead, their attacks were aimed toward Western Europe.

Under Attila, the Huns settled in the flatland of Pannonia (today's great Hungarian plains), where they subdued the Ostrogoths and the Sarmatians. Packs of their warriors entered Dacia looking for plunder, only to find stubborn resistance. When they reached Drobeta, the vengeful Huns destroyed the Daco-Roman city that had proudly survived so much violent history.

It is believed (but not proven), that one of Attila's hordes entered Dacia through the Iron Gates of Transylvania in search of its legendary gold. More likely, they sacked and destroyed Ulpia Sarmizegethusa, but they did not advance beyond that point into Central and Northern Dacia. They rarely fought in dense forests and mountains where their fast horses and war tactics, well-suited for flatlands, were worthless. Instead of fighting further, in 435 Attila asked for a double tribute from Constantinople, a request denied by proud Emperor Marcian (r. 450-457). He replied that he had only iron, not gold, for the Huns.

In retaliation for this affront, the savage Mongols moved along the Danube and devastated the castri, forts, fortresses, and the Roman cities of Illyricum, Dacia Mediterranea, and Dacia Ripensis. The Huns used the sword, fire, and pillage to destroy the beautiful Roman centers of Arcadiopolis, Marcianopolis, Naissus, Philippopolis, Ratiaria, Sardica, Singidunum, Sirmium, Viminacium, and others.

In 442 they raided Thracia with such violence that it never recovered or rose again as a country or a nation. Each Thracian prisoner was released in exchange for twelve gold coins. Those who could not produce ransom, excepting the young women, were killed. Attila thus occupied most of the lands south of the Danube extending all the way to the gates of Constantinople.

Fortunately for the Byzantines, the overconfident Attila sent a good part of his army to conquer the rest of Moesia. He therefore delayed the siege of

Constantinople but asked for tribute in gold and a strip of grazing land of 495 kilometers/308 miles along the Danube, from Singidunum to Novae (exactly half of the Dacian southern fluvial frontier). The Romans were forced to evacuate this area. To obviate against conflict with Free Dacia and the powerful German allies crowded within it, the northern bank of the Danube was not included in Attila's transaction.

Lengthy negotiations followed, and there was no Hunic attack on free Dacians. Finally, Attila received a payment of 2,724 kilograms/6,000 pounds of gold and all the prisoners and deserters from his army, so he retreated from Constantinople. A total tribute of 5,902 kilograms/13,000 pounds of gold was the price to leave the city untouched. The Huns eventually retreated to their main camps in what is now modern Hungary.

The huge equestrian Hunic Empire with five hundred thousand warriors did not have towns or cities, and they did not practice agriculture. Attila's imperial residence was in Attilopolis (probably Obuda/Buda)—a sea of round tents with not a single dwelling of brick or stone. The center of his capital was marked by the log huts in which his concubines lived. These one room dwellings created a circle around the imperial palace, which was also made of wood. After having devastated Europe so thoroughly, the Huns discovered bread, salt, and wine, and they even learned to use wood as a construction material.

Their contacts with the Goths, Scythians, and Sarmatians living on the outskirts of Western Dacia influenced the taste of the Hunic elite, who already ate from wooden dishes. Numerous captured barbarian noblemen lived at the imperial court of Buda as hostages and spoke the seemingly common Scythian language. The remainder of the Huns became more conversant in the Gothic language than their own native tongue. Soon, Attila's chieftains and his courtiers proudly wore royal costumes that were extremely heavy because of the gold and precious stones woven into the fabrics.

Since they had so little respect for the agreements they had made with Rome and Constantinople, the Huns controlled the Danube by cruising it in canoes made from trees. They pirated commercial vessels and killed anyone who tried to avoid taxation. They destroyed Bononia (Vidin), but did not cross the Danube into Central Dacia. The Dacians and their German allies were the only people to fight back, and the Huns left them alone.

Certainly Attila did not want to re-enter Eastern Europe. In 451 he headed to wealthy central Europe and invaded Belgica and Gaul, where he was repulsed by Flavius Aetius who put together a coalition of Franks and Goths. This gifted general had the distinction of being born in Durostorum (Isaccea) in Southern Dacia, and also of being the last successful defender of the Western Empire.

At one point the Huns considered entering Italy and attacking Rome. The idea originated with the sister of Valentinian III, Princess Honoria, who was in love with a servant. The emperor wanted Honoria to marry an aristocrat, and she secretly asked Attila to defend her honor. The desperate message was sealed by Honoria's ring. The present was misunderstood by Attila as an invitation to marry the princess, whom he had already declared his wife and who would bring as a dowry one-half of the Western Roman Empire. Honoria hurried to correct the mistake with a very urgent message that further aggravated the situation.

With his enormous ego deeply wounded, Attila rushed his hordes toward Rome. His orders were for total destruction of the city. Legend has it that Leo the Great and his papal procession dressed in imposing attire and waited outside the capital with singing choirs to meet the Huns, hoping to avoid a doomsday scenario for the city.

It is doubtful that the glitter and authority of the Church convinced Attila not to attack Rome. More likely, Pope Leo made such a tempting offer in gold that he decided to listen to the citizens' pleas for mercy. An alternative explanation is that the cholera outbreak in Rome made the Huns decide to withdraw. Jordanes wrote that the superstitious Attila remembered that "Alaric did not live long after the sack of Rome"[9] and decided not to take a risk. Whatever the reasons may have been, Rome was spared. Nevertheless, Attila left sixty thousand Huns in Italy to keep Roman imperial power in check and collect annual tribute. He led his hordes out of Italy only to loot Western Europe, including the cities of Milan and Paris. Once again, the record of Hunic brutality was written in blood.

Eventually, the Huns regrouped and retreated to the familiar steppes of Pannonia. Because this area was overcrowded, some hordes spanned out into the eastern plains of the Tisza River. This being the case, the Dacians left their threatened locations and withdrew eastward into Transylvania where they would be protected by the Carpathian Mountains. They thus avoided being plundered and killed, as was their case later as well with the Magyar invasion.

Suddenly Attila-the-Terrorizer-of-the-World met a surprising and lamentable end. At age forty-eight he married the beautiful Ildico, the daughter of a German chieftain whose sons he had executed. After a wild party, the aging groom locked himself in his royal palace with his terrified bride. He was later found dead, with a massive nasal hemorrhage and his throat slit, probably by the vengeful young girl. Those who buried Attila were murdered in order to keep the location of his tomb an eternal secret.

Attila's sixty sons succeeded in rending the mammoth equestrian empire that now extended from the Caucasus to the Rhine. Once it was splintered, the countless hordes of barbarians left themselves open to destruction. The first to revolt against the Huns were the Ostrogoths; they were followed by the Alani, Heruli, Rugiani, and most of the Gepidaes, all of whom lived in Free Dacia or near its borders. They were highly motivated in so far as they had the support of Emperor Gratian, who believed that the immense military power of the new German coalition would be able to destroy the Huns.

In the memorable battle of 454 on the Netad River banks of Pannonia, the Hun horsemen thundered into disaster against the heavily armed German cavalry clad in mail, carrying shields, long lances, and broadswords.[10] More than thirty thousand Huns were slaughtered there, including Ellac, the oldest son of Attila. This defeat destroyed the myth of their invincibility. They would never recover and so never again constitute a danger for the nations of Europe. The Dacians lost no time in casting out these horrific invaders from the Transylvanian land.

The Huns subsequently became scattered in all directions. They were pursued by the Germans who killed any Hunic males regardless of their age. The Pannonian fields were occupied by the Heruli and other Goths, and the escaping Huns attempted their last invasion south of the Danube. They entered Thracia in the year 457 but were defeated by the legions of Emperor Leo I (born in Thracia). The head of Dengisich, another one of Attila's sons, was displayed in the center of the Constantinople racetrack.

The rest of the Huns who escaped under Ernac, the youngest son of Attila, moved through the Dacian corridor near the Black Sea toward Scythia, but they were they suffered a crushing defeat by the Avari, a rising military power in Eastern Europe. Others of them were mercilessly intercepted all over Europe and slaughtered by the Germans, Goths, and Romans. Some tribes incorporated into the Hunic hordes, like the Fossatisi and Sacromontisi, entered Dacia, where they unconditionally surrendered. In due time, they vanished without a trace. Still other tribes of Huns found themselves running for shelter toward Dalmatia and the Western Empire. One wandering tribe ended up in the protective wetland along the Adriatic Sea. With a group of Roman deserters, they founded what would become the city of Venice.

The destruction of the Mongolian Empire put Emperor Marcian in full charge of the Danubian lands which he generously appropriated to the coalition of the victors. According to Jordanes, the Gepides were pacified in so far as they were allowed to settle in "all Dacia," meaning north of the Danube: The Goths received Pannonia, where the Huns used to camp. The Alani received Scythia Minor (Dobrudja) and Lower Moesia. As for the remaining Huns, "swarming everywhere, they betook themselves into Romania,"[11] south Moesia above Thracia, where they were quickly displaced by Marcian's legions.

When they, too, regained their independence, the Ostrogoths settled south of Dacia in parts of Moesia and became loyal allies of Constantinople. A few Gothic tribes with their enormous herds of horses and cattle chose the flatlands of the middle Danube and became productive farmers. The Sarmatians who escaped annihilation at the hands of the Goths and Huns found safe haven in Banat, the land of the Dacianized Tribalii.

Like the Getians and Tribalii, the Dacian tribes of Albocensi, Bastarni, Biefi, Buridavensi, Costoboci, Dardani, Getians, Moti, Predavensi, and other Magni Dacians, to name a few, constituted the majority of the population who had never left their ancient Transylvanian and Carpatho-Danubian lands. They adopted Christianity and adorned their candlesticks and fibulas with crosses and Christ signs. Meanwhile, nearly one million Dacians from other tribes thrived south of the Danube, in the small Dacias founded by Hadrian, Aurelian, Diocletian, and other emperors.[12] They became known as Valachians, the ancestors of the present of Balkan Aromanians.

During these turbulent and bloody times, the Germans were the only force that could stop the barbarians coming in from the steppes of Eastern Europe. By rejecting them as neighbors, the Germans prevented the destruction of the traditional people of Europe. Because they were the major source of muscle in the Roman army, they felt entitled to take over the empire. The Vandals left their lands on the Baltic coast and fought their way into Pannonia and Eastern Dacia. In 406, they entered Gaul; later they were bribed by Rome to settle in Spain. There they allied themselves with the Alani, built ships, conquered Carthage, and established a Vandal kingdom in Africa. They then took over the area of the Mediterranean Sea south of Italy, and in 455 they plundered Rome.

This lengthy series of defeats clearly demonstrated one thing—Roman military power was on the wane. Increasingly the empire needed to appeal to barbarian forces to solve even its internal conflicts. The fact that these distant socio-political developments occurred a significant distance from Dacia, as they had four centuries earlier, meant the land and its people were left in peace. Even though the gold of Transylvania continued to strongly tempt Rome, its emperors preferred a Free Dacia north of the Danube. Any further Roman occupation meant that the legions, already thinned to a minimum and spread across three continents, would again be over-extended. Almost by default, the Dacians became the implicit guardians of one-third of the Danube and the most vulnerable western shores of the Black Sea.

With the German military power on the rise, Odoacer, chieftain of the Heruli and now a Roman general, declared himself king of Italy, and Emperor Romulus Augustulus was dethroned in Ravena. Thus in 476 the Western Roman Empire ceased to exist, and the Germans founded their own European empire. In the meantime, a young Roman officer of only eighteen years of age, born in Vienna to a royal Ostrogoth family, refused to serve Rome and returned to serve his people. Leading six thousand warriors, he confronted the Sarmatians of Dacia, who had filled the void left by the Huns and occupied the former Western Dacian territories as far west as Singidunum (Belgrade). The same story was repeating itself again and again: when more than one group of people claimed the same piece of land, the force of arms had to be applied to solve the problem

The Sarmatians were led by kings Babai and Beukan, who dominated the most important tribes of the region but had little military strength. After a bloody battle, both of them were killed and many Sarmatians were captured. Those who avoided slavery retreated to protective Central Dacia. The name of this victorious Ostrogothic cavalry leader who refused to server Rome was Theodoric, the future Roman emperor. He returned to Vienna with many captives and a great deal of war booty, mainly gold.

After 473 the name of the Sarmatians as contemporary people would never again appear in history. It is worth recalling their glorious military tradition. It made six Roman emperors proud to call themselves *Sarmaticus Maximum.* Roman coins and monuments were dedicated to the victories against the Sarmatians who contributed so much to the longevity of the Dacian people.

Theodoric was given many names—"the Ostrogoth" because of his nation, "the Great" because he reigned for thirty-three years, and "the Heretic" because he adopted the Aryan beliefs. This former hostage in Constantinople was also nicknamed "the Second Trajan" because he succeeded in maintaining apparent Roman domination of lands that stretched from Beograd to the Atlantic Ocean and from south of the Danube to Sicily. This barbarian found himself in a position to name bishops and Popes. What history remembers about him is that Theodoric succeeded in transforming Italy into an Ostrogothic kingdom and integrated Germans into the civilized world.

Yet, Rome was still casting a long shadow over Dacia. The great Theodoric respected Free Dacia's borders and even fed the first migratory Slavs who settled below the Danube, under the condition that they would not attack Dacia. Having learned from the past, he did not want the belligerent Dacians to again unleash the type of nightmarish raids they had carried out in Moesia during the previous centuries. The Dacians were not to be challenged or undermined by anyone, especially given that their numbers had been doubled by the now permanent presence of their Gepidaen guests.

While the Dacian people continued to live in peace, the Italic Peninsula fell into further decline, and none of the fifth century's emperors could save it. Wave after wave of Alani, Franks, Vandals, and others headed toward the Roman Empire in order to plunder it. Its emperors raised the prices of goods and increased taxes, attempting to keep their governments and nation alive. At the same time, they lowered the wages of the workers, legionaries, and veterans. Greedy governors and other Roman officials were illegally squeezing incomes from millions of frustrated laborers. The majority of independent farmers vanished, victims of the pressures coming from inflation. Un-repaired roads, bridges, and aqueducts paralyzed the empire's systems of communications and commerce. Rome itself was in ruins and essentially beyond repair. It was declining at an alarming and unstoppable speed.

These deplorable circumstances turned out to have an unexpected impact on the population—the once proud imperial Romans preferred to be dominated by the barbarians rather than suffer the consequences of any more wars. Ironically, it was the barbarians who brought a new humane spirit to Rome by terminating the gruesome gladiator fights in public arenas. Since they were poorly trained, ill-equipped, and underpaid, the Roman legionaries lost interest in fighting in territories or against enemies they had never heard of.

Due to the lack of imperial funds, the legionaries stationed in the far regions, including the Balkans, had to be compensated in land. This transformed soldiers into permanent farmers. Others chose different trades, and some even built boats and became middle class citizens. They constructed strong commercial centers on the outskirts of the empire and became entrepreneurs, small warlords, and the future knights of the early Middle Ages in the Balkans.

Like its emperors and kings, no empire can last forever, and Rome met the ultimate fate of all empires—collapse. It reached too far lands with too few troops and tried to rule barbarians who were too numerous and too strong. Finally, the ancient world of the Roman Empire, one of the longest lasting empires on earth, officially came to an end in the year 493 when Theodoric killed Odoacer; both were non-Latin rulers. From that point onward, all the Dacian lands located at the end of the civilized world would be directly affected only by what happened in Constantinople. Even as a Latin speaking nation, the Dacians were excluded from the influence of Rome and Western Europe. In the middle of the barbarian chaos that generated apocalyptic events, Dacia and its settled people would continue to be the stable cornerstone of Eastern Europe, much as it had been from 500 B.C. to A.D 500.

NOTES

1. Jordanes, *The Gothic History of Jordanes*, ed. and trans. Charles Christopher Mierow (Cambridge: Speculum Historiale, 1966), 74.

2. Romulianum cannot be located on any map. Phonetically, the location closest to it is Romula on the Olt River; in fact his mother's name was Romula. Another

version of the name is Romuliana, which is today near Gamzigrad (east Serbia), where Galerius presumably had one of his palatial residences. Some dispute the claim that Romulianum was near Serdica (Sofia).

3. These two Christian victims commenced the long list of "warrior martyrs." They were followed by Saint George and other military heroes. All are depicted in legion uniforms in Romanian Orthodox churches.

4. It is possible that Constantine renamed the city of Tomis in memory of his sister, Constantia. The new city name of Constantza was adopted en masse by the Dacians who named their girls Constanta and Constantina, and boys Constantin and Costin, names that continue to be popular in today's Romania.

5. Dacian warriors also appear on the Arch of Galerius built in 305 in Salonika, Greece.

6. The gold of Dacia produced the famous treasure, *closca cu pui* (the hen with the chicks), that was found at Pietroasa in Romania almost two millennia later. It was later taken to Moscow, where it was identified as belonging to the Visigoths, who were declared to have been of a Russian origin. Therefore, *closca cu pui* was finally in the right place. Interestingly, during his WWII campaign in the Caucasus, Hitler declared the natives to be Visigoths, therefore part of the German-Aryan race. Thus, he reasoned, their liberation by the Wehrmacht was justified.

7. Jordanes, *Gothic History*, 126-128.

8. Although there is little information on whether Balta Brailei (the Wet Land of Braila) and other similar names have any connection with Alaric's family, Balta did become a common Romanian name.

9. Jordanes, *Gothic History*, 223.

10. The river, also called Nedao by Jordanes, remained unidentified at the time. It was located west of the Danube, inside today's Hungary.

11. Jordanes, *Gothic History*, 266.

12. It is well documented that these "estranged" Dacians, known in the Middle Ages as the Vlachs/Wallachians, were numerous and formed strong communities in what are today Albania, Bulgaria, Macedonia, Yugoslavia, and Greece. In the eleventh century A.D., a dense population of Vlachs lived in northern Albania, the Tarnovo region of Bulgaria, Greece's Thessaly, most of the Herzegovina region, and throughout the Balkan Mountains. They were the former Rhomanoi who spoke a Daco-Roman dialect that was easily understood by modern-day Romanians, much as the Parisians understand Quebequois. Their language identified them as Macedo-Romanians/Aromanians, and today they are dispersed throughout the world.

Epilogue

A certain amount of academic confusion arises each time the subject of Dacia and its people is brought to discussion. This is primarily because the ancient Dacians left no written records of their past. Sometimes their story was passed on in distorted form; misinformation was often included in it. Often, the Dacians are left out of history altogether or replaced with other tribal names. However, while researching this work, I found a surprisingly large number of reliable, written testimonies supported by archeological evidence for the existence of a distinctive Dacian society that endured for more than three thousand years.

The gap of some one thousand years between the Roman occupation of Transylvania and the early Middle Ages was, and still is, replete with ambiguities when it comes to establishing an historical basis for the Romanian people and the continuity of the Daco-Roman culture. Dacia's neighbors, the former Asiatic invaders of the Eastern Europe, were prone to assuming ownership of Romanian territories; even conquering a land does not give the victor the right to inherit.

An undeniable fact is that during Dacian times the Bulgarians, Hungarians, Magyars, Ukrainians, and Serbians were not part of ancient Europe. It was not until after the year A.D. 500 that the first small groups of Bulgars appeared in Dobrudja, some of them settling in Dacia Ripensis between Moesia Inferior and Moesia Superior. Moreover, it was not until two hundred years later that the Magyars and Serbi crossed into Europe. Just like the Avari, Huns, and Turks, the Bulgarians, the Magyars and Serbi were not Slavs, but of Mongolian descent.

Although many waves of these predatory tribes may have swept through parts of post-Roman Dacia, they were forced to look for a homeland elsewhere in the Balkans and Eastern Europe. After the ninth century, the

Bulgarians, Magyars, and Serbs became Christians which gave them legiti-
macy to form new countries in Eastern Europe. But their historians, wittingly
or otherwise, put a lot of personal feelings and patriotic emotions into their
narratives in an effort to substantiate unjustified nationalistic claims. Western
researchers are reluctant to contradict demographic aberrations, and the overall result has been an historic neglect of the role played by the Dacians in the
Balkans during ancient times. Linked with this is an incomplete understanding of the Dacian evolution into a Romanian nation within the perimeters of
their original lands.

A striking example of this ongoing misunderstanding is Hungary's territorial claim over Transylvania. The argument is that Transylvania was
a deserted land when the Magyars occupied it in the earlier Middle Ages.
Hungarians trace this theory to a paragraph of Eutropii's *Historiae Romanae
Breviarium* (*A Brief Roman History*):

> *Idem de Dacia facere conatum amici deterruerunt, ne multi cives Romani bar-
> baris traderentur, propterea quia Traianus victa Dacia ex toto orbe Romano
> infinitas eo copiae hominum transtulerat ad agros et urbes calendas. Dacia
> enim diuturno bello Decibali viris fuerat exhausta.* [1]

This translates as: "Trajan, after Dacia was conquered, transplanted there
a large number of people from the entire Roman world to populate its cities
and cultivate fields, since Dacia was exhausted of its men during the long
war of Decebalus." Clearly, Eutropii (Eutropius) does not suggest that the
entire Dacian population vanished in the war, nor that they were replaced by
the newcomers.

Elsewhere, Eutropii described why Emperor Aurelian was forced to evacuate the non-Dacians from Dacia Felix: "because Moesia and Illyricum had
been entirely devastated, and he settled the Romans brought from the Dacia's
cities and villages in the middle of Moesia and of the area that now divides
the two Moesiae, giving it the name of Dacia, a territory that now is on the
right side of the Danube." [2]

The historian is obviously referring to Dacia Aureliana, which was large
enough to shelter the Roman administration, colonists, and the troops who
withdrew from of Dacia. In no way could it have accommodated almost one
million Dacians from the former Roman province. In fact, that land had been
populated by Dacians since pre-historic times.

Eutropii died in the year 399, having served emperors Julian, Valens and
others as a secretary. In that role, he had to be a royal "pleaser;" he was
charged with making Rome look good regardless of any facts to the contrary.
His manuscript was later copied and translated in many versions by medieval
writers who were not faithful to the original, as was often the case.

Some versions of the two paragraphs cited above were misused by foreign revisionists who tried to demonstrate that the Dacians were exterminated during the Trajan wars of 101-106, and who believed that after the Romans withdrew from the Dacian territories (mainly Transylvania) in the year 275, it was *terra deserta* for the next seven hundred years. In essence, this would mean that today's Romanians have no basis for claiming Dacian heritage and no legitimate claims to their land. This is, however, far from accurate. Three important points contradict the distorted views attributed to Eutropii:

1. He wrote his abridged history one century after the Roman evacuation of Dacia, describing the events associated with it in vague terms and drawing on the same confused pattern of information which Herodotus and Jordanes had relied upon.
2. After the Daco-Roman wars, the Dacians continued to be the largest settled population in all of southeast Europe. The northern and eastern parts of Dacia, more than half of its land, were never occupied by the Romans. Therefore, any "vanishing" population that moved out of Dacia Traiana was to be found in Free Dacia.
3. The Romans surely had no interest in destroying the local Dacian population, who were very productive. Exterminating almost a million people in a few years would have been practically impossible, particularly considering Dacia's terrain. Furthermore, common graves of such proportions have never been found in Romania to support such a theory of genocide. Thus there is neither logic nor evidence to support the theory that the Dacian people "vanished." And, it is known that in a later period, more than ten Roman emperors had Daco-Illyrian origins, a fact that, in and of itself, proves that these ancient tribal nations continued to exist after the Italic Empire had ended.

It is true, many enthusiasts of the "Latin Movement" and "Transylvanian School" focused on the importance of the Roman colonists in creating the Transylvanian Romanians. Even Prince Dimitrie Cantemir was strongly committed to the Latinity of the Romanians as he tried to separate the Romanian heritage from the rapacious Russian and Turkish domination of the Balkans in the seventeenth and eighteenth centuries. By embracing a strong Roman past in the Dacian land, these enthusiasts believed they were giving the Romanians a more favorable identity, one which would be accepted by Western Europe.

Fortunately, the Daco-Roman continuity is confirmed by Trajan's Column, which clearly shows how the Dacian civilians were taken prisoners but returned to their homes after the war was over, and how the Romans used the natives in their building projects. In spite of Trajan's imperial propaganda (*Universa Dacia Devicta Est* 'All of Dacia has been conquered'), he actually occupied only part of Transylvania. He did not "annihilate" the Dacians, nor did they commit mass suicide. In fact, all the emperors and historians who followed Trajan reported fighting against the Free Dacians—some one million of them. More than eight hundred treasures that belonged to the Dacians before and after Roman occupation have been unearthed in Romania, providing evidence of the continuity of Dacian life and clearly establishing their link with today's Romanians.

Equally radical and untenable is the theory that denies that the Dacians were Romanized. It argues that they lived by hiding in the densely forested mountains and never heard Latin because they had no contact with the Romans. It is true that the Dacians did not worship the Roman gods, but the Roman occupation had a huge impact at all levels, one that lasted even after the occupation ended in the third century. Today in Romania there are at least ten locations with the name of Traian/Trajanus and countless others derived from Roman names.

The Latin vocabulary was robustly integrated into the Dacian language, and today a Romanian can speak without using words of other roots, an obvious important effect of the process of Romanization. Equally valid is the theory that the Romans assimilated the culture they conquered. In this way the Daco-Roman people gave birth to the future Romanians and so also to the Wallachians/Vlachs (Latin speaking people) who still live all over the Balkan Peninsula. The Dacians may have vanished as a nation but not as a people.

The end of the sixth century A.D. marked the beginning of the Medieval Era. It was also the time during which Avars defeated the Gepidaes and came to a position of dominance in Dacia for the next two centuries. The Avars opened the road for the Slavs, another diversified tribal people migrating from far Eastern Europe, who settled south of the Danube. Still, regardless of the many demographic changes that took place around them, the Dacians did not leave their lands. They adopted the early feudal system with its *voievozi* (princes) ruling *voievodate* (kingdoms) and with the strong Orthodox Church ruling the society as a whole. Because they were genetically different from their neighbors, their Latinity was fully accepted by the Church community of the Western European nations.

The merciless march of time forced many empires and nations to vanish from Europe, but Dacians were never displaced from their ancient land, although they were assaulted by many Asiatic hordes. Since then, the Daco-Romans have remained a Latin island within a sea of Magyars, Slavs, and Turks.

When the Crusaders tried to revive the shrinking Byzantine Empire, they renamed part of it *Romania,* because the most numerous segment of its population were the Latin speaking people, including Wallachians of Dacian heritage who had lived south of the Danube. The Crusaders' empire with its Roman laws was short-lived in the Balkans, but the name "Romanians" stuck to the former Dacians, already known as Rhomaioi (Romans) to the Greeks.

As mentioned in previous chapters, millions of other Daco-Roman descendents live in what are today Albania, Croatia, Bosnia-Hertzegovina, Bulgaria, Greece, Hungary, Macedonia, Montenegro, Serbia, Slovakia, and the remainder of Eastern Europe. Some of them are known as Aromanians or Macedo-Romanians and often nicknamed Tzintzars; others, Istro-Romanians, and so on. Many of their locations can be identified by the presence of the ancient Dacian *davas* and by the fact that their shepherd's clubs and dagger pummels were decorated with the famous Dacian dragon head. They are a present historical reality, not "previous Balkan inhabitants."

This truly Dacian Diaspora (one of the longest lasting in the world) still speak a Daco-Roman dialect—a proto-Latin, which for centuries was misidentified as the "Thracian" language.[3] The Romanian language, which is close to the coarse Latin retained by the Dacians, belongs to the Romance language tree that includes French, Italian, Portuguese, and Spanish.

By the thirteenth century, the Golden Horde (the Tartars) had scorched Eastern Europe just as their Hunic predecessors had. In Asia, the Ottoman Empire emerged as a global power, backed by Islam and its formidable armies. The Byzantine Empire would continue to exist until 1453, at which time Constantinople was attacked and conquered by the Turks, who later renamed it Istanbul.

The new masters of the Balkans gave the name of *Rumelia* (the Land of Romans) to the former lands of ancient Moesia and northern Thracia because so many of the people of this area spoke a language related to Latin. The name *Romania,* which eventually replaced the ancient name of Greater Dacia, had already been mentioned by Jordanes, who referred to it as a Roman land where Emperor Valens met the embassy of Visigoths in the year 376.[4]

Not many historians realize that Bucharest is located so close to the Danube River because at the time it was founded by Prince Vlad Dracula/the Impaler, it was in the middle of Greater Dacia, whose lands he wanted to recover from intruding neighbors. Those neighbors had savagely taken possession of the Dacian lands and had changed the names of settlements, rivers, mountains, and anything else that related to the true history of the land.

Because the winners of the world's major battles write the history books, it is not surprising that most of the information about the Dacians was passed down through unsubstantiated reports that have to be treated with great caution. In the absence of an alternative explanation, Euro-historians accepted a certain amount of misinformation produced by unreliable documentation of ancient Eastern Europe. Some critical points concerning this history are noted below.

Bulgarians and Hungarians continue to discover ancient artifacts and take pride in identifying them as their own. This requires, however, that they disregard the carbon testing that dates them hundreds and thousands of years before their ancestral tribes reached Eastern Europe. Because the Dacians did not build temples or set up tombstones, the remains of their dead are erroneously attributed to other peoples throughout the area of the Balkans, even when their locations bear the names of Cherna, Gradishte, and Peshtera—duplicates of ancient names still to be found in Romania.

The story of the Wallachian Asan/Asen brothers proves the existence of a majority Wallachian population in the Balkans who established their own kingdom after defeating Byzantine armies at the end of the twelfth century. From 1187 to 1197 Ioan and Petru co-ruled the Second Bulgarian Empire, and in 1204 Pope Innocent III crowned their brother Ioannitsa-Caloian as king of Wallachians and Bulgars, a joint entity which had the right to mint its own coins. One year later the Vlachian emperor crushed an army of crusaders at Adrianople, and two years later he besieged Salonica where he was assassinated. Today the historical achievements of the three brothers are presented as the victorious revolution of Bulgarian boyars.

The equestrian statues of the Assens (the above mentioned Asan brothers who created their own Asen/Asanizi dynasty and *Terra Assani*) adorn the Veliko Tarnovo (a former Dacian *dava*) and they are taken to be Bulgarian national heroes. The fact that when they were in danger the brothers crossed the Danube into Dacia and returned with military help is intentionally minimized. Some historians even hint that "Vlach" means "Bulgarian".

As for the Greeks, they have a hard time admitting that between the years 1100 and 1300 Thessaly was named Megale Vlachia/Large Valachia. Smaller Vlachias (today's Albania and Macedonia) was where the Megleno-Romanian speaking people lived.

The myth that Getians and Dacians were sub-tribes of the Thracians has been perpetuated with the result that the Romanians have been excluded from historical justification altogether. Ironically, Bulgarians do not speak any Thracian dialect, and their national costume is copied from the Romanians, not unlike those portrayed on Trajan's Column. This demonstrates that, like the Serbians, the Bulgarian immigrants needed to blend in with the dense Dacian population of Moesia. Speaking a Slavic language was their way of maintaining a pan-Slavic brotherhood.

In the past, the Hungarians have made hugely exaggerated claims on Transylvania and other Dacian lands. But they did so at the price of historic accuracy: the Great Hungarian Plains were under the rules of Burebista and Decebalus eight centuries before the Magyars arrived in the flat land of Pannonia. According to their historical revisionists, there were almost no Dacians in Dacia. This would mean that no Dacian population existed under the Roman occupation, and so there could also be no descendants of ancient natives. These people also claim that the Dacians were never Romanized and that there is no archeological evidence to support Dacian continuity in Transylvania. In their view, Romanization took place only south of the Danube, and eventually estranged Dacians returned to Transylvania after the Magyars occupied it. Ostensibly, this is how the Romanian language migrated into Dacia from the Balkans. Therefore, the deniers contend, it is unlikely that Daco-Romanians can be associated with the Romanian language. All such claims aside, Romanians do not need any such stamp of approval on their history since they are the living proof of it.

The Middle Age Romanian population of Transylvania was, however, forcibly Magyarized, and Hungarian names replaced countless original Daco-Romanian names, a state of affairs that is comparable to the British in India where they impose their names on certain locations. For this reason on Hungarian maps the Dacian capital of Sarmizegethusa was located at Varhely, Napoca-Cluj was renamed Kolosvar, the Carpathian Mountains were called the Kudzsir Alps, and the name for Transylvania became Erdély.

From the Hungarian perspective, "Romanism" was a historic gimmick, and all sorts of fraudulent data were used to justify Hungarian ownership of Daco-Romanian lands. Numerous claims were developed to support this, such as the "vacuum theory," according to which the Magyars settled in Transylvania because it was an unpopulated area and later the Romanians invaded it. Hungarian archeologists continue to try to prove that Dacia was never Romanized, but they overlook the obvious fact that the Romanian language has the same Latin roots as Italian. Ironically, the most popular Hungarian name *Olah* (which has many versions) means "Valach" (one who speaks Latin), further suggesting that the Magyars encountered Dacians when they migrated to Pannonia.

The Serbians, who wonder why Belgrade is so close to the actual Romanian border, may find the answer in the fact that its ancient site was populated by the Dacians and that today's Romanian and Serbian Banat was once named Dacia Superior—never Serbia Superior. In fact there was a Vlachia Veche /Old Wallachia in southeast Serbia, and there are many smaller Vlachias in Croatia and Moravia.

According to those who would deny the continuity of Dacian culture, the name Valachian describes a group of herders and so identifies economic status, not ethnicity. Far from being "discovered" by Bulgars, Hungarians, and Serbs, the Daco-Valachians constituted the largest indigenous ethnic group in the Balkans. Regardless of the ruling empires and kingdoms, they always acted independently and never adopted either Catholicism or Islam. These Aromanians were dispersed but not destroyed.

During the Medieval Era, the Polish nobility refused to be identified with its Slavic heritage, and, rejecting Ukrainian and Russian claims to its land, the haughty *pani* dressed in Sarmatian costumes. This is a deeply rooted identity problem which the Romanians never had to contend with—and this in spite of the fact that the Sarmatians were so involved with Dacian affairs that historians often interchanged their names.

Over the next centuries, the Austro-Hungarians, Russians, and Turks would reduce the former land of Dacia to less than half its size. However, the Dacian legacy triumphed once again at the 1919 Paris Peace Conference when amputated Romania was given back its ancient territories of Banat, Bessarabia, Bukovina, Dobrudja (part of Moesia), and Transylvania. It took Hitler and Stalin to rip the country into pieces again, but after WWII Transylvania was reattached to Romania, while the Soviet Union incorporated the Dacian lands of Basarabia/Bessarabia and part of Bukovina.

When Soviet leaders twisted historical facts to make them conform to Communist doctrine, Romanian history suffered another setback. Romanians were forced to claim that Russians, not Dacians and Romans, were the backbone of their nation. The Russian language and Slavic culture were imposed on them in an effort to make them assimilate and become Homo Sovieticus.

After the fall of the Soviet Empire, Bessarabia became the independent Republic of Moldova. This meant the loss of its land in the area of the Budjak region with its revered shrine Cetatea Alba (Tyras/Album Castrum) at the mouth of Nistru (Dniester) River and the entire Black Sea costal line. Moldovians continue to fight to revive their Romanian heritage, yet no one seems to remember that the Dacian land of Tyragetae is today's Transnistria. However, the Russians and Ukrainians have always been aware of the fact that the Romanians are inextricably linked to Transylvania, which remained a cornerstone between the Balkans, Eastern and Central Europe.

Historic amnesia tends to clash with the reality of demographics and with actual border claims. This was demonstrated at the beginning of WWI and WWII, and more recently in the Balkans during the devastating civil war in the former Yugoslavia. The ethnic and religious confrontation between Albanians (and other nationalities) and Serbs proved once again that fifteen hundred years of history had not erased nationalistic pride, nor had it resolved the disputes over a land that has changed hands too many times.

After the fall of Communism, these disputes reached a point at which independent Macedonia could not keep its name because its neighbors, especially Greece, were afraid the small nation of Alexander the Great might attempt to reclaim its ancient provinces. When Kosovo declared its independence from Serbia, the ethnic land dispute that erupted there divided the European Union and reignited the Cold War tensions between Russia and the United States. This dispute has tremendous historic implications and is likely to affect both regional security and global economy for years to come. Other historical facts which have been repressed by modern scholarship and made to conform to the dictates of political correctness will undoubtedly resurface in different terms and affect the peace and stability of Eastern Europe as well. As always, nationalism came down to "us and them, the foreigners," and the historical right over land remains highly contested.

Regardless of how modern Italians relate to the Romanians, in the middle of Rome the magnificent Column radiates a clear message from ancient Dacia, to the modern world. It validates the facts of one period in early Eastern European history with a kind of crystal clarity. That is, it documents the events surrounding the Roman war against the Dacians and the effort to conquer Transylvania and, implicitly, Moesia and Pannonia. It is not a testament to the heroism of the Bulgarians, Magyars, Hungarians, and Serbs, who at that time were wandering between Mongolia and Siberia and had never heard of Europe. It is a testimony of the Romanian history written in stone.

The historical references cited in this work are supported by the archeological findings that attest to the continuous existence of the Daco-Romanians from 500 B.C. to the present day. It is my sincere hope that more skilled historians and researchers than myself will choose to address this much neglected scholarly subject and fill in the many blanks and correct historical errors that need attending. Still more scientific precision is requisite for academic acceptance of the main thesis of this work. I am, however, confident that other authors will be inspired to expand the existing body of knowledge about Dacia and the pivotal role it played in the history of ancient Eastern Europe. Let me conclude by expressing my gratitude to them in anticipation of their endeavors.

NOTES

1. Eutropii, *Historiae Romanae Breviarium* (Oxonii. E. Theatro Sheldoniano Impensis AB. Wall & Tim Child, ad insigne Monocerotis in Coemeterio. London: D. Pauli Londini, 1696), bk. 8, 6.

2. Eutropii, *Historiae*, bk. 9, 15.

3. The much publicized Thracians, whom historians believed to be the most dominant mega- tribe of ancient Eastern Europe, in fact vanished as a nation and country
before the Daco-Roman wars. When they adopted the Greek language, they ceased
to exist as a distinct minority. This itself provides additional evidence of the fact that
Dacians and Thracians were different ethnic groups.

4. Jordanes, *The Gothic History of Jordanes, e*d. and trans. Charles Christopher
Mierow (Cambridge: Speculum Historiale, 1966), 131.

Selected Bibliography

INTERNATIONAL SOURCES

The Ancient World. Vol. 2 of *History of Mankind.* New York: UNESCO & Harper & Row, 1965.

Anastasoff, Christ. *The Bulgarians: From Their Arrival in the Balkans to Modern Times: Thirteen Centuries of History.* Hicksville, NY: Exposition Press, 1977.

Bacon, Edward, Ed. *Vanished Civilizations of the Ancient World.* New York: McGraw-Hill, 1963.

Bachman, Ronald D., ed. *Romania: A Country Study.* Washington: Federal Research Division Library of Congress, 1991.

Branston, Brian L. *Gods and Heroes from Viking Mythology.* New York: Peter Bedrick Books, 1994.

Bunson, Mathew. *A Dictionary of the Roman Empire.* London: Oxford University Press, 1995.

Cadzow, John, F., Andrew Ludanyi, and Louis J. Elteto, eds. *Transylvania: The Roots of Conflict.* Kent: Kent State University, 1983.

Carcopina, Jerome. *Daily Life in Ancient Rome.* Translated by E. O. Lorimer. New Haven: Yale University Press, 1958.

Ćirković Sima M. *The Serbs.* Translated by Vuk Tošić Oxford: Blackwell Publishing, 2004.

Coarelli, Filippo. *The Column of Trajan.* Rome: Editore Columbo, 2000.

Cunliffe, Barry. *The Ancient Celts.* London: Oxford University Press, 1977.

Cunliffe, Barry, ed. *Prehistoric Europe.* London: Oxford University Press, 1998.

Dio, Cassius. *Roman History.* Vol. 6, Bk. 51. Loeb Classical Library: 1917. http://penelope.uchicago.edu/Thayer/E/Roman/Texts/Cassius_Dio/51*.html (12 Feb. 2008).

———. *Dio's Roman History.* Translated by Earnest Cary. London: William Heineman; New York: Macmillan, 1914.

———. Press; London: William Heinemann, 1955.

Dixon, Karen R., and Pat Southern. *The Roman Cavalry.* New York: Barnes & Noble Books, 2000.

Durant, Will. *Caesar and Christ.* New York: Simon & Schuster, 1944.

Eliade, Mircea. *A History of Religious Ideas from Gautama Buddha to the Triumph of Christianity.* Translated by William R. Trask. Chicago: University of Chicago Press, 1982.

Eutropii. *Historiae Romanae Breviarium.* Oxonii E. Theatro Sheldoniano Imprensis A.B. Wall & Tim Child, ad insigne Monocerotis in Coemeterio. London: D. Pauli Londini, 1696.

Fine, John V.A. *The Early Medieval Balkans: A Critical Survey from the Sixth to the Late Twelth Century.* Ann Arbor: University of Michigan, 1991.

Gibbon, Edward. *The Decline and Fall of the Roman Empire.* Everyman's Library. New York: Knopf, 1993.

Goffart, Walter. *Barbarian Ties.* Philadelphia: University of Pennsylvania Press, 2006.

Grant, Michael. *A Guide to the Ancient World.* New York: Barnes & Noble Books, 1997.

Grun, Bernard. *The Timetables of History.* New York: Simon & Schuster, Touchstone, 1991.

Hadas, Moses. *Ancilla to Classical Reading.* New York: Columbia University Press, 1957.

Hammerton, John, and Harry Elmer Barnes. *Illustrated World History.* New York: Wm. H. Wise, 1940.

Herodotus. *The History.* Translated by David Grene. Chicago: University of Chicago Press, 1987.

Hinnells, John R. *Persian Mythology.* Library of the World's Myths and Legends. New York: Peter Bedrick Books, 1985.

Jordanes. *The Gothic History of Jordanes.* Edited and translated by Charles Christopher Mierow. Cambridge: Speculum Historiale, 1966.

Juvenal. *Juvenal and Persius.* Translated by G. G. Ramsay. Cambridge and London: Harvard University Press, 1999.

——. *The Satires.* Translated by Niall Rudd. Edited by William Barr. Oxford World's Classics. London: Oxford University Press, 1999.

Keller, Werner. *The Bible as History.* New York: Barnes & Noble Books, 1995.

Keppie, Lawrence. *The Making of the Roman Army: From Republic to Empire.* New York: Barnes & Noble Books, 1994.

Kriwaczek, Paul. *In Search of Zarathustra: The First Prophet and the Ideas that Changed the World.* New York: Knopf, 2002.

Lafferty, R. A. *The Fall of Rome.* New York: Doubleday, 1971.

Lengyel, Emil. *1,000 Years of Hungary.* New York: John Day, 1958.

Liberti, Anna Maria, and Fabio Bourbon. *Ancient Rome: History of a Civilization that Ruled the World.* New York: Stewart, Tabori & Chang, 1996.

Luttwak, Edward N. *The Grand Strategy of the Roman Empire.* Baltimore: John Hopkins University Press, 1979.

Mierow, Charles C. "Jordanes: The Origin and Deeds of the Goths in English Version." Part of a thesis presented to the Faculty of Princeton University for the degree of Doctor of Philosophy, Princeton, 1908.

Millar, Fergus. *A Study of Cassius Dio*. Oxford: Clarendon Press, 1964.

Mommsen, Theodor. *The History of Rome*. New York: Charles Scribner's Sons, 1900.

O'Connor, Colin. *Roman Bridges*. Cambridge, U.K.: Cambridge University Press, 1993.

Ovid. *The Poems of Exile: Tristia and the Black Sea Letters*. Translated by Peter Green. Berkeley: University of California Press, 2005.

Pliny. *Letters, Books I-VII*. Vol. 1 of *Letters and Panegyricus*. Translated by Betty Radice. Cambridge: Harvard University Press; London: William Heinemann, 1972.

——. *Letters, Books VIII – X and Panegyricus*. Vol. 2 of *Letters and Panegyricus*. Translated by Betty Radice. Cambridge: Harvard University Press; London: William Heinemann, 1975.

Pliny the Elder. *Natural History: A Selection*. Translated by John F. Healy. London: Penguin Books, 1991.

Pliny the Younger. *The Letters of the Younger Pliny*. Translated by Betty Radice. New York: Penguin Classics, 1963.

Ptolemaeus, Claudius. *Cosmographia*. Amsterdam: Thetrum, Orbis Terrarum, 1956.

Ptolemy. *The Geography*. New York: New York Public Library, 1932.

——. *Ptolemy's "Geography": An Annotated Translation of the Theoretical Chapters*. Translated by J. Lennart Berggren and Alexander Jones. Princeton: Princeton University Press, 2000.

Roebuck, Carl. *The World of the Ancient Times*. New York: Charles Scribner's Sons, 1966.

Rostovtzeff, Michael Ivanovitch. *Iranians & Greeks in South Russia*. Oxford: Clarendon Press, 1922.

Scarre, Chris. *Chronicle of the Roman Emperors: The Reign-by-Reign Record of the Imperial Rulers of Rome*. London: Thames & Hudson, 1995.

Sekunda, Nicholas V., Simon Northwood, and Michael Simkins. *Caesar's Legions*. Oxford: Osprey Publishing History, 2000.

Steves, Rick, and Cameron Hewitt. *Rick Steves' Eastern Europe*. Berkeley: Avalon Travel, 2008.

Strabo. *The Geography of Strabo*. Edited by G. P. Goold. Translated by Horace Leonard Jones, in Eight Vols. The Loeb Classical Library. Cambridge: Harvard University Press, 1917.

——. *The Geography of Strabo*. Translated by Horace Leonard Jones. Vol. 3. London: William Heinemann; New York: G. P. Putnam's Sons, 1924.

Strohmeier, John, and Peter Westbrook. *Divine Harmony: The Life and Teachings of Pythagoras*. Berkeley: Berkeley Hills Books, 1999.

Tacitus. *The Annales of Cornelius Tacitus, The Description of Germanie*, London: Printed by F. L. for Richard Whitaker, 1640.

———. *The Germania of Tacitus.* Vol. 5 of *History.* The Latin Classics. New York: Vincent Parke & Company, 1909.

———. *Agricola.* Translated by M. Hutton. *Germania.* Translated by M. Hutton. *Dialogus.* Translated by W. Peterson. Cambridge: Harvard University Press, 1992.

———. *The Histories.* Edited by D. S. Levene. Revised translation of W.H. Frye. London: Oxford University Press, 1999.

Thucydides. *The Complete Writings of Thucydides.* New York: Random House, Modern Library, 1951.

———. *A Comprehensive Guide to the Peloponnesian War.* Edited by Robert B. Strassler. New York: Free Press, 1996.

———. *History of the Peloponnesian War.* Translated by Rex Warner. New York: Penguin Books, 1972.

Toynbee, Arnold J., and Jane Caplan. *History.* London: Oxford University Press, 1972; distributed in the U.S. by American Heritage Press.

Toynbee, Arnold J., and Edward D. Myers, *Historical Atlas and Gazetteer.* Vol. 11 of *A Study of History.* London: Oxford University Press, 1959.

Vékony, Gábor. *Dacians-Romans-Romanians.* Toronto and Buffalo: Matthias Corvinus Publishing, 2000.

Watson, Francis. *A Concise History of India.* New York: Charles Scribner's Sons, 1975.

Williams, Derek. *The Reach of Rome: A History of the Roman Imperial Frontier 1ˢᵗ – 5ᵗʰ Century A.D.* New York: St. Martin's Press, 1996.

———. *Romans and Barbarians.* New York: St. Martin's Press, 1998.

ROMANIAN SOURCES

Blaga, Lucian. *Zalmoxis.* Iasi: The Center for Romanian Studies, 2001.

Campulung Mic Îndreptar Turistic. Bucureşti: Editura Meridiane, 1968.

Cluj-Napoca. Cluj: Editura Studio, 1997.

Daicoviciu, Constantin. *Dacia Libera si Dacia Romana.* Bucureşti: Editura Didactica si Pedagogica, 1964.

Daicoviciu, Hadrian. *Dacia - de la Burebista la Cucerirea Romana.* Romania: Editura Dacia, 1972.

Dicţionar de istorie veche a României. Bucureşti: Editura Ştiinţifică Enciclopedică 1976.

Histria - Monografie Arheologica. Bucureşti: Editura Academiei R.P.R., 1960.

Ionita, Ion. *Din Istoria si Civilizatia Dacilor Liberi.* Romania: Editura Junimea, 1982.

Macrea, Mihail. *Viata in Dacia Romana.* Bucureşti: Editura Ştiinţifică 1969.

Rusu, Ion I. *Dacia si Panonia Inferior.* Bucureşti: Editura Academiei R.S.R., 1978.

Sanie, Silviu. *Din Istoria Culturii si Religiei Geto-Dacicei.* Iasi: Editura Universitatii Al. Ion Cuza, n.d.

Parvan, Vasile. *Dacia.* Bucure□i: Editura □iin□fic□ 1967.

Tudor, Dumitru. *Oltenia Romana.* Bucure□i: Editura Academiei, 1968.

Vulpe, Radu. *Columna lui Traian.* Bucure□i: Editura Sport-Turism, 1988.

Zahariade, Mihail. *Moesia Secunda, Scythia si Notitia Dignitatum.* Bucure□i: Editura Academiei R.S.R., 1988.

Index

13577932R00165

Made in the USA
Lexington, KY
08 February 2012